SUPER TENANT

Books by John M. Striker and Andrew O. Shapiro

Mastering the Draft:
A Comprehensive Guide for Solving Draft Problems

Super Tenant
New York City Tenant Handbook—Your Legal Rights and How to Use Them

Super Threats:
How to Sound Like a Lawyer and Get Your Rights on Your Own

By Andrew O. Shapiro

Media Access:
Your Rights to Express Your Views on Radio and Television

New and Revised Edition

NEW YORK CITY TENANT HANDBOOK

SUPER TENANT

YOUR LEGAL RIGHTS AND HOW TO USE THEM

John M. Striker & Andrew O. Shapiro

A Brownstone Book

HOLT, RINEHART and WINSTON
New York

Published simultaneously in Canada by Holt, Rinehart
and Winston of Canada, Limited.

Library of Congress Cataloging in Publication Data

Striker, John M.
Super tenant.

"A Brownstone book."
1. Landlord and tenant—New York (City)
2. Leases—New York (City) 3. Rent control—
New York (City) I. Shapiro, Andrew O., joint
author. II. Title.
KFN5145.S76 1978 356'.7471'04342 77-72336
ISBN Hardbound: 0-03-021101-8
ISBN Paperback: 0-03-021096-8

Second Edition

Designed by Brownstone Publishers, Inc.
Printed in the United States of America
10 9 8 7 6 5 4 3 2 1

To our good friend

Leonore Fleischer

Acknowledgments

Natalie Chapman of Holt, Rinehart and Winston was a moving force behind the revision of this book. Early on, she became convinced of the need for updating the book thoroughly and bringing it out in a new edition. Thanks to Natalie's patience, perseverance, sense of humor, and sound editorial judgment, this book will continue to serve New Yorkers.

We gained many valuable insights into the rent-control system and the rehabilitation of the city's housing stock from Barbara Cohn, Deputy Commissioner of Rent Control, and Joseph Shuldiner, Director of the Litigation Bureau, Housing and Development Administration.

Charles Poidomani, Director of Operations, and Edward Jirak, City-wide Chief Inspector, generously took time from their demanding schedules to answer numerous inquiries regarding the Office of Code Enforcement.

We are indebted to Ellis Frank, Executive Director of the Conciliation and Appeals Board, and attorneys Benjamin Binder and Jane Gropper, for discussing key legal issues that have arisen under the Rent Stabilization Law. Attorney Charles Mehlman of the Rent Stabilization Association supplied us with important research materials.

New York State Assemblyman Peter Sullivan (92d District, Westchester County), who sponsored the bill for the state's new plain English law, was most forthcoming and informative in his views about the kind of language that ought to be used in standard form leases.

For providing clear answers to many technical questions, we wish to thank Phoenix Ingraham, Chief Clerk, Civil Court of the City of New York; Harry Joslin, Clerk of the County of Bronx; and clerks Tom Crawford and Stan Isaacs.

Many attorneys with whom we spoke gave us the benefit of their experience in various aspects of housing law. For their guidance, we are grateful to Mark Fresco; Lawrence Grosberg, Robert Anderson, and Judith Lacoff of the Mobilization for Youth; Stephen Shulman; Alan Pekelner; and Jane Rosenberg of the Small Claims Action Center.

Roz Post of the Department of Rent and Housing Maintenance responded promptly and cheerfully to all our inquiries.

We are grateful for the cooperation we received from all the tenants' groups that answered our inquiries about their activities and interests.

For the fifth time, we find ourselves indebted to the staff of the law library at New York University School of Law for facilitating our research on a book. Our special thanks go to Julius Marke, Ed Bander, and Jerry Leone.

Many people with diverse talents contribute to the making of a book. In particular, we wish to thank Fran Shuman, who cast a sharp editorial eye over the manuscript.

Preface

In the five years since its initial publication, this book has, we believe, served a useful purpose. It established a common ground where landlords and tenants can meet to resolve their differences—calmly, rationally, and often without resort to attorneys. The mail we receive indicates that many tenants have used this book to help themselves negotiate what one of our readers aptly termed a "stoop settlement"—that is, an acceptable understanding with the landlord, often worked out on the front stoop of the apartment building. It is our conviction, borne out, we believe, by the response to this book, that once tenants know their rights, they are more likely to act dispassionately and, as a result, help themselves with a minimum of rancor and frustration. For those who haven't been able to do it themselves, they have, at least, learned enough to know when they should seek outside assistance—whether from a tenants' organization, a city agency, or an attorney.

There is much new material in this second edition, reflecting recent developments in landlord–tenant law. The controversial vacancy decontrol law was repealed and replaced by the Emergency Tenant Protection Act of 1974. As a result of this legislative change, hundreds of thousands of formerly rent-controlled apartments have become rent stabilized. Accordingly, we have increased our coverage of rent-stabilization law.

We have also greatly expanded our discussion of the warranty of habitability—the legal guarantee on the basic fitness of an apartment. Five years ago, the warranty of habitability was only a gleam in some judges' eyes. By 1975, it had become an important state statute.

We have gone into much greater detail on leases because so many readers told us they didn't understand the document they had signed. In 1976, the state legislature passed the unconscionability law, authorizing judges to crack down on unfair lease provisions. One year later, the so-called plain English law was enacted; it may eventually rid leases of legalistic gobbledygook. In response to numerous requests, we have explained how a tenant can break a lease if he has to. (One technique makes use of the state's new right-to-sublet law.)

Shortly after the first edition was published, the city's new housing court began operation. We have explained the new system the court employs for resolving complaints about housing violations. We have even told tenants how they can take their landlords into housing court on their own—without hiring a lawyer.

Turning to a different court, we have added an extensive discussion on how to sue a landlord in small claims court.

We have also discussed an important new line of court cases, under which a landlord may be held personally liable if his tenants are victimized by criminal intruders.

Even from these brief highlights, it should be evident how many changes have occurred since the first edition was published. Clearly, this book can do no more than describe laws and cases as they exist today. While most of these laws are not likely to undergo major revision, there is always the chance that some laws will be amended and new ones enacted. Therefore, if the reader needs legal advice designed for his individual problem, he must consult an attorney.

J.M.S.
A.O.S.

New York City
September 1977

Preface to the First Edition

For too long landlord–tenant law has been the private preserve of landlords and their lawyers. The great mass of tenants are left to grab at scraps of information about their rights—a news story here, a television interview there. Consequently many tenants are reduced to talk rather than action. They swap rumors, wonder what the law is, and, understandably, wind up doing nothing to improve their living conditions.

This book seeks to change the imbalance of power between landlord and tenant. Not that any secret plan or foolproof formula is revealed. Instead, we have organized hard information that you can understand easily and put to work without a law degree.

More importantly, this book is written for New York City tenants only. Any wider scope would have lessened the book's utility. Landlord–tenant law varies greatly from city to city and state to state, so a book that strains for the big picture must necessarily render the useless picture.

Bear in mind that your rights are only what you make of them. They will not serve you automatically. They must be stretched and strengthened through your individual and group efforts. Then you stand to fulfill the aim of this book: to take the lord out of landlord.

J.M.S.
A.O.S.

New York City
January 1973

Contents

Part II
Rent Control and Rent Stabilization

Part III
Maintenance and Repairs

Part IV
Court Actions

Appendix

SUPER TENANT

CHAPTER 1

General Principles

RENTING AN APARTMENT

Apartment hunting in New York City yields slightly more pleasure than root-canal work. You schlepp from building to building, where superintendents (who must invariably be summoned up from some basement grotto) take you grudgingly on tour and tell you everything the apartment "doesn't come with." It may offer you some small comfort to know that even as a prospective tenant you already have certain legal protection.

Undoubtedly, most of you know that a landlord is not permitted to discriminate in renting on the basis of race, creed, religion, or color. Do you know, however, that it is illegal for a landlord to refuse to rent to you solely because you have children? It is also illegal for a landlord to refuse to rent an apartment solely because the prospective tenants are an unmarried couple—whether of the same or of the opposite sex. If you're ever refused an apartment on what you feel are discriminatory grounds, complain to the Division of Human Rights of the State of New York; division offices are located at 2 World Trade Center, New York, N.Y. 10047 (Tel.: 212-488-5750).

Special legal protection is extended to handicapped persons. A landlord can't refuse to rent to a prospective tenant because he is blind and has a seeing-eye dog, nor can a landlord withhold an apartment from any severely physically handicapped person solely on the grounds that the person owns a dog or a cat that will be staying in the apartment.

Suppose a landlord is not unwilling to rent to you; he just wants you to show your gratitude—say, by slipping him a few hundred dollars. (Superintendents have been known to engage in this practice.) What's being squeezed from you is supposed to give you an edge over other prospective tenants who want the same apartment. The payment is popularly known as "key money"; legally speaking, it's "rent gouging," which is a crime and can lead to prosecution. If this happens to you, report it to the district attorney's office.

Once you actually rent an apartment in New York City, the landlord owes you more than four walls and a ceiling. You're entitled to a definite package of benefits and services:

- *A fair lease* A lease is supposed to be an agreement between equals—not a trap where the stronger party (the landlord) takes unfair advantage of the weaker one (you). In Part I of this book you will learn just how much leeway you have, despite whatever oppressive terms you may have been forced to accept.
- *Enjoyment of your apartment* Broadly speaking, you can satisfy your tastes, living standards, and lifestyle, as long as you do not cause harm to others—like the landlord or the neighbors.
- *Maintenance and repairs* You have the right to adequate heat, hot water, sanitation services, painting at regular intervals, and the maintenance of essential building services. If the landlord fails to deliver, you can get your rent reduced or withhold payment of it altogether.
- *Safety* The law prescribes certain equipment that a landlord must install (such as dead-bolt locks) for your personal security. In chapter 16 you will read about landlords' liability for crimes committed inside apartment buildings.

These legal benefits, as well as many others, belong to all New York tenants. Certain other rights and protections are enjoyed only by tenants whose apartments fall under special New York laws. For example, maximum rent levels are set for many New Yorkers, based upon the legal status of their apartments. These tenants may also gain important rights when it comes to building services and lease renewals. Since so much of the law explained in this book varies according to the legal status of your apartment, it is essential at this point to lay out the basic legal systems that apply to different tenants.

THE RENT LAWS: A HISTORY

While there are many laws in New York City that give tenants rights, by far the most important are the rent-control and rent-stabilization laws, which limit the amount of rent a landlord can charge. They also dictate the kinds of services a landlord must provide and restrict his right to evict tenants. The majority of New Yorkers are entitled to the benefits of either one of these laws but never to both. This section and the next two will help you figure out which, if either, of these laws protects you.

We must begin by learning the language of the rent laws. A tenant who has the protection of the rent-control law is called a *rent-controlled tenant*—he lives in a *rent-controlled apartment;* a tenant who has the protection of the rent-stabilization law is a *rent-stabilized tenant*—he lives in a *rent-stabilized apartment*. A tenant who does not have the protection of either of these laws is an *uncontrolled tenant*—he lives in an *uncontrolled apartment*.

The majority of rent-controlled tenants are referred to technically as *statutory tenants*. These tenants do not have leases, but they are entitled to remain in their rent-controlled apartments solely because a statute (the rent-control law) gives them that right. Hence, they are statutory tenants.

A rent-controlled or rent-stabilized apartment can, under certain circumstances, lose the protection of whichever law applies. A rent-controlled apartment that loses the protection of the rent-control law becomes *decontrolled*. A rent-stabilized apartment that loses the protection of the rent-stabilization law becomes *destabilized*.

Now that you know the basic language of the rent laws, you are prepared to ask some questions: What am I—rent controlled, rent stabilized, or uncontrolled? Has my apartment been decontrolled or destabilized? To answer these questions we must first take a brief look at the history of the rent laws, and then look more closely at the laws as they exist today.

In 1947 there was only the rent-control law (technically, the City Rent and Rehabilitation Law), which applied to apartments in buildings built before February 1, 1947. However, it did not cover tenants in buildings that were financed and operated by the city, the state, or the federal government—e.g., housing projects run by the New York Housing Authority.

The number of rent-controlled apartments has been decreasing since the late 1960s. In 1968 a law was passed that decontrolled some high-rent apartments. The theory was: people who could afford high rents didn't need the protection of the rent-control law. As a result, a small number of rent-controlled apartments were decontrolled.

The following year, as the rent-control law showed early signs of fading, the Rent Stabilization Law of 1969 was passed. This law covered apartments excluded from the rent-control law. Thus, apartments in buildings completed *after* February 1, 1947, were covered. Also, as rent-controlled apartments became decontrolled because of their high rents, they became rent stabilized. There was only one catch: the only apartments covered by the law were those in buildings that contained at least six apartments. If you lived in a small building—one with fewer than six apartments—you received no benefits from the rent-stabilization law; your apartment remained uncontrolled.

Through 1969, 1970, and the first half of 1971, the situation remained stable. A few apartments became decontrolled and most ended up rent stabilized. And then along came the *vacancy decontrol law*. This law was very simple. Any apartments vacated on or after June 30, 1971, lost the protection of the rent-control or rent-stabilization laws. They became decontrolled or destabilized (and, therefore, uncontrolled). Landlords were free to charge whatever rents they wanted. (Of course, apartments that did not become vacant remained rent controlled or rent stabilized.)

This situation persisted for three years, with more and more apartments becoming uncontrolled. However, on May 29, 1974, the Emergency Tenant Protection Act of 1974 (ETPA) became law. This act picked up the pieces left by the vacancy decontrol law. All apartments that had been decontrolled or destabilized by the vacancy decontrol law (which was in effect from June 30, 1971, through June 30, 1974) became rent stabilized by the ETPA. However, there was one exception—apartments in buildings that had fewer than six apartments: those tenants were, and still are, left out in the cold.

The result was that on the morning of July 1, 1974, all the apartments that had been decontrolled or destabilized became rent stabilized (with, of course, the exception of apartments in buildings with fewer than six apartments). There were also some rent-controlled apartments (about three hundred thousand) that had weathered the vacancy decontrol law simply by not becoming vacant after June 30, 1971. Apartments that had been rent stabilized in 1969 and had also weathered the vacancy decontrol law remained rent stabilized.

While the ETPA swelled the ranks of the rent-stabilized tenants, it did little for the remaining band of rent-controlled tenants. Any rent-controlled apartment that becomes vacant on or after July 1, 1974, becomes decontrolled. However, if the apartment qualifies, it immediately becomes rent stabilized.

Today, the majority of New York apartments are rent stabilized. There are still a few rent-controlled apartments around, but as they become vacant they become decontrolled, and many of them then become rent stabilized. Obviously, the future is in rent stabilization.

THE RENT CONTROL LAW

The rent-control law is administered by the Office of Rent Control, which is part of the Office of Rent and Housing Maintenance, which is, in turn, part of the Department of Housing Preservation, which is, in turn, part of the city's superagency, the Housing and Development Administration. The Office of Rent Control sets maximum rents, approves rent increases and decreases, regulates decontrol, grants and/or denies certificates of eviction, and settles disputes over the rent-control law. Presently, there is one main office and six district rent offices (see Appendix A).

If your apartment is rent controlled, you probably know it because you have received letters from the Office of Rent Control at one time or another over the past few years. However, if you have any doubt, visit your district rent office. (Be sure to bring along proof that you are the tenant of the apartment in question; your lease or a rent receipt from your landlord will do.) You will be told if your apartment is rent controlled.

THE RENT STABILIZATION LAW

The first rent-stabilization law went into effect on March 10, 1969. Basically, it covered three groups of tenants: (1) those who lived in buildings constructed after February 1, 1947, and before March 10, 1969; (2) those whose apartments were decontrolled under the rent-control law; (3) those who lived in buildings that were built after March 10, 1969, and that have received special tax abatements.

The law also specified that it did not cover: (1) apartments in buildings that contained fewer than six apartments; (2) apartments in buildings owned by city, state, or federal agencies; (3) apartments in buildings financed by loans from a public agency or a public-benefit corporation; (4) apartments in hotels (a different law covers hotel tenants).

The second rent-stabilization law (the ETPA) went into effect on July 1, 1974. This law extended the coverage of rent stabilization to: (1) apartments in buildings built between March 10, 1969, and December 31, 1973; (2) apartments decontrolled or destabilized under the vacancy decontrol law; (3) rent-controlled apartments that became (or become) vacant on or after July 1, 1974.

While extending the coverage of the rent-stabilization law, the ETPA also eliminated some apartments from rent stabilization. Specifically, the act eliminated apartments in buildings owned or operated by hospitals, convents, monasteries, asylums, public institutions, schools, and any exclusively philanthropic institutions. Also, apartments in buildings with fewer than six apartments were still left unprotected.

A number of court cases have arisen over exactly which apartments are covered by the first and second rent-stabilization laws. For example, is an apartment in a building that is financed by a loan from the Federal Housing Administration covered by the law? What about an apartment in a building that is owned by a church but is operated for profit? The answers to these questions are beyond the scope of this book. However, if you have any doubt as to whether you are rent stabilized, we strongly suggest that you contact a local tenants' group (see Appendix C), the Rent Stabilization Association, or the Conciliation and Appeals Board (see Appendix A). Ask them for assistance in determining whether you are rent stabilized.

THE RENT STABILIZATION SYSTEM

The rent-stabilization law established a curious system of administration. Rather than create another governmental organization to administer the law, it provided a system of self-regulation. Landlords were given the opportunity to form their own organization, the rules of which would be dictated by the stabilization law. If a landlord joined the organization and agreed to follow its rules, his apartments would become rent stabilized. *If he failed to join the organization, his apartments would become rent controlled.*

Obviously, landlords wanted to get away from the low rents on rent-controlled apartments, so they formed an organization, which is called the Rent Stabilization Association. To determine whether your landlord is a member, call the association (see Appendix A).

We know of many landlords who should have joined the Rent Stabilization Association but never did. What is the status of apartments in buildings owned by these landlords? At present, the answer is not clear. Technically, in buildings where the landlord did not join the association, apartments should be rent controlled. Yet, whenever the Office of Rent Control seeks to assume control, the landlord is not only permitted to join the association but his membership is made retroactive to the beginning of rent stabilization. Retroactivity foils the efforts of the Office of Rent Control.

By what authority is the Rent Stabilization Association allowing landlords to receive retroactive membership? That question has now been posed in a court case. As this book goes to press, the outcome of the case is not yet clear. However, any tenant whose landlord has not joined the Rent Stabilization Association (or if he was permitted to join late) should remain alert for any new developments. These tenants should keep in touch with a tenants' group for any court decisions affecting their apartments.

If your landlord did join the association and you are rent stabilized, your landlord must abide by the rules of the Rent Stabilization Code. The most important part of this system is the Conciliation and Appeals Board (CAB), which is responsible for enforcing the rules of the association. The board determines the proper rent on apartments, grants and/or denies rent increases, and decides which services a landlord must supply to tenants. (The address and phone number of the CAB are in Appendix A.)

Tenants may complain to the CAB if they feel they are not receiving all their rights under the code (the complaint procedures are described in chapters 9 and 10). The CAB will interpret the code and decide exactly what the tenant's rights are. It will order the landlord to provide them, and if the landlord refuses, the board has the authority to assess a fine. Also, if a landlord becomes a chronic offender, the board may kick him out of the Rent Stabilization Association. If that happens, all of the landlord's rent-stabilized apartments become rent controlled!

The final component of the rent-stabilization system is the Rent Guidelines Board. This board, which is an independent group, determines how much rent a landlord may demand from a rent-stabilized tenant. Chapter 9 explains how the board functions.

THE PRIMARY RESIDENCE DECONTROL LAW

As if there were not enough laws already buffeting the status of apartments, there is still one more we must consider. In May 1972, the primary residence decontrol law went into effect for both rent-controlled and rent-stabilized apartments. The purpose of this law is to prohibit any tenant from reaping the benefits of the rent-control and rent-stabilization laws when he is not, in fact, using his apartment as his primary residence. The rationale is that a tenant should not have the protection of these laws for what amounts to a second home.

Because of this law, both the rent-control and the rent-stabilization laws now have provisions for dealing with apartments not occupied as primary residences. However, each law uses a different enforcement technique.

Under the rent-control law, a tenant whose apartment is shown, to the satisfaction of the district rent office, not to be his primary residence will have his apartment decontrolled. Once it has been decontrolled, the landlord is free either to evict the tenant or to sign a lease with him at prevailing free-market rents.

Under the rent-stabilization law, the enforcement technique is different. If a landlord can convince the Conciliation and Appeals Board that an apartment is not being used by a tenant as his primary residence, the landlord has the right *not* to offer the tenant a renewal lease. Once the present lease expires, the tenant can be evicted.

The law, whether for rent-controlled or rent-stabilized apartments, provides guidelines for determining which of two or more residences is the tenant's *primary* one.

In general, the law considers the primary residence to be at the address specified as the tenant's residence on any tax return, motor vehicle registration, driver's license, voter registration card, or any other document filed with a civil agency. However, the cases we have read indicate that any information that tends to prove the location of the tenant's primary residence will be considered.

A survey of the cases reveals that the district rent office (for rent-controlled tenants), or the Conciliation and Appeals Board (for rent-stabilized tenants), generally gathers extensive information, usually of the type described in the guidelines, and then renders a logical decision. For example, if you have a home in Florida, vote in Florida elections (but not in New York), have a car registered in Florida, and have a Florida driver's license, kiss your New York apartment good-bye. On the other hand, merely having a second home does not mean that your rent-controlled or rent-stabilized apartment is something other than your primary residence. The question is: *Which home is the primary one?*

Another guideline used in determining the location of a tenant's primary residence is whether he sublets the apartment in question. If a tenant sublets his apartment for an extended period and establishes a new home elsewhere, the apartment may become decontrolled or destabilized. However, short sublets (such as for the summer months) would probably not be considered sufficient evidence that the apartment has ceased to be the tenant's primary residence.

It would seem, therefore, that extended sublets are impossible without constantly running the risk that the landlord will seek to decontrol or destabilize the apartment. In fact, an extended sublet does raise the possibility that you, the primary tenant, will lose your right to occupy the apartment. However, your subtenant is in a different position: he does occupy the apartment. The landlord might be able to use the law to get you out of the apartment, but he will run into some trouble if he tries to evict your subtenant.

A rent-controlled tenant who sublets his apartment has transferred to the subtenant his right to possess the apartment. Likewise, a rent-stabilized tenant who sublets his apartment for the remainder of his lease has transferred to the subtenant his right of possession. While the primary tenant no longer has a right to possess the apartment, the subtenant does. The law says only that a "tenant in possession" who is not using the apartment as his primary residence may be evicted. A subtenant can qualify as a "tenant in possession"; therefore, if the subtenant *is* using the apartment as his primary residence, the landlord will have a serious problem invoking the law.

Thus, if you run into a problem with the primary residence decontrol law because you sublet your apartment, you might want to give your subtenant the option to claim the apartment as his own. However, if he accepts that option, you might lose your right to occupy the apartment. In other words, if, in order to fend off an attack under the primary residence decontrol law, you have your subtenant claim that he is actually the tenant in possession, you just might become the former tenant, with no right to return to the apartment.

Another way to get around the primary residence decontrol law is to share your apartment. As long as there is one tenant in your apartment, using it as his primary residence, the law will not work for the landlord. If you can share your apartment and be sure that one tenant will use the apartment as his primary residence, you can return to the apartment at any time. (See chapter 6 for a full explanation of ways to sublet and share your apartment.)

FEDERAL PREEMPTION

The United States government has an interest in certain buildings in New York City. For example, some buildings' mortgages are insured by the Federal Housing Administration (FHA). If the FHA decides that the income a landlord is receiving is not sufficient to keep the building profitable, the FHA has the power to issue an order of preemption to protect their interest in the mortgage of the building.

This order removes the apartments in the building from any regulation by the city. In effect, the building becomes uncontrolled, and therefore rents can be raised. The federal government "preempts" the city and the state. And, as every student who has taken a basic course in government knows, if the interests of the federal government are in conflict with those of a city, the feds usually win out.

We don't know how far the preemption doctrine will go. However, because of the impact of preemption on the rents in a building, tenants in a preempted building should consider seeing a lawyer. It's not yet clear what a lawyer can do, but, considering the consequences of preemption, a legal consultation would probably be worthwhile.

PART I

Apartment Living and the Law

CHAPTER 2

Your Rights vs. Your Lease

YOUR LEASE AND THE LAW

Often, when a landlord hands you a lease he will tell you not to worry about what you're signing because it's just a standard "cigar store" lease. (He will probably be smoking a cigar as he tells you this.) Don't believe him. *A lease is a serious legal document; under no circumstances should it be signed without a thorough reading.*

If you find things you don't like when you read the lease, point them out to the landlord. The time to protest and ask for a change in terms is *before you sign;* afterward, it's too late. Don't let yourself be hoodwinked by a landlord who tells you that he never enforces certain lease provisions—say, a prohibition against keeping a pet. If the landlord is unwilling to change, delete, or add a lease provision *in writing,* then you're a fool if you believe *anything* he says. You'll have a devil of a time if you later try to prove in court that your written lease ought to be interpreted according to what the landlord *said* to you; generally such evidence isn't even admissible in court. Furthermore, your lease probably states (somewhere near the end) that it can't be changed orally and that the landlord has made no promises to you other than those set forth in the lease. So if you want to be assured of the right to sublet, or to install an air-conditioner, or to have a roommate, etc., insist that the lease provide for these things *in writing* before you sign.

No matter how careful you are, you probably won't get everything you want; even worse, you undoubtedly will get much that you don't want—some of which you may not fully understand. Does that mean all hope is lost and you're locked into a lousy deal? Not necessarily.

For one thing, the landlord can't throw you out just because of any little violation of your lease. Mere technical violations usually are not sufficient grounds for eviction. Rather, most judges will demand proof of a *substantial* violation of the lease. As one judge recently stated the key issue: "The question presented is whether the violation is substantial enough to justify so drastic a remedy as the eviction of the tenant. One must ask: 'Is the violation of real substance? Is it material, important, and consequential? Is the violation sufficiently serious in character to warrant the tenant's ouster and a forfeiture of the lease?' All the . . . facts and surrounding circumstances must be examined." Unless you have committed a substantial violation, you will not be evicted. In chapters 3, 4, and 6 you will read about a number of eviction cases in which the judge found either no violation of the lease or only an insubstantial one.

In addition to the gloss added to your lease through favorable judicial opinions, there are laws that affect provisions in your lease. *Affect* is actually too mild a word, because certain laws can invalidate part of your lease. (Some of these laws are discussed in the latter portion of this chapter.)

The key point to remember is: *your lease is not the law*. True, we've seen that a lease is, by and large, a binding legal document, which must be taken seriously. Still, it may contain provisions that are difficult to enforce or only partially valid or even totally void. Knowing what these provisions are and how far you can push them or ignore them are essential to being an informed tenant.

Let's look now at two new laws that may have a potentially far-reaching effect on all leases. The first is called the plain English law; the second is known as the unconscionability law. (In the final section of this chapter we'll run down a list of lease provisions and question their legality. Other lease provisions will be discussed throughout chapters 3, 4, and 6.)

THE PLAIN ENGLISH LAW

On August 5, 1977, Governor Hugh Carey signed a law that may greatly simplify and clarify apartment leases. Popularly known as the *plain English law,* it is contained in section 5-701 of the state's General Obligations Law. The plain English law applies to every written apartment lease (e.g., printed form leases) entered into after June 1, 1978. Under the law, these leases must be written in nontechnical language and in a clear and coherent manner, using words with common everyday meanings. The leases must also be divided into appropriate sections, which are properly captioned.

The law does not go beyond these general guidelines. It offers no definition of nontechnical language or examples of words with common everyday meanings. Presumably, the legalese in which leases have always been written will be replaced by much simpler terms. (For example, "the demised premises" will become "the apartment.") The final arbiters of this transformation will be New York judges. They will have to decide on a case-by-case basis whether particular leases abide by the plain English law.

If a landlord violates the new law, he can be held liable for any loss that a tenant suffers as a result of the violation. However, the amount of the loss will probably be difficult to establish; it will simply be too speculative a matter for a tenant to prove that a loss of a particular magnitude resulted from the existence of certain technical language in his lease. The law does, however, provide a penalty of fifty dollars whenever a violation occurs. Indeed, a group of tenants can take advantage of this penalty provision, because the law provides for a penalty of up to ten thousand dollars in any class action (i.e., a lawsuit brought by a group of tenants against their landlord).

The penalty provisions will not be enforced against a landlord who has attempted in good faith to comply with the plain English law. Thus, if a landlord has employed an attorney to simplify a lease (assuming attorneys are capable of such reverse magic!) or has used a form lease specially designed to meet the requirements of the new law, he may have a good defense in any lawsuit brought to collect penalties.

The plain English law can't be used as a defense by a tenant. If a landlord sues to enforce a lease or for breach of a lease, the tenant can't defend himself on the grounds that the lease violates the plain English law.

A lease that violates the plain English law is by no means void. It remains valid and enforceable, even though the landlord may be liable for damages and penalties.

It is too early to predict the total effect of this new law. Undoubtedly, though, the printers of standard form leases will be selling a new series of much more intelligible leases to landlords for use after June 1, 1978. And organized tenant groups may bring class actions to help speed the elimination of all legalistic gobbledygook from leases. Once leases become comprehensible, some landlords may actually be too ashamed to state in plain English the more outrageously one-sided clauses now common to most leases. If so, the plain English law could result in fairer, as well as clearer, leases.

THE UNCONSCIONABILITY LAW

For years landlords had tenants over a barrel when it came to signing leases. The parties rarely if ever met in a setting where free bargaining was possible. The landlord was invariably in control of a scarce commodity—housing—and unless the prospective tenant wanted to risk winding up out in the cold, he was in no position to start haggling over undesirable lease terms. Even if the tenant was prepared to shop around, he usually had little time in which to do it; often, his current lease was due to expire, so new arrangements had to be finalized—whatever the terms.

Besides being in a superior bargaining position, the landlord possessed superior knowledge and resources. These latter advantages became painfully evident to the prospective tenant when he was presented with a ten-thousand-word form lease covered with fine print and written in legalistic boilerplate language.

"The lessees in situations such as this," observed Judge Edwin Kassoff in 1972, "are usually occasional customers, not acquainted with the carefully drafted legal terms set forth in such printed form leases. The landlord and his agents, assisted by expert legal counsel, carefully draft the lease in language designed solely for the landlord's protection. When the landlord presents the lease to the lessee for acceptance and execution he is usually fully cognizant of the fact that the other party has not read or bargained for many of the incidental terms of the contract. The terms of the printed contract are usually nonnegotiable. In most cases the tenant is not represented by counsel." The inevitable result for the tenant was a rotten deal. Like it or not—indeed, understand it or not—the tenant had no choice but to sign a binding legal document that slipped all the aces to the landlord.

Such unfair, one-sided leases offended the judicial conscience of many New York judges. They found it unconscionable—that is, unfair and unjust—that a landlord should be able to use his superior resources and bargaining position to ensnare an unwitting tenant in a legal trap. Until recently, however, concerned judges could only improvise legal arguments as to why a tenant should be relieved from the onerous provisions in his lease.

On July 26, 1976, Governor Hugh Carey signed a law that specifically empowers New York courts to pass judgment on whether a lease is unconscionable. This new *unconscionability law* is section 235-c of the state's Real Property Law, and it applies to all leases, regardless of when they were executed. Basically, section 235-c establishes the legal grounds of unconscionability as a shield that tenants can raise in any landlord-tenant case. Whenever a tenant claims—or a judge decides on his own—that a lease is unconscionable, in whole or in part, the judge will allow both sides to present evidence regarding the setting, purpose, and effect of the disputed lease provision. Based upon this evidence and his sense of fair dealing, the judge will determine whether the lease is unconscionable.

Section 235-c authorizes three basic forms of relief if the judge finds the lease unconscionable in whole or in part: (1) the judge can refuse to enforce the entire lease; (2) the judge can enforce the remainder of the lease without enforcing the unconscionable provision; (3) the judge can limit the application of the unconscionable provision in order to avoid any unconscionable result. For example, say you've successfully defended yourself in an eviction action by proving that the lease provision under which the landlord sought to evict you is unconscionable. By way of relief, the judge could simply refuse to order your eviction, thereby severely restricting the unconscionable provision of your lease.

Obviously, the pivotal aspect in the operation of the new law is the concept of *unconscionability*. This concept is not defined in section 235-c, leaving judges free to exercise their discretion. So far there have not been many reported cases that indicate the ways in which judges will use the new law. However, a look at these cases—as well as some older ones in which judges tried to develop a doctrine of unconscionability prior to the enactment of section 235-c—will give some indication of the effect that the new law is likely to have on landlord-tenant relations.

• *Lockout* In a 1977 case, *Pine Hill Associates* v. *Malveaux,* the tenant fell two months behind in his rent payments. One day while the tenant was not home, the landlord changed the lock on the apartment; when the tenant returned, the landlord refused to let him reenter. The landlord then sued the tenant for all the rent due on the remainder of the lease ($3,795), plus attorney's fees ($1,000), plus redecorating and rerental expenses ($525). The tenant claimed that the landlord had no case because the lockout constituted an unlawful eviction and therefore relieved the tenant of all further obligations under the lease.

In pressing his case, the landlord relied upon a particularly one-sided clause in the lease. The clause provided that "after a default by the tenant in the payment of rent, the landlord may 'immediately' or [at] any time thereafter reenter the demised premises and remove all persons and property thereupon, either by summary dispossess proceedings, or by any suitable action or proceeding at law, or by 'force or otherwise,' without being liable for indictment, prosecution or damages therefor." Translation of this tooth-busting legalese yields the following: the landlord had the right to enter the apartment, without any notice, if the tenant was even one minute late with the rent; further, the landlord could expel the tenant and his belongings either through a court proceeding or by physical force; and to top it all off, the landlord could not be held liable to the tenant even if the landlord's own bookkeeping error accounted for the apparent rent deficiency.

Did this clause authorize the landlord to bypass eviction proceedings and lock the tenant out? The court said no: "This court is of the opinion that orderly procedure and preservation of the peace require that actual possession shall not be disturbed except by legal process. The fact that the lease by its terms might sanction this type of activity by the landlord is of no consequence, as the court finds the . . . lease provision unconscionable and unenforceable . . . pursuant to . . . section 235-c." So, the landlord's lockout constituted an illegal eviction and his claims against the tenant were dismissed. What's more, the court ruled that the tenant was entitled to collect damages (money) from the landlord because of the illegal eviction. Since the lease provision was unenforceable, it did not shield the landlord from liability for taking the law into his own hands.

• *Breaking a lease* In a 1976 case, *Lefrak* v. *Lambert,* the tenants moved out of their apartment before their lease expired. Seventeen months elapsed during which the lease was still running and the apartment remained vacant (the landlord apparently made very little effort to find a new tenant). After the apartment was finally rerented, the landlord sued the tenants for all the rent due while the apartment had been vacant.

The lease provided that in situations of abandonment by the tenant, the landlord was under no obligation to rerent the empty apartment, nor even to try to rerent it, in an effort to cut his losses. The court concluded that this provision "is so unconscionable on its face that even without the recently enacted statute [section 235-c], this court would have ruled it unenforceable."

• *Attorney's fees* In *Weidman* v. *Tomaselli* (decided just before enactment of section 235-c), the landlord tried to collect fixed attorney's fees from the tenant whenever court proceedings were instituted. Virtually anytime the landlord's attorney sneezed, the tenant was bound to pay one hundred dollars under the following lease provision: "Notwithstanding any provision of this agreement to the contrary, in the event that the tenant defaults with respect to any of the covenants of this lease, the tenant agrees to pay forthwith as additional rent to the landlord

$100 attorney's fees, plus court costs and disbursements, in . . . connection with any action or proceeding instituted by the landlord against the tenant by reason of such default; said amount shall be due and payable upon the commencement of any proceedings."

Talk about oppressive clauses! This one automatically exacted a hundred-dollar penalty from the tenant whenever the landlord instituted legal proceedings—regardless of whether the landlord ultimately won or lost. The court refused to enforce this unconscionable lease provision.

• *Landlord's liability for lack of services* Form leases that list the building services to be supplied by the landlord often seek to insulate the landlord from any liability for interruption in these services (e.g., lack of hot water or lack of elevator service). Thus, the list of services may conclude: "Interruption or curtailment of any service or services shall not constitute or be deemed to be an eviction by the landlord, in whole or in part, actual or constructive, nor entitle the tenant to any compensation or to any diminution or abatement of rent, nor subject the landlord to any liability for damages or otherwise." The lawyer behind this legalese is being really cute—he's eliminating any means for the tenant who is deprived of services to abandon his apartment or to get his rent reduced or even to sue the landlord for damages.

At least, that's what the legal draftsman thought he was accomplishing through this clause. In two cases decided before the enactment of section 235-c—*Harwood* v. *Lincoln Square Apartments,* and *Groner* v. *Lakeview Management Corporation*—courts ruled that the clause was unconscionable. (Indeed, one judge labeled the clause a "classic example of unconscionability.") In both cases, tenants won the right to sue their landlords for damages based upon interruptions in essential services.

• *Prohibition against dogs* A heartwarming 1974 case, *Belmar Realty Corporation* v. *Brown,* demonstrates how handy the concept of unconscionability can become when a judge really wants to decide a case in favor of a tenant but has very little to go on. The tenant kept a dog named "Little Jim" in his apartment, without getting the landlord's permission. Little Jim was well behaved and was well liked by the other tenants, and he never dirtied up the apartment building. Nevertheless, the landlord sought to evict the tenant for violating this lease provision: "No animals of any kind shall be kept or harbored in the demised premises unless the same in each instance be expressly permitted in writing by the landlord, and such consent, if given, shall be revocable by the landlord at any time."

Since the tenant had never obtained the landlord's consent, he had violated the clause. What's more, in 1973 New York's highest court, the Court of Appeals, had decided a case (*Pollack* v. *J. A. Green Construction Corporation*) that was highly adverse to tenants who had pets. In essence, the Court of Appeals had ruled that the strict prohibition against pets that is found in many leases is enforceable—by eviction if necessary.

But where there's a will there's a way, and the judge in the *Belmar Realty* case was obviously determined to avoid throwing Little Jim and his master out on the street. The judge got around the Court of Appeals case because he felt that it involved a flat prohibition against pets as opposed to a provision allowing the landlord to consent to pets and later revoke that consent if he so chose. Referring to this latter type of clause, the court ruled: "This court finds [the clause] requiring consent expressly in writing but permitting the landlord to revoke . . . consent, once given, at any time thereafter, to be unconscionable in view of the special relationship of landlord and tenant under the law and [in view of] man's unique relationship to man's best friend. The court notes that the revocability clause is absolute and no reason or cause need be given by the landlord before revoking the prior consent. . . .

" 'Little Jim' the mongrel dog in question is one of the more than 25 million dogs who live in the United States. They have earned man's love and respect for their faithfulness and devotion. . . . A dog and master once attached to each other develop a bond that is not easily broken. . . . It would be unconscionable to place in the hands of a landlord a power that may be used arbitrarily and capriciously to the detriment of a tenant who harbors an animal grown attached to him."

From these examples we get some idea of the ways in which judges are likely to apply the concept of unconscionability under the new statute. Virtually any unfair lease provision might be declared unconscionable. Indeed, tenants are likely to raise section 235-c, almost as a matter of course, whenever an unfair lease provision comes into issue.

If there is any guiding principle in the application of section 235-c, it would seem to be the prevention of oppression and unfair surprise. Leases that arrogate to the landlord unrestrained rights and arbitrary powers, or insulate him from legal responsibility, will have difficulty passing muster under section 235-c. If tenants regularly invoke section 235-c, and judges apply it liberally, the once-ironclad standard form lease may wind up looking like legal swiss cheese.

LOOPHOLES AND BOILERPLATE

If you've ever whiled away a winter's eve curled up before the fire, reading your lease, you know that the document is of, by, and for landlords. It's hammered together out of boilerplate clauses—all designed to protect the landlord's interests. Despite the determined draftsmanship of generations of landlords' lawyers, however, the standard printed lease is not ironclad. Let's run down some typical lease provisions to see what's really effective boilerplate and where the loopholes lie.

• *As is* Some leases state that you're renting the apartment "as is." Translated freely, "as is" usually means that the apartment needs a lot of repairs but the landlord doesn't intend to lift a finger, so if you want the place badly enough, you'll just have to suffer along with it or do the work yourself. In all likelihood, such a provision is void and, therefore, not binding on a tenant. Under the state's new *warranty of habitability law,* your apartment must be maintained in habitable condition by the landlord (see page 171). The law specifically provides that any agreement you might make to the contrary is automatically void; an "as is" or similar clause would seem to fall squarely under the new law.

• *Attorney's fees* The typical lease says that you have to pay attorney's fees incurred by the landlord whenever he has to bring an action against you for failure to perform some provision of the lease (for example, if you don't pay the rent and the landlord sues you). Although such a provision is enforceable, state law turns the tables on your landlord. If your lease allows your landlord to recover his attorney's fees, then, under section 234 of the state's Real Property Law, you automatically get the same right, even though the lease doesn't say so. In other words, you can recover your attorney's fees from your landlord if the fees were incurred as a result of the landlord's failure to perform some obligaton of his under the lease.

In a 1972 case the landlord failed to return the tenant's security deposit of $550. The tenant sued the landlord for this violation of the lease, seeking not only his deposit but also $250 for attorney's fees. The court ruled that the tenant was entitled to recover both, because the lease had provided for the landlord's recovery of attorney's fees in any action brought against the tenant.

Under section 234 of the Real Property Law, the tenant can also recover his attorney's fees if he successfully defends himself in an action brought by the landlord. In a 1976 case the landlord sued the tenant for nonpayment of rent. The tenant was put to the expense of hiring a lawyer to file an answer; attached to the answer was a photocopy of the tenant's canceled rent check. After receiving this rather convincing answer, the landlord quietly dropped his case. The court awarded the tenant fifty dollars for attorney's fees, because the lease would have given attorney's fees to the landlord if he had not lost.

Assuming that you do acquire the right to attorney's fees under section 234 because your landlord has already grabbed this right in the lease, your right cannot be taken away. Section 234 specifically provides that any waiver of your right to attorney's fees—say, in some lease provision—is void.

• *Children* If you run into a really nasty landlord, or just one who demands total peace and quiet, your lease may provide that during your tenancy you agree not to have children. Disregard this clause. Not only is it unenforceable, it constitutes a misdemeanor. So, if your landlord threatens to enforce the clause, tell him politely that if he agrees to forget the clause, you won't report him to the district attorney.

• *Counterclaims and setoffs* If a tenant withholds payment

of rent and the landlord wants to take the tenant to court swiftly and expeditiously, it's in the landlord's interest to steamroll the tenant, without facing any arguments about lack of services or other grounds that might justify the withholding of rent. So, many leases state that if the landlord brings a nonpayment proceeding, the tenant agrees not to raise any counterclaims against the landlord or to seek any setoff (i.e., deduction) from the rent due.

Although some courts have enforced this type of heavy-handed clause against tenants, other courts have more recently refused to do so. When a tenant has withheld rent because of lack of repairs or essential services, he should be allowed to raise these issues in the ensuing nonpayment proceeding. To hold otherwise is to take the teeth out of laws that are designed to assure that landlords provide maintenance and repairs. Besides, a clause that sandbags counterclaims and setoffs may not pass muster under the state's new unconscionability law.

• *Interruption in building services* Most landlords insist on having their cake and eating yours too. So, they employ a lease clause that requires you to continue paying full rent even if full services aren't being provided. Usually this provision is slipped in right after a list of all the services that the landlord agrees to provide (heat, hot water, elevator, etc.). The provision states that interruption or curtailment of any of these services will not entitle you to any compensation or abatement in rent. In other words, the landlord wants you to pay for what you don't receive.

Courts rightfully take a dim view of such gross overreaching. Recently, courts have held that this type of lease provision is unenforceable. Tenants are not required to pay for services that are promised but are not delivered. Besides, the state's new warranty of habitability law requires a landlord to maintain your apartment in fit condition. Thus, it is illegal for the landlord to deprive you of essential services and make you pay for them nonetheless.

Another variation of the interruption-in-service clause seeks to protect the landlord in case labor strikes prevent him from providing building services. This clause got a legal workout following the May 1976 strike by the building employees' union (local 32-B). A number of irate New Yorkers withheld their rent and sought rent abatements based upon the deprivation of building-wide services during the strike. In one such case, *Goldner v. Doknovitch,* the landlord argued that no rent abatement could be granted because the interruption-in-service clause specifically covered strike situations. The court rejected this argument. Allowing the landlord to get off scot-free, after the tenants had suffered through a long strike without adequate building personnel, would have been contrary to the warranty of habitability law. So, the tenants won rent abatements despite the contrary provision in their leases.

• *Jury trial waiver* The Seventh Amendment to the Constitution guarantees you the right to trial by jury, but few landlords do. Invariably, form leases contain a clause in which you and the landlord "agree" to waive (that's legalese for "give up") the right to trial by jury. For example: "It is mutually agreed by and between Landlord and Tenant that the respective parties hereto shall and they hereby do waive trial by jury in any action, proceeding or counterclaim brought by either of the parties hereto against the other on any matters whatsoever arising out of or in any way connected with his lease, the Tenant's use or occupancy of said premises, and/or any claim of injury or damage."

The landlord's reason for forcing you to throw away your constitutional right is obvious. In all likelihood, many jurors will also be tenants. What landlord wants to have a jury decide questions like whether you should be evicted or whether you were justified in withholding your rent?

Is the jury-waiver clause valid? Unfortunately, yes, although there are some important exceptions. Generally, New York courts will honor the waiver and enforce it, as long as the tenant waived his right knowingly, intelligently, and voluntarily. The fact that you didn't read the lease before signing it, or couldn't understand the lease if you did read it, is no excuse. Nor is the fact that the lease was offered to you on a take-it-or-leave-it basis sufficient to make your signing of the lease involuntary. As yet there is no requirement that, before you sign, the landlord must call to your attention the valuable right you're waiving.

The waiver of the constitutional right to trial by jury is an ideal area for New York judges to start testing out the state's new unconscionability law. Judges who have always found the jury waiver repugnant now have a legal peg to hang their conscience on if they decide to shoot down a jury-waiver clause.

The state legislature has already punched one important loophole in the jury-waiver clause. Section 259-c of the state's Real Property Law invalidates the jury-waiver clause in any lawsuit between landlord and tenant involving personal injury or property damage. (Section 259-c applies only to leases executed after July 2, 1965.) New York courts differ on the scope of section 259-c. It's given a narrow application in the state's second judicial department, which covers Brooklyn, Queens, and Staten Island. There, the courts insist that in order for section 259-c to apply, the lawsuit not only must concern personal injury or property damage but must arise out of the so-called law of negligence. Negligence is the area of law under which people, including landlords, may be forced to pay damages for the consequences of their carelessness.

For instance, say you sue your landlord because he neglected to repair a leak in your apartment, and, as a result, your apartment was flooded and you suffered extensive property damage. In such a lawsuit, your waiver of the right to a jury trial would be void under section 259-c. Suppose, however, that your landlord sued you for violating your lease by leaving your apartment dirty or in a state of disrepair. Here, second-department courts would not apply section 259-c to your jury waiver. You would not be entitled to a jury trial, because the lawsuit, although admittedly involving property damage, arose out of a breach of contract (i.e., the lease), rather than out of negligence.

Pretty technical, eh? Things are much more straightforward in the first judicial department, which covers Manhattan and the Bronx. There, as long as the lawsuit involves personal injury or property damage, a jury-waiver clause will be void under section 259-c—regardless of whether the action is based on a claim of negligence.

For example, a landlord sued a tenant for three thousand dollars. The landlord alleged that the tenant had damaged the building by installing a security gate, which was prohibited by the lease. The tenant wanted a jury to hear the case, and the court granted his request, despite a jury-waiver clause in the lease. Since the lawsuit was for property damage, the waiver clause was void under section 259-c—even though a lease violation, rather than an act of negligence, was the issue at stake.

• *Landlord's liability for personal injury or property loss* Many leases contain a so-called exculpatory clause. The purpose of this clause is to protect the landlord from liability if his carelessness causes harm to a tenant or to his property. If your lease contains such a clause, don't worry. All such clauses are void. Section 5-321 of the state's General Obligations Law states that every provision in a lease "exempting the lessor from liability for damages for injuries to person or property caused by or resulting from the negligence of the lessor, his agents, servants or employees, in the operation and maintenance of the demised premises shall be . . . void . . . and wholly unenforceable." So, even if your lease has an exculpatory clause, you can still sue your landlord for negligence.

• *Locks* A lease prohibition against the tenant installing his own lock in his apartment door is void; similarly, a provision charging the tenant money for the privilege of installing his own lock is void (see page 63).

• *Objectionable or improper conduct* Here's a honey of a lease provision: the landlord claims the right to terminate your tenancy if he "deems objectionable or improper" any of your conduct. If this clause were worth the paper it's written on, you'd have to tiptoe on eggshells, never knowing when the landlord might deem your conduct objectionable. Fortunately, courts won't allow landlords to play God, regardless of what your lease says (see pages 34–39).

• *Organized tenant action* A really uptight landlord might try to ensure that you'll be a Caspar Milquetoast whenever other tenants start talking about organizing. He'll slip a clause into your lease under which you agree not to join any tenant organization or participate in any type of rent-strike action. Such an oppressive restriction is clearly illegal. New York law bars a landlord from interfering with your right to participate fully in the lawful activities of a tenant organization (see Appendix C). One such lawful activity is a proper rent strike, and any lease provision that says you can't join in is void under state law (see page 218).

• *Pets* Here, Benji! Here, Morris! All you furry New Yorkers gather round; and bring the master of your apartment with you. Unfortunately, there's bad news. In 1973 the highest court in New York State, the Court of Appeals (of which there is, as yet, no canine or feline member), decided *Pollack* v. *J. A. Green Construction Corporation,* a case that's about as much fun as being left alone in an apartment with a bowl of dry pet food.

Basically, the *Pollack* case says that a lease prohibition against keeping pets in an apartment is reasonable and enforceable. Violation of this prohibition constitutes grounds for eviction. Further, the fact that the landlord has, in the past, accepted rent from the tenant without objecting to the tenant's pet does not necessarily mean that the landlord is prevented from objecting in the future. This is so because most leases, like the one enforced in *Pollack,* contain a "no waiver" clause. Under such a clause, the landlord may waive his right to insist upon the tenant's compliance with the lease, *but only if he does so in writing;* actions alone don't constitute a waiver.

Because of the *Pollack* case, tenants who have pets would be well advised to read their leases carefully before signing. If there is a provision that clearly and unequivocally prohibits pets, don't plan on sneaking yours in with you; you may be forced to get rid of the pet or face eviction. If there's a discrepancy between what the lease says and what some rental agent promises you, believe the lease.

It's conceivable that some courts may find that certain lease prohibitions against pets violate the new unconscionability law (passed three years after the *Pollack* case). There has been at least one case—*Belmar Realty*—that suggests that such an application of the new law might be possible (see page 22).

• *Rent* Needless to say, one of the first things that a lease states is the amount of rent that you will pay. In the case of uncontrolled apartments, the sky's the limit. If, however, your apartment is rent controlled or rent stabilized, the *law*'s the limit: the law sets maximum rents. If the rent specified in your lease exceeds the legal maximum, you're paying too much rent.

(See chapters 7 and 9 to determine what your maximum rent should be.)

• *Repairs to be made by tenant* Some leases provide that the tenant must make any repairs in his apartment that are necessitated by his misuse or neglect. Such provisions are of questionable legality. The city's Housing Maintenance Code clearly imposes the duty to repair upon the landlord, even in situations where the tenant's misuse or neglect created the need for repairs (see page 171).

• *Security deposit* Virtually every lease provides for the payment of a security deposit by the tenant. (A security deposit is the lump sum that you pay a landlord when you move into an apartment.) The deposit is like a ransom. It protects the landlord from losing money if you skip out on an unexpired lease or damage the apartment. You will get the security money back when you leave only if you have lived up to the terms of the lease and have not damaged the apartment.

In principle, the security deposit makes sense. In practice, it has been a windfall for landlords. They have taken one or two months' rent from every tenant as security and have that money for years, returning it only when the tenant leaves. Sometimes the money sat in a bank, piling up interest for the landlord; in other instances, the landlord would spend it on his building—or for his personal use.

In 1970, however, the state legislature blew the whistle on landlords who played fast and loose with tenants' security money. Now, when you pay a security deposit, your landlord must place the money in a separate bank account *and must inform you of the name of the bank.* He cannot mingle your money with his own, nor can he spend your money. He must hold it in trust for you. This rule applies to all landlords.

In addition, if your building has at least six apartments, your landlord must add to your security deposit the interest that it earns. And he must pay you all accrued interest when the security money is returned to you. *If a clause in your lease says the landlord can keep the interest, that clause is void.* The landlord is, however, permitted to keep 1 percent of the interest, as payment for managing your money.

If you are a rent-controlled tenant, your landlord is not permitted to demand more than one month's rent as security. If your landlord has more, you have the right to demand that he return the excess. If he refuses, ask your district rent office for two copies of form A-60 (Tenant's Statement of Violations); complete the forms and return them to your district rent office.

The maximum amount of security required from rent-stabilized tenants is, in general, one month's rent. However, in those rare cases in which a landlord was holding two months' security when an apartment became rent stabilized, the landlord is permitted to retain the two months' security, but only for the duration of the lease that was in effect when the apartment became rent stabilized and for renewals of that lease. However, when the apartment is vacated and a new tenant moves in, the landlord is not permitted to seek more than one month's security.

• *Use of apartment as a private dwelling by tenant and his family* A lease usually begins by describing the apartment and stating that it is to be occupied as a strictly private dwelling by the tenant and his immediate family only. While such a limitation is pretty solid boilerplate, there are, nevertheless, some loopholes in it. Chapter 6 explains how guests or others outside the tenant's immediate family may, under certain circumstances, live in the apartment despite a contrary provision in the lease.

What about use of the apartment for something other than a private dwelling? Certainly, the tenant shouldn't plan on running a commercial business in the apartment. Any enterprise that generates a lot of traffic (e.g., clients, customers) is not likely to be tolerated. On the other hand, suppose the tenant does live in the apartment but also uses it to practice a musical instrument or to write or paint for a living. It's doubtful that such use will cause the apartment to be considered something other than a private dwelling.

In a Brooklyn case, *Diament* v. *Isaacs,* the tenant ran a daycare center in her apartment, even though the lease provided that the apartment was "to be occupied as a strictly private dwelling . . . by said tenant and the tenant's immediate family." You would probably agree that a daycare center is not a ''strictly private dwelling''; and daycare children are not members of the tenant's ''immediate family.'' Clearly, the landlord thought so, because he instituted an eviction proceeding. Although the judge conceded that there had been a technical violation of the lease, the violation was not substantial enough to warrant an eviction. So, there is some flexibility when it comes to interpreting use-and-occupancy clauses.

CHAPTER 3

The Right to Enjoy Yourself

ARE YOU AN OBJECTIONABLE TENANT?

When you were a child, your parents told you to behave. At school, your teachers took over. Then, maybe, there were camp counselors and later army sergeants. Well, now you've got a landlord to deal with. And the lease he had you sign probably says that he can get rid of you if he decides you're an "objectionable" tenant. Don't take the lease too seriously, though—most judges don't. You see, you have the right to enjoy your own lifestyle, do your own thing, without a hassle from the landlord.

This idea has been summed up quite clearly in *Moss* v. *Hirshtritt*. Judge Hilda Schwartz ruled: "A landlord may not constitute himself a censor of the personal tastes, choice of friends or preferences in interior decoration of his tenant, unless these [inflict] serious and substantial injury upon the landlord." Judge Schwartz was faced with a curious dispute over a four-room rent-controlled apartment at 337 East Eighty-eighth Street in Manhattan. The landlord had saved up a grab bag of petty gripes, which he finally unloaded in one large, futile attempt to evict the tenant.

First, he charged violation of the lease provision that limited occupancy to the tenant and his immediate family. The basis for this charge was deemed insubstantial. Apparently, on one occasion the tenant had had some visitors, one of whom was a young man with—of all things—a beard! Also, the super testified, sometimes a guest of the tenant actually stayed overnight. (Horrors!)

Next, the landlord complained about some photographic supplies, tripods, lights, and a dark windowshade that the tenant had installed. In court the landlord displayed a business card with the tenant's name, address, phone number, and the word *photography*. The landlord protested that a commercial photography studio was being illegally maintained in the apartment.

The tenant admitted that he was a professional photographer and did have in the apartment an enlarger, a tripod, three small cameras, some trays, and some chemicals. But he explained that the equipment was all for his hobby, not for his actual profession. His work as a freelance photographer and film editor was conducted at a separate office and the home number on his business cards was simply to allow calls after business hours.

Still, the landlord pressed his attack. The lease forbade exposing any sign or advertisement, and the landlord had removed from the tenant's mailbox a small adhesive strip that read "Hirsch Enterprises." According to the tenant, this sign and another one, which was on his apartment door, were intended solely as a prank to amuse his friends. (Anyway, both signs had been removed before the eviction action began.)

Finally, the landlord had a few things to say about the tenant's homemade furniture—a sofa and two tables constructed from boards and boxes. One of the tables was suspended by a chain that hung from the ceiling. To add a unique touch, the tenant had decorated his walls with antique washboards.

The whole case smacked of the proverbial tempest in a teapot. All the evidence seemed to boil down to one, unstated premise: the landlord was not particularly fond of the tenant's whole lifestyle. But mere disapproval was not—and is not—legal grounds for eviction. Although there had been a few technical violations of the lease, they were not substantial. Judge Schwartz denied the eviction.

In this day of increasing concern for senior citizens, the lifestyle of elderly tenants is entitled to as much respect as that of young tenants. Recently Judge Nat Hentel stood up for an elderly tenant in *Truncali* v. *Kusstatscher*. A landlord was trying to evict an eighty-eight-year-old woman, alleging that she had assaulted him, used profanity, left on an unlit gas burner, accumulated garbage in her apartment, and kept a cat that had unhygienic habits. According to the landlord, she was a nuisance.

The old woman was hard of hearing and enfeebled. She lived alone with her cat. In Judge Hentel's words: "She has no family and other than two local friends who look in on her regularly she lives the unrelentingly lonely and grinding life of an elderly person who has outlived family, friends, and usefulness in a cold society which appraises usefulness on whether or not an individual still has something to give. Apparently, once a person has been drained dry of good looks, nimble mind, clear eye and skin, the resultant dregs are ready to be cast upon the scrap heaps of homes for the aged or other institutional devices for getting rid of unuseful people."

In reviewing the evidence, Judge Hentel found that only one of the landlord's charges had been substantiated: apparently the tenant had left on an unlit gas burner on one occasion. However, this single instance fell far short of proving that she was objectionable enough to warrant eviction.

"To sustain the charge of nuisance," Judge Hentel explained, "or that the tenant is objectionable, a landlord must show a course of conduct over a period of time performed by the tenant, and which poses a threat to the safety, health, and peaceful enjoyment of the premises by others lawfully using the premises. As a general rule, to make a tenancy objectionable, the use of the property by the tenant must be unwarranted, unreasonable, or unlawful, to the annoyance, inconvenience, discomfort, or damage of another. . . . An isolated instance of objectionable conduct will be insufficient, as a general rule, to warrant the removal of a tenant as objectionable. . . .

"This court is convinced that the tenant should not be torn from the surroundings familiar to her for the past thirty-four years. Certainly there is no other comfortable place she could go at a more reasonable rent. [She paid sixty dollars a month.] Her life, which is just as precious to her as is life to the landlord, can best be preserved and extended by insuring that she be allowed to live her life out peacefully and with dignity in familiar surroundings; and that she be permitted to continue to do and fend for herself as long as she possibly can. The ability of the elderly to live independently is what keeps their human machinery going. I find that the tenant is not a nuisance merely because of the burden of her many years."

Judge Hentel made an important point when he warned that an "isolated instance of objectionable conduct" does not make a tenant objectionable. The law does not require a tenant to adjust his lifestyle according to the personal likes and dislikes of his landlord. And tenants are entitled to falter in their personal lives without being damned by some avenging landlord.

This point was dramatically upheld by the state supreme court in a novel 1946 case. The act in question was an attempted suicide. Apparently, the tenant became severely depressed after she had given birth. In an attempt to asphyxiate herself, she turned on the gas in her kitchen. Medical treatment led to full recovery, and the prognosis was that there would be no recurrence.

Nevertheless, the landlord delicately launched an eviction proceeding. He charged that the woman had, by her conduct, created a nuisance. But the judge thought otherwise: " 'Things merely disagreeable, which displease the eye, or offend the taste, or shock an oversensitive or fastidious nature, no matter how irritating or unpleasant, are not nuisances.' . . . An isolated instance of an attempt at self-destruction cannot be classified as a nuisance even though it might have endangered others. Another situation would be presented if it was shown that the tenant was continuously attempting suicide through means which might endanger the life and property of others or interfere with their comfort and enjoyment; but I do not see that a single attempt, in a moment of despondency, can be held to be a nuisance." So there were no grounds for eviction.

The reasoning in this decision applies equally to less drastic situations. For example, New York courts have decided that a single conviction for disorderly conduct does not make a tenant a nuisance. Neither does a single tantrum during which a tenant kicked and scratched the elevator doors. And in another case, a tenant who fought with several of his neighbors all in one day was deemed not a nuisance. The moral seems to be: you're entitled to one "bad day."

Although a judge may be willing to overlook one bad day, or one conviction for disorderly conduct, or even an attempted suicide, eventually a tenant may build up quite a record and wind up out in the street. Not so long ago in Nassau County, an eight-year-old vandal succeeded in making a genuine nuisance of himself. His parents' lease contained a typical warning: "If Landlord or Landlord's agents shall deem objectionable or improper any conduct on the part of Tenant . . . Landlord may . . . give to Tenant three days' notice of intention to end the term of this lease." Which is precisely what the landlord did, because the eight-year-old boy was wrecking the building.

One day he threw a brick through the plate-glass window of the lobby. He defaced the lobby walls with snow and mud, and in the basement he broke six light bulbs with an umbrella. On three or four occasions he let the shower overflow and leak into the luncheonette on the floor below.

The judge observed that one or two of these mishaps might have been regarded as boyish pranks. But when the misconduct persisted to the point of wanton vandalism, and the parents seemed incapable or unwilling to control their child, then the landlord was entitled to curb the objectionable behavior. An eviction was granted. So, parents, be vigilant, lest your children take the roof from over your heads!

Perhaps the most classic example of objectionable conduct is the famous case of the eviction of the "pigeon lady." For more than a quarter of a century she had lived in a large building on Manhattan's West Side. Every day she fed pigeons from her apartment window—not just once a day, but four or five times, starting at five-thirty in the morning. These feedings consisted of more than a few handfuls of corn or crusts of bread. The pigeon lady was the Julia Child of birdland. She treated her airborne gourmets to twenty-five or thirty pounds of feed daily! Imagine the flapping, squawking storm that descended four or five times a day as more than a hundred pigeons gorged themselves outside her window. A sleepless opera singer who lived next door complained that even earplugs were no defense against the feathery sorties.

Needless to say, the pigeons left a veritable monument of excretion, which, blown about by the wind, threatened neighbors with parrot fever, histoplasmosis, encephalitis, and meningitis. In addition, the combination of pigeon droppings and leftovers exuded a stench that was indescribable.

The pigeon lady kept her door locked to complaining neighbors. Even representatives of the health department were refused admittance. When the landlord telephoned, the pigeon lady threatened to report him to the ASPCA. Finally, the police got into the apartment, where they discovered pigeons inside. One of the birds walked around behind an officer, and the pigeon lady called to it with the name "Bravo"!

From all the evidence, the judge had little trouble concluding that the pigeon lady was creating a nuisance. She had interfered substantially with the health, safety, and comfort of the other tenants. An immediate eviction was fully justified.

PRIVACY AND LOVE

Have you ever had a cozy little candlelit supper interrupted by an unexpected knock at the door and a brusque: "This is the landlord. I want to check out a few things in your apartment"? Can a landlord get away with this kind of meddlesome, unannounced visit anytime he wants to know what's going on in your apartment? Legally, no. In effect, the law hangs a sign on your door that reads: NO TRESPASSING: LANDLORD TAKE NOTICE. Your apartment is not Grand Central Station for the landlord or for any of his employees or agents. Only in the case of legitimate inspections, repairs, or emergencies can your privacy be invaded, and even then, the intrusion must be made at reasonable hours and arranged in advance.

Of course, you can't refuse to admit the landlord if he has to make a bona fide inspection or maintenance visit. Under the city's Housing Maintenance Code the "unreasonable refusal to afford access to the dwelling unit to the owner or his agent or employee for the purpose of making repairs or improvements" that are required by law can be grounds for eviction. The point is that the landlord's right to access must be exercised *at a reasonable time and in a reasonable manner*.

What's reasonable? That depends on the circumstances. Generally, you're entitled to notification from the landlord *before* he or his crew shows up at your door. In the case of inspections to determine whether your apartment is in compliance with legal requirements, the landlord is supposed to give you notice of his planned visit at least twenty-four hours in advance. If the landlord needs to get into your apartment to make improvements or repairs required by law, you are entitled to notification one week in advance. All advance notices must be in writing and must state the nature of the improvements or repairs to be made.

Emergencies are another matter. Whenever repairs are needed to prevent property damage or personal injury, the landlord doesn't have to give any notification. Emergencies that demand immediate attention might include a leaking pipe or roof, a stopped-up drain, or a broken ceiling or one that is in dangerous condition.

When an authorized agent or employee of the landlord shows up to make an inspection or repair, technically, he's supposed to show you written authorization from the landlord before entering your apartment.

Barging in at ungodly hours is definitely verboten. Ordinarily, access to your apartment is limited to weekdays, from 9:00 A.M. to 5:00 P.M.; you don't have to admit the landlord at all on weekends and legal holidays. (Of course, forget the time limits if there's a genuine emergency that requires the landlord's immediate access to your apartment.)

Since no one is allowed to intrude upon you at his whim, generally you can enjoy yourself without worrying about having to admit a nosy landlord or super. What you do in the privacy of your apartment is your business, unless you're using your apartment for illegal purposes. Such illegal use, in order to be grounds for eviction, must be habitual and continuous; isolated incidents don't count. So, if a few of your friends drop by and you all get mellow puffing on some funny-smelling cigarettes, you haven't *used* your apartment for illegal purposes. Indeed, the mere fact that you get a visit from the cops one day does not, in and of itself, mean that you are using your apartment for illegal purposes.

You have the right to make love in your apartment. No doubt you take this right for granted, but, as recently as 1971, in

Edwards v. *Roe,* a landlord dragged one of his tenants into Manhattan civil court and tried to evict her for using her apartment for "illicit relations." The tenant, who was unmarried, had been engaging in sexual intercourse with one particular man over a period of several months. She was not a hooker and her conduct was not disorderly.

"The question for decision," announced Judge Irving Younger, "is whether chastity is a prerequisite to maintenance of the landlord-tenant relationship. . . . What I must decide . . . is whether an unmarried female who, in her apartment, privately engages in sexual intercourse thereby subjects herself to eviction."

Judge Younger decided that there had been no illegal use of the apartment. The tenant was not a prostitute, nor was she running a bawdy house. And New York law does not prohibit sexual intercourse carried out in private between unmarried consenting adults.

"So much for illegality," said Judge Younger, turning to the less definite problem of immorality. "With respect to immorality, one should say little precisely because there is so much to say. . . . If the test be personal to me, I hold that, without a showing—and there is none—that she has harmed anyone, [the tenant] has done nothing immoral. And if the test be the response of the 'ordinary' or 'average' man or woman . . . I hold that, given the ethical standards of the day, [the tenant] has done nothing immoral." So, there was no eviction.

STEREOS, PIANOS, AND OTHER NOISES

If you live in a New York City apartment building, you must be getting used to the sounds of neighbors walking over your head, arguing under your feet, playing a stereo to your right, a television on your left, flushing toilets down one wall, and getting steam up another. After all, no New York tenant is an island; in this city you're not even a peninsula. You must learn to live with a certain amount of noise, and you have a right to make some of your own.

Start with what must be the most common noise in New

York: those millions of footsteps New Yorkers make each night back and forth between their televisions and their refrigerators. Have you ever asked yourself whether you have the legal right to walk to your refrigerator during a television commercial? The question sounds absurd, until you check out your lease. While it cannot restrict eating between meals, it probably prohibits making noise that disturbs other tenants. What if the guy downstairs is going nuts listening to you walk back and forth? Suppose he complains to the landlord. Can you be evicted for having feet?

These burning questions were answered recently in a Queens civil court case, *Louisiana Leasing Company* v. *Sokolow*. The Levin family lived below the Sokolow family. The Levins could hear children playing upstairs, even though the Sokolows kept shoes off their children to lessen the noise. Mr. Sokolow often walked back and forth from the refrigerator to the television, and he assumed that his footsteps made nothing more than the everyday level of noise.

Not so, claimed the landlord. He pointed out the Sokolows' lease: "No tenant shall make or permit any disturbing noises in the building by himself, his family, servants, employees, agents, visitors and licensees . . . that will interfere with the rights, comforts or convenience of other tenants." Both the landlord and the Levins felt that this clause had been violated, so the landlord tried to evict the Sokolows.

Moved by this human dilemma, Judge Daniel Fitzpatrick gave voice to the understandable frustration many New Yorkers feel: "The tenants below, the Levins, are a middle-aged couple who go to business each day. They are like many others of our fellow citizens, who daily go forth to brave the vicissitudes of the mainstream of city life. At the end of the toilsome day, like tired fish, they are only too happy to seek out these quiet backwaters of the metropolis to recuperate for the next day's bout with the task of earning a living.

"They have raised their own children and are past the time when the patter of little feet overhead is a welcome sound. They say they love their new apartment and that it is just what they have been looking for and would hate to have to give it up because of the noise from above. . . .

"Mr. Sokolow, one of the upstairs tenants, is reported to

have said, 'This is my home, and no one can tell me what to do in my own home.' This is a prevalent notion that stems from the ancient axiom that a man's home is his castle.

"The difficulty of the situation here is that Mr. Sokolow's castle is directly above the castle of Mr. Levin. That a man's home is his castle is an old Anglo-legal maxim hoary with time and the sanction of frequent repetition. It expressed an age when castles were remote, separated by broad moors, and when an intruder had to force moat and wall to make his presence felt within. The tranquillity of the King's peace, the seclusion of a clandestine romance and the opportunity, like Hamlet, to deliver a soliloquy from the ramparts without fear of neighborly repercussions, were real.

"Times, however, change, and all change is not necessarily progress, as some sage has perceptively reminded us. For in an era of modernity and concentrated living, when high-rise apartment houses have piled castle upon castle for some twenty or more stories in the air, it is extremely difficult to equate these modern counterparts with their drawbridged and turreted ancestors. . . .

"[Today's apartment buildings] contain miles of utility and sanitary piping which convey sound throughout the building with all the gusto of the mammoth organ in the Mormon Tabernacle at Salt Lake City. Also, the prefabricated or frugally plastered walls have their molecules so critically near the separation level that they [pose] almost no barrier at all to alien sounds from neighboring apartments. This often forces one into an embarrassingly auditory intimacy with the surrounding tenants. Such are the hazards of modern apartment house living. . . .

"Weighing the equities in this difficult controversy, the court finds that the Sokolows were there first, with a record as good tenants. The Levins underneath seem to be good tenants also. This was attested to by the superintendent who was called upon to testify. He made the understatement of the year when he said: 'I kept out of the middle of this fight. It's near Christmas and this is no time for me to fight with tenants'—a piece of homely pragmatism which would have gladdened the heart of William James. . . .

"The evidence . . . shows that . . . the . . . Sokolows

were already in a fixed relationship to the landlord. The Levins, on the other hand, were not—their position was a mobile one. They had the opportunity to ascertain what was above them in the event they decided to move in below. They elected to move in and afterwards attempted to correct the condition complained of. Since upon the evidence the overhead noise had been shown to be neither excessive nor deliberate, the court is not constrained to flex its muscles and evict the [Sokolows].''

The Sokolows had not violated the lease provision about making noise. Contrary to the landlord's contention, there was no substantial violation of the lease. (A substantial violation would have been grounds for eviction.) So Judge Fitzpatrick refused to let the landlord evict the Sokolows.

Judge Fitzpatrick's live-and-let-live attitude should make sense to most New Yorkers—except those who get along without television, radio, stereo, and, in some cases, conversation. A tenant is not required to take a vow of silence, regardless of what his lease says. So don't be too worried if neighbors complain about hearing you through the floor or the walls. (They should be satisfied that they can't see you.) Nowadays, courts recognize that the construction of a building can reduce eavesdropping from an art form to a dull routine.

Without a doubt, the majority of noise problems concern the ''food of love''—music—wafting up between the floorboards, creeping under doors, seeping out of vents, and vibrating through New York City's tympanic walls. In general, New York courts give fairly free rein to your right to play music. This judicial forbearance is summed up best in an oft-quoted remark: ''The peace and quiet of a rural estate or the sylvan silence of a mountain lodge cannot be expected in a multiple dwelling.'' A wise city-court judge said this twenty years ago in the case *Twin Elm Management Corporation* v. *Banks*.

The Banks family lived in Queens. Their sixteen-year-old daughter had played the piano since age seven. She was an accomplished concert pianist and had performed in several eastern cities. The Bankses' neighbors, however, were treated to something less than keyboard rhapsodies. They heard plenty of thumping sounds and scales after scales. Apparently, nothing resembled a complete musical composition. For twelve hours a day this practicing crept into the neighbors' ears.

The Bankses' lease permitted piano playing during reasonable hours, but the landlord still attempted to lower the final curtain. He took the Bankses to court, claiming that they were objectionable tenants because their daughter was creating a nuisance. Instead of an encore, the landlord wanted an eviction.

The judge seemed sympathetic: "The court is not unmindful of the fact that continuous piano practicing can become nerve racking, particularly to elderly persons and those with a nervous temperament." Nevertheless, the judge refused to evict the Bankses. "On this record," he reasoned, "I cannot find that the piano-playing was exceptionally loud or noisy or that the piano was used at unreasonable hours. To constitute a nuisance, the use of one's property must be unwarrantable, unreasonable or unlawful [and be] to the annoyance, inconvenience, discomfort or damage of another. Mere annoyance in and of itself does not create a nuisance or make the tenancy of the occupant undesirable. Of necessity, the practice work of a talented pianist would require some finger-exercising on the keyboard together with the playing of musical compositions."

If the Bankses' lease had not permitted any piano practicing, would the judge have reasoned differently and, perhaps, granted an eviction? Most likely not, according to the case of *Douglas L. Elliman & Co., Inc.,* v. *Karlsen.* The Karlsen family lived in Manhattan. Their elder son used to practice playing drums. When the landlord asked him to stop, Mrs. Karlsen wrote to him: "As a mother I must protect my son's interest. Music is not just a passing fancy to him, it is indeed his whole life. My son practices a maximum of one hour per day . . . usually between two and three P.M. If an earlier or later hour would be more convenient for others, we will be happy to cooperate in any way possible." (The Karlsen boy did not practice at all on weekends.)

Unsatisfied with this response, the landlord sought to evict the Karlsens. In court, he argued that drum practice violated the lease. Indeed, the lease did prohibit any practicing—but in a confusing manner: "No tenant shall play . . . any musical instrument . . . between the hours of eleven o'clock P.M. and the following eight o'clock A.M. if the same shall disturb or annoy other occupants of the building. No tenant shall conduct . . . instrumental practice . . . at any time." The last sentence, prohibiting practice, seemed inconsistent with the prior sentence, which allowed musical instruments to be played. The judge resolved this conflict in favor of the Karlsens: if they could play an instrument, they could also practice playing an instrument. So, they were acting reasonably, and within their rights, by allowing their son to practice the drums for one hour each weekday.

Undaunted, the landlord tried another tack. The lease gave him authority to end the tenancy if he "shall deem objectionable or improper any conduct on the part of the Tenant . . . or shall deem Tenant . . . objectionable." Seizing upon this clause, the landlord argued that he could evict the Karlsens as objectionable tenants.

Of course, this vague word, *objectionable,* could have meant practically anything—especially when left to the discretion of the landlord. But the judge was not about to surrender his role as official interpreter. "As a general rule," he declared, "to make a tenant objectionable, his use of the [apartment] must have been unreasonable or unlawful [and] to the annoyance, inconvenience, discomfort or damage of others.

"While the court can sympathize with the [Karlsens'] neighbors who may be annoyed with the sound of the drums . . . that is the price they must pay to live in a city apartment.

"The city is filled with the sounds of life and the living and some of the more civilized sounds are those of children learning to make music. . . . 'Where people indulge their inclination to be gregarious they must not expect the quiet that belongs to solitude.'

"The [Karlsens] have demonstrated a reasonable consideration for the comforts of their neighbors. The court feels reasonably certain that they will exercise their rights with restraint and with due regard to the rights and comforts of others." Clearly, the judge had not been convinced that the Karlsens were objectionable tenants. Therefore, they could not be evicted on that basis.

You should not conclude from the *Twin Elm* and *Karlsen* cases that music-playing tenants are always protected by the law. In September 1972 Judge Bentley Kassal wisely observed: "The sound of a musical instrument is not by definition immune from classification as a 'nuisance' to others; it is the nature, volume and duration of the sound that is important." Judge Kassal had to decide an eviction suit—*O'Connor* v. *Lahm*—brought against a French-horn player who lived in Stuyvesant Town, on Manhattan's East Side. The case led Judge Kassal to draw some important distinctions between various musical instruments.

The Stuyvesant Town musician practiced her French horn every day for several hours. While she thought of her playing as "dark, muted, mellow and veiled," her neighbors had different opinions: "Piercing sound like an auto horn"; "heard it over the radio and vacuum cleaner"; "drives you up the wall"; "makes me so tense I am unable to sleep."

After five months of complaints from other tenants, the landlord brought an eviction action. He claimed that the practicing was a substantial violation of the lease, which provided: "Tenants shall not make or permit any disturbing noises in the buildings or elsewhere . . . that will interfere with the rights, comforts, safety, or convenience of other tenants. . . . Tenants shall not play upon, or permit to be played upon, any musical instrument . . . in such a manner or at such time as may disturb or annoy tenants or other occupants." The issue for Judge Kassal was not whether the horn playing was good or bad but whether it was a nuisance that violated the lease.

Judge Kassal carefully contrasted the case before him with the promusician decisions in the cases of *Twin Elm* (piano) and *Karlsen* (drum): "The situation in *Twin Elm* . . . must . . . be distinguished. There the court found that the piano playing of tenant's daughter was not exceptionally loud or noisy nor [was it conducted] at unreasonable hours. [The judge] concluded that although it may have been an annoyance to some tenants, it was not a 'nuisance.' Tenant's horn practice, however, is more than a mere annoyance and unreasonably discomforts others, not only in its cacophony but in its excessive duration. These elements also distinguish the [horn] playing from the [*Karlsen*] case, where the drums were practiced one hour a day between 2 P.M. and 3 P.M., never on weekends, and did not disturb most of the neighbors."

So the key here is *unreasonableness*. The French-horn practice was an unreasonable interference with the other tenants' comfort. The practicing was a nuisance and a substantial violation of the lease. But Judge Kassal did not issue a warrant of eviction. He withheld that final sanction, providing that the tenant would limit her practicing. On weekdays she could play for one hour between noon and 2:00 P.M. and two hours between 4:00 P.M. and 8:00 P.M. On Saturdays she could play for three hours between noon and 6:00 P.M., and no playing at all was allowed on Sundays.

You can see how Judge Kassal struck a balance between the competing interests before him. This balancing approach is equally suited to noise cases in which music is not the noise at issue. In general, an objectionably loud tenant is one who persists in making too much noise too often. For example, in a 1946 case, the tenant's wife frequently came home drunk early in the morning. Swearing and other noise always followed. The police were summoned on three different nights to break up noisy quarreling. Given these repeated disruptions, the landlord had no difficulty proving that the tenants were a nuisance, and the court granted an eviction. On the other hand, in a 1961 case, the tenants could not be evicted, because all they had done was thrown a noisy housewarming party for twenty guests.

So far we have looked at noisemaking solely within the context of eviction proceedings. Suppose, however, the landlord won't initiate such an action; suppose he won't even attempt to quiet the tenants who are driving you nuts with their noise. What can you do on your own?

The first thing to do is try to have a rational talk with your noisy neighbor. Don't just sit there stewing in your apartment, and don't assume that your neighbor knows that he's causing a disturbance. He may not realize how far his noise carries. So, reason with him and try to settle things amicably.

If friendly persuasion fails, try New York's Finest (call your police precinct and report a noise complaint). The cop who is dispatched to check out your complaint can issue the noisemaker a summons, which is answerable in criminal court. Frequently, a police visit in itself, or the mere threat of calling the precinct, will instill a little self-restraint in an excessively noisy tenant.

A tenant who is victimized by a noisy neighbor can sue that

neighbor or the landlord who failed to quiet the neighbor. The usual approach in a lawsuit against a noisy neighbor is to seek a court-ordered injunction restricting the neighbor's disturbing activities. Just such a case, *Ryan* v. *Steele,* arose in a Manhattan co-op near Fifth Avenue. The trouble began when a tenant, Alfred Steele, embarked upon an ambitious remodeling project. Imagine what the tenant downstairs, Marjorie Ryan, heard: overhead, a stairway was torn down, exterior walls and windows were redesigned, and even the roof was replaced; the laying of parquet floors was yet to come, and that, for Ms. Ryan, would have been an exquisite form of torture rivaling even a dentist's drill.

When it became apparent that the noise would continue for quite some time, Ms. Ryan went to court to enjoin Mr. Steele, the upstairs tenant. The judge set the stage for his decision: "It is beyond dispute," he warned, "that repairs in one apartment may, and if they be extensive do, cause some annoyance to the occupants of nearby apartments. To the extent that this annoyance does not cause serious harm and is of reasonably short duration, a balance of necessities and conveniences ordains that the neighbors are without redress and must accept the situation as one of the penalties of living in that particular type of urban dwelling. However, the annoyance can reach a degree that entitles the sufferer to relief. This relief may take the form of regulating the time of work and manner of performance or even of limiting it."

Was Mr. Steele's work annoying enough to entitle Ms. Ryan to relief? The judge said yes. He ordered Mr. Steele to work on his apartment only on weekdays and only between 9:00 A.M. and 5:00 P.M. Steele also had to take all reasonable precautions to minimize noise, vibrations, and dirt.

A noise victim whose landlord won't restore peace and quiet can also sue the landlord for failing to do his duty. Just such a lawsuit may be brought under the state's new *warranty of habitability statute*. Basically, this statute requires your landlord to provide you with a habitable apartment. New York courts have held that an apartment may become nonhabitable if the occupant is exposed to excessive noise; and the landlord violates the statute if he neglects to maintain habitability by failing to eliminate that noise. An important 1976 case, *Pekelner* v. *Park West Management Corporation,* ruled that a noise victim could sue his landlord to collect damages for violation of the warranty of habitability statute (see page 227).

Sometimes, regardless of whatever steps a noise victim takes, the situation becomes unbearable. If noise is so bad that you really can't stand to live in your apartment anymore, you might want to consider moving out. Noise that literally forces a tenant out of his apartment can be legal grounds for breaking a lease and vacating an apartment. The legal theory that operates here is known as *constructive eviction* (see page 77).

Some special noise problems often face New York's co-op tenants. Generally, a co-op tenant's lease binds him to house rules adopted by the board of directors of the cooperative corporation. The board may exercise its authority to limit noise-causing activities.

In one case, *Justice Court Mutual Housing Cooperative* v. *Sandow,* the tenants, Mr. and Mrs. Sandow and their two daughters, moved into their co-op apartment in 1959. The Sandow girls were musicians—one played the flute, the other the violin. Each practiced her instrument three and a half hours a day. For six years the music flowed freely. Then, in response to complaints, the board of directors passed a new rule:

"Be it resolved, the playing of musical instruments shall be prohibited except during the following hours:

"a) Between the hours of 10:00 A.M. to 8:00 P.M. during weekdays.

"b) Between the hours of 11:00 A.M to 8:00 P.M. during Saturdays, Sundays and Legal Holidays.

"Be it resolved," the rule continued, "[that] the playing of musical instruments in excess of an hour and one-half per day by any one person is prohibited unless special approval is requested and received in writing by the Board of Directors."

When the Sandows refused to change their daughters' ways, the co-op took them into the state supreme court, seeking an injunction. Judge Irwin Shapiro refused to enjoin the Sandows, because the co-op's rule was unreasonable and, therefore, unenforceable. "If the [co-op's] regulation restricting the playing of musical instruments to one and a half hours per day were strictly enforced, it is doubtful that any of [the] tenants could ever acquire or maintain expertise as a musician, for even those who are fortunate enough to be born with an aptitude for music must, in order to maintain the necessary proficiency . . . engage in extensive training and practice.

"The one-and-a-half-hour provision of the regulation bears [an] arbitrary character. Take as an example the [Sandow family]. Together they constitute four occupants of the apartment. If each one of them individually [exercised] the right to play a musical instrument for one and a half hours a day, the total playing time . . . would be six hours. That would not be prohibited because the regulation provides only that 'the playing of musical instruments in excess of an hour and a half per day *by* [*any*] *one person* is prohibited.' It is obvious the [co-op's] other tenants would not be less disturbed if the musical playing over a period of six hours were accomplished by four people instead of by two or by one. Under the circumstances, the limitation to one and a half hours bears no reasonable relationship to the . . . mischief sought to be met. . . .

"The other portion of the regulation prohibits the playing [of] 'musical instruments' after 8:00 P.M. It is just about that hour that most city dwellers, after having returned from work or school, finish their dinner and have an opportunity for the first time during the day to engage in avocational pursuits. Under the circumstances, to ban the playing of musical instruments after 8:00 P.M. is in effect tantamount to banning [playing] completely. To uphold this 8:00 P.M. regulation would mean that no tenant could have a party or social gathering accompanied by piano playing and singing in the evening. So, too, under the broad category of 'musical instruments' the playing of stereophonic equipment might well be banned. And if this 'musical instrument' regulation were to be held valid, it would necessarily follow that a similar regulation prohibiting the playing of a television set or radio after 8:00 P.M. would be valid. . . . The 8:00 P.M. regulation is therefore held void as being arbitrary and unreasonable."

Of course, a co-op rule will be enforceable as long as it is reasonable, in which case a tenant's suit to enjoin enforcement of the rule will fail. Such was the case in *Baum* v. *Ryerson*

Towers. The Baums tried to enjoin their co-op from allowing noisiness in the building's community room. Under co-op rules, the room could be used by tenants on Monday through Thursday nights until 11:30 P.M.; on Friday and Saturday nights until 2:00 A.M. Sunday morning; and on Sunday night until 1:00 A.M. Monday morning. Music in the room had to end by 1:00 A.M. on Friday and Saturday nights and by midnight on Sunday night.

The state supreme court decided that these rules were reasonable and should not be enjoined: "The mere showing that on one occasion a noisy party lasted beyond the permissible hours hardly warrants [an injunction]. After all, [the Baums] together constitute but a single co-operator among more than one hundred others. They are practically alone in their grievance that the community room is misused. . . . Undoubtedly [the Baums] were more disturbed than were others, since their apartment is close by [the community room]. . . . They must abide the minor inconvenience, provided, of course, that their fellow co-operators . . . do not resolve upon a course of action leading to a true breach of the peace or [to a] nuisance."

CHAPTER 4

Remodeling and Appliances

REMODELING

"It's got such great potential!" you reassure yourself as you take occupancy of your new apartment. Perhaps you envision a shelf system on the living-room wall, enlarged closet space in the hall, a sleeping platform on the bedroom floor, and bright enamel paint in the bathroom. Your decorating ideas are boundless, until you encounter resistance from your landlord; his taste in interior decoration inclines toward "early bomb shelter." Does this mean that you'll be condemned to serve out your tenancy staring at four bare walls? Not necessarily.

Check your lease. There's a chance that it does not contain any restrictions about making alterations. If this is the case, you'll be fairly free to implement your own decorating scheme—notwithstanding the landlord's more conservative views—as long as you don't commit *waste*. That's legalese for a significant alteration (usually structural in nature) that permanently changes the physical character of the apartment. Frequently, such alterations do serious damage to the building and to the landlord's investment in his property. But even if the alterations actually improve the building, waste might still be the result, and committing waste is grounds for eviction.

The difference between waste and permissible alterations was at issue in *Rumiche Corporation* v. *Eisenreich*. Charles Eisenreich did not have to contend with any lease restrictions about making alterations. He was a statutory tenant under rent control and he had never had a lease on his studio apartment. When the landlord declined to repair the falling ceiling in Charles's apartment, he decided to help himself. He replaced the old ceiling with one constructed of three-eighths-inch Sheetrock. He also had a licensed electrician install a new ceiling-light fixture and a wall switch to replace the old-fashioned pull chain, which was not working. In addition, Charles attached a single wooden closet to a wall and erected a small, decorative wooden frame around the only window in the room. All this work was done without the landlord's permission and without filing any plans or obtaining any permits.

While the new ceiling was of the composition required by the city's fire code, it was not, alas, as thick as the code required (namely, five eighths of an inch). The landlord sought to evict Charles for damaging the landlord's property. The case went all the way up to the Court of Appeals, where the issue boiled down to whether Charles had committed waste. The answer from New York's highest tribunal was no.

"In the case before us," reasoned the court, "there was insufficient proof of any repair or alteration which could be characterized as one causing permanent or lasting injury to the premises. The apartment in issue remains a one-room studio. Its four walls are intact and remain in place. The closet and windowframe built by the tenant are merely nailed to and not built into the walls; there was no showing that either cannot be taken down and removed at minimal, if any, expense or damage. They are clearly consistent with the tenant's use of the apartment as a residence. The ceiling light fixture is a straight replacement of the old and unworkable one by a new and functioning equivalent; the addition of a modern wall switch could hardly have been more [insignificant]."

With regard to the illegal ceiling, the Court of Appeals found no harm caused to the landlord: "The replacement of the defective ceiling itself, though . . . not as thick as that required by the fire code, was of the required composition, and, interestingly, no violation because of it had ever been issued by the city. More pointedly, the landlord made no showing whatsoever . . . that the thickness of the falling ceiling which it replaced was any greater than the one . . . complained [about] in this proceeding."

Therefore, Charles could not be evicted for having made the alterations without the landlord's consent. His alterations were readily removable at no great expense—except for the illegal ceiling, about which the court seemed remarkably undisturbed.

Suppose that, unlike Charles Eisenreich, you have a lease and it contains a blanket prohibition against driving in nails, drilling holes, changing the color of the paint, or making any alterations without the landlord's permission. There is always the possibility that you can get permission to make the alterations you desire. You should seek such permission from your landlord before you start work. Often, the landlord's chief concern is that the alterations be executed in a workmanlike manner, without violating any building codes. In order to satisfy your landlord, you may have to hire a licensed electrician or contractor.

If the landlord refuses to give the permission provided for in the lease, you'll have to decide how far you can go in ignoring your lease without committing waste. The leeway you have here is less than that of the tenant whose lease does not restrict alterations. (If Charles Eisenreich had had a lease prohibiting alterations, he probably would not have received such a favorable hearing in the Court of Appeals.) On the other hand, a broad, heavy-handed lease is not likely to be rigidly enforced to the letter of the law. As a New York judge once quipped: "I regard the lease prohibition against the driving of picture or other nails in the walls or woodwork as unreasonable and unenforceable. . . . The apartment was leased for living purposes and not as a monastic cell."

In *Lansis* v. *Meklinsky,* the tenant's lease prohibited any alterations unless the landlord first gave written consent. Without obtaining consent, the tenant removed both a sink and a stove from his apartment and stored them in the basement. Then he installed his own sink and stove. The appellate division of the state supreme court refused to grant an eviction, because the changes effected by the tenant did not even amount to an alteration under the lease—let alone an alteration calling for eviction.

In 1965 the Office of Rent Control had occasion to decide that a tenant could not be evicted for installing a peephole in his apartment door. The landlord had threatened to evict the tenant for violating this lease provision: "The tenant will not drive nails, drill into, disfigure or deface any part of the building . . . and not make any alterations.'' The rent-control commissioner decided that the tenant had not violated his lease: ''The installation of a peephole or window-type viewer in the entrance door of the apartment at a location in the door which is consistent with the purpose for which such installation was made (i.e., to identify callers) serves a legitimate purpose.'' Four years later, a New York court refused to evict a tenant for drilling a small hole in his door and also installing a burglar alarm, despite contrary provisions in his lease.

In a 1968 case the tenant removed two closets from the bedroom and built a new closet there. He also removed two doors within the apartment and replaced the stove. The appellate term of the state supreme court dismissed an eviction action against the tenant, ruling that he had not made any structural changes in the apartment.

In another protenant alteration case, *Sigsbee Holding Corporation* v. *Canavan,* the tenant removed some old cabinets and replaced them with new, built-in ones. He did not bother to get the landlord's consent. The landlord cried waste and promptly sought an eviction.

''The importance of this matter cannot of course be disregarded,'' warned Judge Arthur Wachtel in Bronx civil court. ''Countless tenants would be affected by the decision in this case, for if this [alteration] were a basis for eviction . . . the door would be opened to evictions in almost every case where a landlord refused to permit the tenant to improve the apartment, perhaps even to drive nails into the wall to hang shelves, pictures, curtains or medicine cabinets. The law obviously cannot permit such [absurdity]. Nor is this the law.''

Judge Wachtel admitted that waste could result if a tenant tore down walls, doors, lighting fixtures, or plumbing, thereby seriously diminishing the value of the property. But there was no proof that the tenant's new cabinets damaged the property. The built-in cabinets replaced old ones that had hung from two nails below a hole in the ceiling where some BX electrical cable had been exposed. Even though the new cabinets were built in, the character of the apartment had not been substantially or permanently changed. There was no waste. The tenant could not be evicted just because the landlord had not consented to the alteration.

The difficulty even that judges sometimes have in distinguishing waste from permissible alterations was dramatically illustrated by the four conflicting judicial opinions rendered recently in *Freehold Investments* v. *Richstone*. The lease prohibited any alterations without the landlord's consent and specified that even papering the walls or changing the color of the paint constituted a substantial violation of the lease. Despite this provision, the tenant embarked upon an ambitious remodeling scheme, without getting the landlord's consent. In both the bedroom and the living room the tenant put up metallic wall-covering material. He built a box canopy over the bed. False bulkheads were installed along the living-room ceiling to conceal the addition of ten recessed lighting fixtures. Finally, the tenant removed a series of painted cabinets from the kitchen walls and replaced them with a set of new, oak-veneer cabinets. Having exhausted his creative urge, the tenant rested.

Whereupon the landlord roused himself and sought an eviction. In civil court, where the case was tried, the judge ruled in favor of the tenant, because the alterations were "purely decorative in nature and cannot be regarded as structural, or alterations which required the landlord's consent."

On appeal, however, the supreme court's appellate term reversed and held for the landlord. The court clearly disagreed with the trial judge's assessment of the alterations as purely decorative. Referring to the "extensive and substantially imbedded ceiling and wall reconstructions and lighting arrangements," the court was plainly disturbed by the magnitude and expense of the tenant's alterations, completed "at a cost of no less than $5,500, with a minimum removal (not restoration) cost estimated by tenant's expert at no less than $250 and two days' labor." In conclusion, the court declared: "The compelling weight of the evidence makes inescapable the conclusion that we have here a misuse of rented premises, by material alteration in removing and adding fixtures, resulting in prejudice to the present and prospective interest of the owner and substantial injury to the [property]."

Not about to give up his designer's den too easily, the tenant appealed to the supreme court's appellate division, which turned the case upside down for a second time, reversing the appellate term and holding for the tenant. As if the case had not already demonstrated amply the diversity of opinions that a close case can arouse, the Court of Appeals reversed the appellate division. The state's highest court reinstated the order of the appellate term (favoring the landlord) in the following brief opinion: "The evidence persuasively demonstrates, as a matter of law, that the alterations were sufficiently substantial to constitute a significant injury to the [landlord's interests], entitling [the] landlord to possession of the premises." In short, an eviction was warranted.

The moral of the *Freehold* case seems to be: if your lease prohibits alterations and your landlord won't consent to them, don't blithely launch a major renovation scheme. Hammering in a few nails to hang up pictures is one thing—as is, no doubt, switching new appliances for old ones, or installing shelving systems that require only simple screw holes. As long as you don't tear out permanent fixtures—or install new ones that can't be removed without considerable expense or labor, or leaving gaping holes—you're probably a safe distance from committing waste. But when you start breaking into, or building into, the very heart of your apartment—i.e., the walls, the floor, the ceiling, or any fixture permanently attached to them—you distinctly run the risk of being evicted for waste.

A common problem with many alterations is that they last longer than do the tenants who made them. So, when you vacate your apartment, the question of restoration may arise. You have no duty to restore the apartment to its original condition, unless your lease says so. Offhanded or indirect statements in your lease are not binding. Either the lease says you must restore your apartment to its original condition, or it doesn't; and if it doesn't, you don't.

For example, your lease might say: "Upon the expiration of the term of this lease, tenant shall surrender the premises to landlord, broom clean, in good order and condition, ordinary wear excepted." The phrase *good order and condition* does not mean "original condition." You would have no obligation to remove your alterations and make a restoration.

Of course, the picture changes if your alterations damaged the property—that is, if you committed waste. Generally, a landlord can win a money judgment against you for the damage. Consider the case of a dentist who rented an apartment at 1081 Astor Avenue in the Bronx. To adapt the apartment for professional use, he installed wall-to-wall closets, linoleum, lighting fixtures, and special gas lines for dental equipment. The landlord never objected to these alterations and the dentist was not bound by a lease to restore the apartment to its original condition. But, when the dentist vacated, he removed some of his alterations, leaving behind a hole in the living-room floor, damaged ceiling and walls, and a live gas-pipe outlet in one closet. So, the landlord sued. While he could not compel the dentist to restore the apartment, he did win a judgment for three hundred dollars to compensate for the damage to his property.

APPLIANCES

When it comes to appliances, a New Yorker usually counts himself lucky if he can just get a working stove and refrigerator from the landlord. Beyond these basics, tenants must fend for themselves, unless they live in a luxury building outfitted with all the amenities of electric living. Not surprisingly, many tenants who get fed up with dishpan hands, or trips to the laundromat, or stifling summer heat, finally consider installing their own dishwasher, or washing machine, or air-conditioner. Then comes the moment of truth: the landlord (or his eyes and ears, the super) objects to the new appliance. Can the tenant be forced to give it up or, even worse, be evicted for keeping it?

To begin with, if your lease contains no prohibition against appliances like washers, dryers, air-conditioners, etc., you won't be violating your lease if you install such appliances. Of course, the landlord might protest; he might notify you to get rid of the appliance "or else"; he can even institute eviction proceedings if you refuse to give up your appliance. However, you won't be evicted unless your appliance is causing real harm—say, to the building's electrical or plumbing system or to the other tenants.

In *A & B Cabrini Realty Company* v. *Newman,* the tenant, Arthur Newman, had no lease at all. For fifteen years he had lived in a rent-controlled apartment as a statutory tenant. Without getting the landlord's permission, Arthur bought a movable Whirlpool washing machine for his apartment. The machine was stored in the closet and, when needed, rolled out on casters to the kitchen sink, where it was connected to the water faucets by means of rubber hoses; another hose was placed in the sink to carry wash and rinse water out of the machine and down the sink drain. The machine plugged into a regular electrical outlet. In no way was the Whirlpool permanently attached to either the plumbing or the electrical lines.

When Arthur ignored the landlord's notice to stop using the machine, the landlord tried to evict him for committing a substantial violation of his statutory tenancy. The court held for Arthur and his Whirlpool. As a general legal principle, in the absence of any contrary lease restrictions, a tenant has the right to use and enjoy his apartment for all the purposes of normal, everyday living—as long as he doesn't in any way damage the landlord's property. In Arthur's case there were, of course, no contrary lease restrictions on washing machines—there was no lease at all—and the landlord had offered no proof that the Whirlpool was causing any damage or nuisance (e.g., clogged drains, water backup, noise). Therefore, Arthur's right to enjoy his apartment in accordance with modern living standards prevailed.

The *A & B Cabrini* case indicates how a tenant will fare if his lease (if he has one) doesn't restrict the use of appliances but he installs one against the landlord's wishes. But what happens if your lease explicitly prohibits appliances? For example, your lease might broadly provide: "The tenant shall not install or use a laundry machine, dish-washing machine, air-conditioning or ventilating equipment, or other mechanical equipment, without the consent of the landlord in writing. The violation by the tenant of any restriction contained in this paragraph shall be deemed a violation by the tenant of a substantial obligation of this lease and shall entitle the landlord to terminate the tenancy." Now you're in trouble: you've made a formal, legal agreement with the landlord; you've consented not to use specifically identified appliances without first obtaining the landlord's permission; you've even consented that unauthorized use of such appliances will constitute a substantial violation of your lease—that is, grounds for eviction. The higher appellate courts in New York generally enforce such clauses against the tenant, even to the extent of eviction. The rationale behind these pro-landlord decisions is, basically, that the parties to the lease have entered into a binding agreement and therefore it should be given full legal effect. (In practice, however, usually the actual issuance of an eviction order will be stayed—say, for thirty days—to give the tenant an opportunity to get rid of the unauthorized appliance. If the tenant does so, issuance of the order will be stayed indefinitely—that is, the tenant won't be evicted.)

Despite the strict legalistic approach taken by the appellate courts, some lower trial-court judges have persisted in looking beyond a lease to determine for themselves whether there really was a substantial violation. Regardless of the hard line taken by the higher courts, the lower courts seem willing to overlook technical lease violations as long as the unauthorized appliance is not causing any harm. Thus, tenants have been allowed to run air-conditioners and portable washing machines when there was no evidence of an overload on the electrical or plumbing system of the building. It seems that at the trial-court level, judges are more prepared to accommodate a tenant's needs for modern conveniences than is the case at the higher appellate level. Nonetheless, you can't really count on being able to install and maintain a major appliance in your apartment unless your lease specifically permits you to, or unless you get your landlord's permission.

Is your apartment one of the hundreds of thousands in New York City that fall under the protection of the rent-stabilization law? If so, you have some valuable rights regarding appliances. You might not even know about these rights, because they derive from the law itself rather than from your lease (see pages 136–139).

CHAPTER 5

Crime Protection and Safety

All tenants in New York, whether rent controlled, rent stabilized, or uncontrolled, have the following rights guaranteed by the Multiple Dwelling Law and the Housing Maintenance Code:

• *Peepholes* Every apartment must have a peephole in the entrance door. The peephole must be "in such a place that the person in each dwelling unit may view from the inside any person immediately outside the entrance door."

• *Elevator mirrors* The elevators in your apartment building must be equipped with convex mirrors to "enable persons to view [the elevator's] interior before entering."

• *Door locks* The door to your apartment must be equipped with a "heavy duty latch set and a heavy duty dead bolt" lock. The lock must be operable by key. On the inside there must be a "thumb turn" operation to the dead bolt. In addition, your door must have a "chain door guard so as to permit partial opening of the door."

You also have the right to install your own lock on the entrance door to your apartment. You are permitted to install "a lock, separate and apart from any lock installed and maintained by the owner." The cylinder of the lock must not be more than three inches in circumference. If you install a lock, you must give your landlord a duplicate of the key if he asks for it.

Sometimes landlords will insert in their leases a clause that prohibits tenants from installing their own locks. Such clauses are absolutely void—therefore, disregard them. A landlord is not permitted to take away a right that the law specifically grants you.

Your landlord is not permitted to charge you for the right to install your own lock. For example, Morris Berkowitz moved into his apartment under a lease that gave him the right to install his own lock if he paid the landlord thirty-five dollars. Morris paid the money, installed the lock, and then sought to get his money back. Since his apartment was rent stabilized, he resorted to the Conciliation and Appeals Board.

The board decided that the law "provides that any provision of a lease which requires the payment [by a tenant] of any additional rent, bonus, fee or other charge . . . for the right or privilege of installing or maintaining any . . . lock shall be deemed void as against public policy and wholly unenforceable." The board ordered the landlord to return thirty-five dollars to Morris.

• *Lighting* You are entitled to safely lighted hallways. There must be at least 10 watts of light for every 25 square feet of floor space in the hall. For example, if the hall is 10 by 15 feet, the floor space is 150 square feet and a 60-watt light bulb is required. If the landlord uses fluorescent lights, they must provide at least 4 watts for every 25 square feet of floor space.

The lights must be kept on twenty-four hours a day. However, if there is a window in the hall, the lights have to be on only from sunset to sunrise.

Your landlord must also light the area directly in front of your building. If the front of your building is not more than 22 feet wide, there must be at least a 50-watt bulb; if the front is more than 22 feet wide, there must be at least 100 watts. And if the entrance door is more than 5 feet wide, there must be *two* lights on the front of the building—one at each side of the door; together, these lights must provide at least 150 watts. All lights on the exterior of the building must be on from sunset to sunrise.

• *Bell and buzzer systems* Buildings that contain at least eight apartments and were erected after January 1, 1968—or were converted into apartment buildings after that date—must have an intercom system connecting the front entrance with each apartment. "Such intercommunication system shall be located at an automatic self-locking door giving public access to the main entrance hall or lobby . . . and shall consist of a device or devices for voice communication between the occupant of each apartment and a person outside [the] door to the main entrance or lobby . . . The apartment occupant [must be able] to release the locking mechanism of [the front] door from the apartment.''

If your apartment building was built before January 1, 1968, you can compel your landlord to install a bell-and-buzzer voice-communication system. A landlord *must* install the system if the tenants occupying a majority of the apartments consent, in writing, to the installation. To petition for an intercom system, contact your local division of the Office of Code Enforcement (see Appendix A for the addresses) and ask them for form RC-1. If you live in a rent-controlled or rent-stabilized apartment, your landlord is permitted to increase your rent slightly, depending upon the type of system he installs.

• *Tenant-operated lobby-attendant service* Tenants in buildings that contain at least eight apartments have the right to operate their own lobby-attendant service. The attendant must be ''stationed at and remain in the entrance halls or public lobbies of the building adjacent to the main entrance.'' The only acts that the attendant may perform are those directly related to the safety and security of tenants and their visitors.

If the tenants in your building want to operate a lobby-attendant service, you are permitted to perform the service yourselves, or hire someone, or provide a combination of the two. If your landlord interferes with the attendant, he is committing a violation and can be fined up to fifty dollars. Keep in mind, however, that the service you set up is your own responsibility. If the attendant causes unjustified injury to someone (or is himself injured), the landlord is not in any way responsible. The extent to which you are responsible depends on the facts of the particular case. If you have any concern, contact a lawyer before you set up any service.

If you have difficulty securing any of the rights described in the preceding part of this chapter, contact your local division of the Office of Code Enforcement, or use the central complaint number (see Appendix A).

• *Window guards* A recent health code regulation requires landlords to install window guards in apartments in which there is a child under eleven years old. This regulation applies only to buildings that contain at least three living units.

There is a timetable by which landlords must install the guards. Exactly when you are entitled to the guards depends on where you live in the city. If you have not yet had them installed, contact the Window Falls Prevention Program at the New York City Department of Health (Tel.: 212-566-8082). Bear in mind that in 1976, 217 children fell from windows in New York City. The window guards might not be beautiful, but they just might save your child's life.

CHAPTER 6

Sharing, Subletting, and Breaking a Lease

Most people cannot make the ups and downs of their lives coincide with the terms of their leases. The newly married couple who signs a three-year lease can't know that they will hate each other after only two years. The young man coming to New York City can't anticipate that he will fall in love after only one year has elapsed on his two-year lease. The young executive can't predict that he will be made a senior vice-president in the Houston office after only three months on his three-year lease. In each of these cases, the problem can be solved by sharing the apartment or subletting it, or by breaking the lease.

SHARING YOUR APARTMENT

Who is permitted to live in your apartment? According to most leases, only the "tenant and his immediate family." This raises an important question: Who, exactly, is considered a member of your "immediate family"? The answer depends on whether you are a rent-controlled or a rent-stabilized tenant.

• *The "immediate family" under rent control* If your apartment is rent controlled, your immediate family definitely includes your spouse, children and/or stepchildren, parents and/or stepparents, parents-in-law, and grandparents. Thus, these members of your family are permitted to live with you in your apartment. There is, however, some confusion about whether your aunts, uncles, and siblings are included. This confusion arises because the rent-control law has more than one definition of *immediate family*. Depending on which definition is used, the size of your immediate family can change.

• *The "immediate family" under rent stabilization* The Rent Stabilization Code defines the immediate family as spouse, children and/or stepchildren, parents, and parents-in-law. However, one court has expanded the list, pointing out that children-in-law should rightfully be included (but only if they are living with their spouses).

Assuming your lease permits occupancy by members of your immediate family, what happens if the person with whom you want to share your apartment doesn't belong to your immediate family? And what if your lease contains no provision for your immediate family, thereby allowing no one but you to live in the apartment? You do not have the right to share your apartment with anyone whose occupancy is not authorized by the lease. However, there are two rules of the rent-stabilization law that permit a tenant to share his apartment even though the sharing would be in technical violation of the lease. These rules will be referred to as (1) the insubstantial breach rule and (2) the waiver rule.

• *The insubstantial breach rule* We have seen repeatedly, in chapters 2, 3, and 4, that a tenant won't be evicted for violating his lease unless he has committed what lawyers call a substantial breach or substantial violation of the lease. Is it possible that sharing an apartment in violation of a lease could be considered an insubstantial breach? The answer is a qualified yes. The court cases seem to say: You can't bring in a stranger or a distant relative, but you can share your apartment with someone with whom you have a closer relationship. The courts also seem to be saying that the length of time during which you share your apartment determines whether there has been a substantial breach.

Let's look at *Park East Land Corporation* v. *Finkelstein,* a case that is especially important because it was decided by the highest court in the state, the Court of Appeals. Mr. and Mrs.

Bennie Bell and their son lived in the Bronx, in a two-room, rent-controlled apartment. Their lease expired, so they were statutory tenants. After Mr. Bell died, Mrs. Bell married a Mr. Alper, who at that time was living with his daughter and son-in-law. When the new Mrs. Alper moved in with Mr. Alper, his daughter and her husband moved into the Bells' old apartment, in which the Bells' son was still living. Thus, the Bells' apartment contained only one of its original occupants—the Bells' son—plus two new occupants—Mr. Alper's daughter and her husband.

The Bells' landlord, Park East Land Corporation, sought to evict all three. But the judge pointed out that a tenant may not be evicted for a breach of his lease unless the breach is of a "substantial obligation." He then concluded: "Substantial is a word of general reference which takes on color and precision from its total context. Having little if any meaning when considered in abstract or in vacuum, it must be defined with reference to the peculiar legal and factual setting in which it occurs. . . . Of the three persons who originally occupied the apartment, one remains. . . . [There is] no increase in the total number of tenants, no increase in the landlord's burdens or costs, no increase in wear and tear upon facilities shown." The judge decided that the landlord could not evict them.

In *Stio* v. *Miniaci,* the facts were much simpler. Here's how the court saw the case: "The facts are that the tenant's sister-in-law and her family migrated from Italy to settle permanently in the United States. They had never before set foot in this country. While they were here and seeking a permanent abode, they were temporarily the guests of the tenant. They found an apartment for themselves the following month and immediately moved into it. . . .

"Obviously the guests from Italy were not the tenant's immediate family. The issue is whether under the circumstances herein the tenant violated a substantial obligation of his tenancy which would authorize his eviction. . . . I think not. There was no evidence here of overcrowding or the creation of a dangerous or unhealthy condition, no increase in the landlord's burdens or costs, no increase in ordinary wear and tear, no evidence of illegality or that under the guise of hospitality the tenant had sublet part of the premises or taken in boarders. The tenant did nothing more than was his privilege. He extended the hospitality of his home to his wife's sister and her family for a temporary period. That does not constitute a substantial violation of the provisions of the lease limiting the occupancy of the apartment to the tenant and his immediate family.

"Surely it would not be seriously contended that the putting up of a guest for the night would constitute a substantial violation of the standard occupancy clause of an apartment lease. . . . The stay was definitely within normal limits under the circumstances. Hence there was no violation of a substantial obligation under the lease."

The preceding cases show that a tenant might reasonably expect not to be evicted either when near relatives move in or when the stay is of limited duration. But what about a more common situation in New York City: sharing your apartment with a friend.

For a while it appeared as though the courts were going to extend the term *immediate family* to include lovers. Indeed, in the case of *Fraydun Enterprises* v. *Ettinger* one lower-court judge made the extension: he ruled that the tenant's fiancée, who had been living with him for three years, was a member of his immediate family. However, the case was reversed by the appellate term of the state supreme court. The appellate term held that a tenant who shares his apartment with a person who is not a relative, regardless of the nature of their relationship, violates a lease that limits occupancy to the tenant and his immediate family. A lover simply is not part of the family. However, in this case, the court gave the couple sixty days in which to get married and thereby create a "family."

The message is clear: If you plan to share your apartment, make your plans known before you sign the lease. The courts will not sanction a tenant sharing his apartment with a person who is not a relative unless his lease permits such sharing. Indeed, there are court decisions in which a godson and a third cousin were declared persona non grata.

• *The waiver rule* If a landlord knows that a tenant is sharing his apartment in violation of his lease and continues to accept rent without objecting to the violation, he waives (i.e., gives up) his right to object. And if the landlord can't object, the sharing becomes legal.

The simplest way to apply the waiver rule is to tell your landlord outright that you are sharing your apartment; if he still cashes your rent checks, he has, in effect, approved the sharing. He is not permitted to later change his mind and object.

If you are certain that your landlord would object if you told him about your sharing, try a more subtle application of the rule. The courts have held that under certain circumstances a landlord will be treated as though he did know about your sharing even if he wasn't directly notified. The "certain circumstances" arise when: (1) the landlord accepts rent from the person with whom you are sharing your apartment, or (2) an agent of the landlord, such as the superintendent, knows about the sharing. The following examples show how these rules operate.

Assume you decide to have a friend move into your apartment with you, but your lease permits sharing only with immediate family. After your friend moves in, you each send in half of the rent. If your landlord cashes your friend's check, the waiver rule swings into action. The landlord is presumed to know who is paying the rent. If he accepts half the rent from a stranger, the court will assume that he knows the apartment is being shared. The longer he accepts the rent, the harder it will be for him to prove that he ever voiced any objection to the sharing.

It is also possible to inform the landlord of your sharing merely by telling the superintendent. Most courts agree that the superintendent is the agent of the landlord. The landlord is presumed to know what the super knows. So, if your super helped your friend move in, he certainly knows that you are sharing your apartment. If after the move your landlord accepts your rent check, the waiver rule again comes into play. In this case, there is no need for your friend to pay half the rent. The landlord is presumed to know that you are sharing your apartment (because the super knows); and, knowing what he is presumed to know, the landlord gave his legal blessing by accepting your rent check!

SUBLETTING YOUR APARTMENT

A couple from the Bronx wants to spend the winter in Miami. A Brooklyn College professor wants to take his sabbatical in Europe. A secretary wants to move in with her boyfriend for an indefinite stay. Each tenant wants to keep an apartment to return to. The options: pay rent on a vacant apartment, or sublet it.

Subletting is a procedure in which you, as a tenant, rent your apartment to someone else. You become his "landlord," but you remain a tenant of the owner of the building. You are the *sublessor,* and the person to whom you rent your apartment is the *subtenant* or *sublessee*.

In general, your right to sublet depends on permission from your landlord. In most cases, the terms upon which subletting is allowed are contained in your lease. But if you are a rent-controlled tenant without a lease (a statutory tenant), you must look to the rent-control law for your rights.

• *Getting the landlord's permission* If you have a lease, it probably has a sublet clause. For example: "Tenant may sublet apartment with the written permission of the landlord, which permission shall not be unreasonably withheld." Often, landlords mistake this clause as a license to refuse any and all sublet requests. Yet, the clause states that consent to sublet "shall not be unreasonably withheld," and your landlord is not the final judge of what is or is not reasonable.

Consider the case of *Cedarhurst* v. *Milgrim.* Sally Milgrim had a standard sublet clause in her lease. She assumed it meant what it said. So, she found responsible subtenants—the Goodmans—and presented their credentials to her landlord, requesting permission to sublet. The landlord said no. He needed the apartment for a business partner and preferred to have her vacate. However, Milgrim was not impressed: over the objections of her landlord, she sublet to the Goodmans. The landlord immediately went to court to get rid of this obstinate tenant-subtenant annoyance, but the judge decided that the landlord had "withheld his consent to the subleasing . . . unreasonably and arbitrarily and therefore . . . the action of Milgrim in subletting the apartment to the . . . Goodmans was legal and permitted."

In short, you have the right to sublet to any person against whom the landlord could have no reasonable objection. If the landlord refuses to give you written consent, you still have the right to sublet your apartment. What would be reasonable grounds for refusing permission to sublet? One New York court, in the case of *American Book Co.* v. *Yeshiva University,* decided that "the reasons for refusal of consent by a landlord fall into two broad categories—objective and subjective. By 'objective' are meant those standards which are readily measurable criteria of a proposed subtenant's . . . acceptability from the point of view of *any* landlord." Thus, objective grounds for refusal—such as financial irresponsibility—might be valid; however, they must not be based upon the unique circumstances of the landlord. They must be grounds that *any* landlord would use in refusing a sublet.

Subjective criteria are not permissible as grounds for refusal. "Arbitrary considerations of personal taste, sensibility, or convenience do not constitute the criteria of the landlord's duty under a [sublet] agreement." Thus, your landlord cannot refuse a sublet because he does not like the race, color, occupation, looks, etc., of the prospective subtenant.

From this rule, you can see how Sally Milgrim was illegally refused permission to sublet. The landlord's refusal was based entirely upon his personal needs. It had nothing whatsoever to do with the prospective subtenants. The landlord's grounds for refusal were, therefore, legally insufficient. The reasonableness of refusing consent cannot vary with the identity and activities of the landlord.

A "reasonable consent" sublet clause can be quite useful. Your landlord may have realized this before you last renewed your lease; if he did, it's possible that he removed your sublet clause. However, if you live in a rent-stabilized apartment, you can fight the removal. Under the rent-stabilization law, your landlord must renew your lease on the same terms as those of your expiring lease. So, if you had a sublet clause in your expiring lease, you are entitled to have it in all lease renewals. If your sublet clause has disappeared, complain to the Conciliation and Appeals Board and demand that it be reinserted in your lease (see page 100).

• *Subletting without permission* A tenant who has no

lease—e.g., a statutory tenant under rent control—has no right to sublet. He's in the same position as a tenant who has a lease that contains an absolute prohibition against subletting. The only way for such a tenant to sublet legally is to get permission from the landlord or to use the waiver rule.

In *Melroy Realty Corporation* v. *Siegel,* Siegel lived in Melroy's building, and his lease prohibited subletting. Undaunted, Siegel requested permission to sublet. The landlord refused. But Siegel's subtenants moved in anyway. They immediately paid one month's rent to Melroy. Melroy cashed the check and then brought an eviction proceeding. The court refused to throw the subtenants out. It decided that Melroy's "acceptance of rent . . . after [learning] of the violation of the lease prohibiting [subletting] constituted a waiver. . . . Having accepted rent, there is a waiver of the provision of the lease against subletting." Though Melroy did not intend to approve the sublet, he did so unwittingly, by cashing the subtenants' rent check.

A landlord's reason for accepting rent from an unauthorized subtenant may not always be ignorance. Consider the case of *Messinger* v. *Chung Eng* in which a nice landlady found an unauthorized sublet in her building. Rather than evict the subtenants, she accepted rent from them, because "she did not wish to put 'them on the street with three small children.' " But all good things come to an end. When the sublet dragged on, she finally commenced eviction proceedings.

Guess what the court decided. "Humane though her motives may have been in not seeking to evict this family, nevertheless as a matter of law she waived her right [to object to the subletting]." The nice landlady was compelled to continue honoring the sublet.

In each of these cases, the landlord personally knew of the unauthorized sublet. However, personal knowledge is not necessary, because the waiver rule operates even if only an agent of the landlord knows (see page 70). The agent most likely to know of the sublet is the superintendent. According to one case, if the super knows of your sublet, and the landlord accepts the rent, you're in business. The landlord has just approved of your sublet, whether he likes it or not.

• *Rights of subtenant* If you are a subtenant, your landlord himself is a tenant. There is a tendency to assume that he is not bound by the rent-control or rent-stabilization laws. False. When the tenant sublet his apartment to you, he became a landlord and was therefore subject to the law.

• *Sublet of rent-controlled apartments* If you are the sublessee of a rent-controlled apartment, the amount of rent you pay is strictly controlled by the law. You should not pay more than the amount that the sublessor was paying to his landlord. However, there is one exception to this rule: If the sublessor is subletting his apartment with his furnishings in it, he may apply to the Office of Rent Control for permission to increase the rent that he charges you. He may then apply to his district rent office on form A.33.1C (Landlord's Application for Increase of Maximum Rent), which requires the sublessor to state in detail the type of furnishings in the apartment.

The district rent office will determine how great a rent increase it will permit for the duration of the sublet. You should pay only the amount specified in the rent-increase order. If you think you are being overcharged by the sublessor, visit your district rent office (the addresses are listed in Appendix A). Bring some proof that you are a subtenant (e.g., a rent receipt). Ask the office to verify the amount of rent you should be paying.

• *Sublet of rent-stabilized apartments* The sublessor of a rent-stabilized apartment is not permitted to charge a subtenant more than the rent he himself was paying to the landlord. There is only one exception to this rule. If the sublessor provides furnishings that were not provided by the landlord, he may charge a reasonable amount for this added service. The amount he charges must be determined by the Conciliation and Appeals Board. The amount of rent which the sublessor must pay to the landlord (and consequently what the sublessee must pay to his sublessor) may be increased if there is a subletting. The amount of the rent increase and the terms under which it may be collected are discussed in chapter 9.

• *Subletting and the primary residence decontrol law* Both the rent-control and rent-stabilization laws have sections known popularly as the primary residence decontrol law. Basically, the law provides for the decontrol of an apartment that is not being used by the tenant as his primary residence. A rent-controlled apartment that has been decontrolled loses the protection of the rent-control law and, if it qualifies, becomes rent stabilized. If a rent-stabilized apartment becomes decontrolled, the landlord is allowed to refuse to renew the tenant's lease. And if the landlord does agree to renew the lease of the rent-stabilized tenant, he is allowed to charge the rent increase as is permitted for a vacancy lease.

A potential problem arises when an apartment is sublet, because the sublet apartment clearly is no longer the place where the sublessor is living—and it might no longer be his primary residence. Therefore, it is possible that your landlord would seek to decontrol your apartment if you sublet it. We are raising this potential problem only to alert you to its existence; a full discussion, including possible solutions, is included in chapter 1.

• *The right to sublet law* You may be wondering why we have waited until this point in the chapter to discuss a law called the right-to-sublet law. There is, indeed, such a law, and it was passed in 1975. The problem is that the title is a misnomer: the law is not, in our judgment, a right-to-sublet law.

Under this law, every tenant has the right to request permission to sublet. However, if the landlord refuses, even if this refusal is unreasonable, all the tenant can do is terminate his lease. There is no absolute right to sublet. Is this law a total loss? Absolutely not. It may not be useful for subletting, but it's terrific for breaking a lease. Therefore, we have discussed this law in the next section, Breaking Your Lease.

BREAKING YOUR LEASE

Leases are like lobster traps: easy to enter but difficult, if not impossible, to get out of. When signing a lease, a tenant hardly ever thinks about having to break it and get out. Yet, time and again tenants later find themselves in the position of asking: How can I get out of my lease?

Let's start with a basic time-honored rule of law: When you sign a lease, you obligate yourself to pay rent for the full term of the lease. If you move out of the apartment before the term ends, the obligation to pay rent remains with you. Now, if that were all the law there was on this subject, we would have to end this section right here. But there is more. The ways to break a lease that we are about to discuss are makeshift at best. They should be avoided if at all possible. So, the next time you sign a lease, remember the rule of law and try to have a clause inserted in your lease allowing you to break the lease or sublet your apartment. Build yourself a way out *before* you sign your lease; afterward, it may be too late.

For those of you who are thinking that this is all fine advice, but I've got a lease and I want a way out, let's get down to business. How can you break your lease? There are two possible avenues: the constructive eviction rule and the right-to-sublet law.

• *Constructive eviction* When you rent an apartment, you agree to pay for the right to use and enjoy one or more rooms in a building owned by the landlord. If the landlord fails to supply you with an apartment that you can use and enjoy, he has reneged on his part of the deal. And if, because of the landlord's failure, you are forced to move from your apartment, you have been "constructively evicted." In other words, while the landlord did not *actually* seek to evict you through a formal legal proceeding, his action in not providing you with an apartment that you can use and enjoy, in effect (i.e., constructively), forced you to move out (i.e., evicted you).

If you are constructively evicted, you are under no obligation to pay rent once you have vacated the apartment. This is true regardless of when your lease actually expires. In one case a Queens tenant was confronted with an apartment that was infested with vermin. The tenant refused to occupy the apartment, claiming that it was unfit and that the landlord's failure to get rid of the roaches amounted to a constructive eviction. He went to court to sue his landlord for return of his security deposit.

The court decided that " 'The presence of . . . vermin, and other like pests in a building . . . may constitute such a nuisance as to justify a tenant in abandoning the [apartment] even without direct proof that such pests came from or through a part of the building under the landlord's control' . . . The Court having found that the condition is as contended by the [tenant] and that it constitutes a breach of the lease by the [landlord], the [tenant] is entitled to a return of his security.'' Thus, this tenant was entitled to break his lease and also was able to compel his landlord to return his security deposit.

The recent case of *Voso* v. *Lentnek* provides another example of a constructive eviction. On Saturday, July 6, 1974, the tenants' kitchen drain backed up and flooded their first-floor apartment; waste water even overflowed through to the lobby floor. The tenants contacted the landlord in the vain hope of getting repairs. The drain continued to back up, causing more problems, and for five days the tenants were left without repairs. They then decided to leave the apartment for good.

The court decided that ''to constitute a constructive eviction the wrongful acts of the landlord must substantially and materially deprive the tenant of the beneficial use and enjoyment of his right to possession of the [apartment]. In moving out, after five days of non-activity on the landlord's part to correct the obnoxious conditions that persisted, the tenant acted with reasonable promptness.'' Of course, if the tenants had lived with the poor conditions for a number of months, their case would not have been as strong. It's hard to argue that you've been forced out of your apartment when you've managed to live with the problem.

In *Cohen* v. *Werner*, the problem the tenant had was noise created by other tenants in the building. The noise was so loud and constant that the apartment was uninhabitable. While the landlord did not create the noise, ''he did nothing at all to try to stop it although he had ample time to do so before [the tenant] finally moved out after having complained.'' When the landlord tried to sue the tenant for the rent, he was met head on with the defense of constructive eviction, which the court upheld: ''Although the landlord had ample notice of the existent conditions, he did little or nothing to [stop it]. Therefore, [tenant] sustained his claim of constructive eviction.'' The tenant was not liable for any rent for the period after he had moved out.

These cases demonstrate how the concept of constructive eviction can be used to break a lease when the tenant's desire to move is motivated by poor conditions in the apartment. Of course, the reasons for breaking the lease are not limited to roaches or water damage or noise. Any condition such as no heat, falling plaster, etc., may be grounds for arguing a constructive eviction.

A word of caution is in order at this point. The only way a tenant can raise the issue of constructive eviction is by vacating his apartment. He can then either sue for any unreturned security deposit or wait for the landlord to sue him for the rent. Either way, if the tenant loses his case—i.e., cannot prove that he was constructively evicted—he may be liable for the rent on the unoccupied apartment. Therefore, consult an attorney for advice before concluding that the conditions in your apartment justify breaking your lease. An attorney may also be useful since any tenant who has been forced out of his apartment as a result of the landlord's neglect may be able to sue his landlord for damages.

Finally, if you do move out, be sure to notify the landlord, preferably in a letter, sent via certified mail, return receipt requested.

• *The right to sublet law* In 1975 the New York State Legislature enacted a new section (226-b) in the lengthy Real Property Law and labeled it "Right to Sublease." This is a misnomer. The law does not give you the right to sublet. It does give you the right *to request permission* to sublet or assign. If that permission is unreasonably refused, you have the right to break your lease. We believe this law should be called the "right to break your lease" law. Here's how it works:

First, the law applies only to buildings that contain at least four residential units. Second, the law applies only to leases entered into (or renewed) on or after June 3, 1975. And third, the law does not apply to public housing or cooperatives.

You probably have noticed that this law gives you the right to request to sublease *or assign* your lease. You should understand the difference between assigning a lease and subletting. The term *subletting* technically applies only when you give someone else the right to occupy your apartment for *less than the full amount of time remaining on your lease*. Thus, when you sublet, the subtenancy will end before your lease does—you will be the tenant in occupancy when the lease expires. However, if you turn over the *entire remainder of your lease* to someone else, you have *assigned* your lease; you no longer have any right to return to the apartment before your lease expires.

The law itself begins as follows: "A tenant renting a residence in a dwelling having four or more residential units shall have the right to sublease or assign his premises, subject to the written consent of the landlord given in advance of the sublease or assignment. Such consent shall not be unreasonably withheld. If the landlord unreasonably withholds consent for such sublease or assignment, the landlord must release the tenant from the lease upon request of the tenant." Thus, under the law, every qualified tenant has the right to request permission to sublet or assign his lease. If the landlord *unreasonably* withholds his consent, he must let the tenant break the lease.

In order to use the law, the tenant must follow these steps: First, he must send a registered or certified letter to his landlord requesting permission to sublet or assign. The letter must include the name, business address, and home address of the proposed sublessee or assignee. Everyone who signed the lease (or guaranteed it) must take part in the request and, therefore, should sign the letter. For example, if two friends both signed a lease that was guaranteed by the father of one of the friends, three people should sign the request—both friends and the father.

Within ten days after you mail the letter, the landlord may ask for further information about the prospective subtenants or assigness. You must provide the information as long as it would be reasonably necessary to determine whether consent for the subletting or assignment should be given.

If the landlord does *not* ask for additional information, he must tell you whether he is consenting to the sublet or assignment within thirty days after you mailed your request for permission to sublet or assign. If the landlord does ask for additional information, he must let you know his decision within thirty days after you mailed him the additional information.

If the landlord agrees to the subletting or assignment, you may go ahead. However, under the law, you remain liable if your subtenant or assignee violates your lease. If the landlord refuses permission to sublet or assign, he must tell you why.

Now, if the landlord agrees to the subletting or assignment, you're in business. However, if he refuses, you've got to determine whether that refusal was reasonable. If it was reasonable, you have no right to break your lease. If it was unreasonable, you may break your lease. How do you make this determination?

You will already know the reasons for the landlord's refusal, since he must tell them to you. To determine whether his reasons are valid, consult the cases dealing with reasonable consent to sublet (see pages 71–72). We believe these cases should apply here. And, if your landlord did not act reasonably, you are permitted to break your lease. However, if you have any doubts, we suggest you consult a lawyer.

• *The cost of breaking a lease* If you have no grounds to claim a constructive eviction because your apartment is in good condition and you don't qualify for the benefits of the right-to-sublet law, you've got a problem.

Let's assume you move out of your apartment after only one year on a three-year lease. In theory, you are liable for the rent for the remaining two years. This is a sizable price to pay for breaking a lease. However, some courts have recently begun to attack the theory. They have pointed out that a landlord who knows he has a vacant apartment (because you moved out) should, in good faith, seek to rerent the apartment. As soon as the apartment is rerented, your liability for rent on the apartment should end. This line of reasoning has given rise to the landlord's so-called duty to mitigate damages—i.e., his duty to attempt to cut his losses.

A recent lower-court case, *Lefrak* v. *Lambert,* utilized the duty to mitigate in the following set of facts. The tenants were a young couple living in Lefrak City. They moved out of their apartment in November 1974 because the birth of their son and consequent loss of the wife's income made the apartment too expensive. After they moved out, the apartment remained vacant for seventeen months, during which time the couple's lease was still running. When the apartment was finally rerented, Lefrak sued the couple for $5,462!

The court was confronted with a dilemma. On one hand, the law clearly holds a tenant liable for the rent due on his lease. It imposes no clear duty on the landlord to mitigate his damages by reletting the apartment as quickly as possible. On the other hand, justice is not served by applying this strict rule.

Judge Herbert Posner of the Queens civil court decided that

justice should prevail: "There is something basically unjust, basically unreasonable and, therefore, basically not legal about a landlord in an urban society with a housing shortage having no obligation to try to re-rent an apartment and mitigate damages. There is something unfair about permitting tenants to be in a different category than other persons entering into a contract. To be sure, a tenant should be required to pay every penny of damage actually sustained by a reasonable landlord acting to mitigate damages, but to allow what is really a draconian remedy is foreign to our modern concept of justice." Judge Posner found that Lefrak did not act in good faith in failing to rerent the apartment for seventeen months. The judge decided that a reasonable period of time in which to rerent would have been three months, so he awarded Lefrak only three months' back rent.

One of the problems encountered by the young couple in this case was that it was hard to prove that Lefrak had failed to use its best efforts to rerent the apartment. There may be a way around this problem. When you notify your landlord that you are vacating your apartment, offer to find a suitable tenant to take over your apartment. Indicate that you believe you can find such a tenant, and request that the landlord let you know whether he wants your assistance. If the landlord does want your help, give it to him; if he doesn't, at least it will be on record that you offered to provide someone to fill your apartment. It will then be difficult for the landlord to justify keeping the apartment empty for many months because he could not find a new tenant.

While the duty to mitigate damages is a growing concept, it certainly is not established law. However, if you have no choice but to break your lease, you might find some protection in it.

PART II

Rent Control and Rent Stabilization

CHAPTER 7

The Rent Control Law

The primary function of the rent-control law is to regulate rent increases while maintaining services. Rent increases are controlled under what has come to be known as the "MBR system." In addition, the rent may be increased if new services are added. The maintenance of services is accomplished through a concept known as "essential services."

THE MBR SYSTEM

Prior to 1970, the rent on a rent-controlled apartment could be increased by 15 percent whenever new tenants moved in. Apartments that had a frequent turnover had high rents, while those that had the same tenant for many years had low rents. Two identical apartments could have vastly different rents. This rather bizarre system lasted until 1970.

In 1970 the city council passed local law number 30, which created what has come to be known as the MBR system. It was designed to remedy the inequities of the old system. As so often happens, the cure was almost worse than the disease.

The first few years of the MBR system were a nightmare. We won't recount for you what happened (or didn't happen). Those people who remember don't want to, and those who don't remember are better off. However, we will describe how the system was supposed to work and, more important, how it works now.

Every rent-controlled apartment has a "rent base," a "maximum base rent (MBR)," and a "maximum collectible rent."

The rent base is the amount of your monthly rent as of December 31, 1971. For example, if the monthly rent on your apartment was $100 in December 1971, then your rent base is $100.

Your maximum base rent (MBR) is the result of a long, complex formula that adds, subtracts, multiplies, and divides facts and figures about your building and apartment. The MBR for your apartment is the "fair rent" that the Office of Rent Control, in its attempt to equalize rents on all rent-controlled apartments, thinks you should be paying.

There may be a considerable gap between your old rent base and your new MBR. How does the law raise your rent from the rent base to the MBR? The answer is: in stages. Each year, beginning with 1972, your rent is increased by a maximum of 7½ percent until the rent you are paying equals the prescribed MBR. (You will never have to pay more than the MBR.) The rent you are required to pay each year en route to the MBR is your maximum collectible rent (MCR).

Take one example that employs all three terms—rent base, MBR, and maximum collectible rent. Assume your rent base is $100.00. The Office of Rent Control has decided that your 1972 MBR is $110.00 per month. Beginning in 1972, your landlord was not entitled to collect the full MBR; he could collect only your rent base plus the maximum 7½ percent increase toward your MBR. In other words, your maximum collectible rent for 1972 was $107.50—not the full $110.00. Beginning in January 1973, your landlord was permitted to raise your rent again. However, this time he was not permitted to get another 7½ percent, because that would exceed your MBR. Since your landlord cannot charge more than your MBR—here, $110.00—he was limited to a monthly increase of $2.50 during 1973.

Every tenant is supposed to be informed of his MBR and maximum collectible rent on a special form, the Tenant's Order of Maximum Base Rent, popularly known as the MBR order. Upon receipt of his MBR order, a tenant should simply pay the specified maximum collectible rent. Each year the tenant should receive a new MBR order. Every two years the Office of Rent Control should recompute a tenant's MBR.

In order to qualify for a new MBR rent increase, a landlord must fix all serious (''rent impairing'') violations and 80 percent of all other violations that were on record against the building prior to the rent increase. If the landlord does not make the necessary repairs, he is not entitled to any rent increase.

The MBR system is not operating quite the way it was planned. The primary problem is that the Office of Rent Control did not recompute the MBRs every two years since 1972. They had a hard enough time computing them in 1972. Trying to do it every two years would have been sheer lunacy.

So, they simply raised the 1972 MBRs by a fixed percentage for all rent-controlled apartments. Your 1974–75 MBR is 8½ percent higher than your 1972–73 MBR. The 1976–77 MBR is 22 percent higher than your 1974–75 MBR. Thus, if your 1972–73 MBR was $100.00, your 1974–75 MBR would be $108.50. And your 1976–77 MBR would be $108.50 increased by 22 percent, or $132.37.

Because the Office of Rent Control did not prepare new MBRs, they did not send out new MBR orders. So, landlords who qualified for an MBR increase were sent a Landlord's Order of Eligibility. This form entitled the landlord to raise the MBR. Before a landlord was entitled to raise the 1976–77 MRB, he was required to have sent you a copy of the eligibility order he received. This form had to have been signed by a director of a district rent office. In addition, the landlord had to have sent you the Notice of Increase in 1976–1977 Maximum Base Rent and Maximum Collectible Rent Computation. This notice showed you how the landlord computed your 1976–77 MBR and your maximum collectible rent.

If you feel your landlord should not receive any rent increase, ask your district rent office for form A-94 MBR, known as the Challenge Re: Maximum Base Rent Order. This form is used to contest the MBR. The two most common grounds for contesting the MBR are: (1) the landlord did not correct the required number of violations existing on the building, and (2) the landlord is not supplying all essential services. (Essential services are discussed later in this chapter. If you are not receiving all essential services, the landlord should not receive any MBR increase.)

The protest to your MBR must be made within thirty-three days after you receive your copy of Landlord's Order of Eligibility. It's probably too late for most of you to file a protest to your 1976–77 MBR. However, when any future MBR is issued, you might want to consider a protest.

The most important point for a rent-controlled tenant to remember is that the rent cannot be increased by more than 7½ percent in one year, regardless of how high the MBR goes. This rule, however, has an exception. It's called the Labor Cost Adjustment.

• *Labor cost adjustment* Section 33.8 of the rent-control regulations permits the Office of Rent Control to increase rents on apartments in buildings where the payroll for building employees is excessively high. In 1977 section 33.8 was used to pass on to the tenants (in the form of a rent increase) the cost of a wage settlement reached with the union representing building employees. The rent increase is called a labor cost adjustment.

The rent increase permitted by the adjustment affects only a small percentage of rent-controlled tenants. The actual increase must not exceed 7½ percent of the tenant's rent. However, many tenants will not receive the maximum increase.

A landlord qualifies for the increase by filing an elaborate series of forms. Unfortunately, the complexity of these forms makes it impossible for us to explain them to you. In theory, each of the forms was reviewed by the Office of Rent Control, and if any errors were made by the landlord, the tenant was notified. However, there is no guarantee that the landlord's computations—even as reviewed by the Office of Rent Control—are correct. Just about the only way to check them out yourself is to hire an accountant and have him review all the data submitted by the landlord. If the rent-controlled tenants in your building are organized, you may all want to go to the trouble of checking the landlord's figures. However, if you are acting alone, we frankly don't see how you can tackle the complex information that the landlord used to justify his labor cost adjustment.

As this book goes to press, the legality of the adjustment is being challenged in the courts. Therefore, tenants should be on the alert for any court decisions that might strike down the labor cost adjustment.

There is one category of tenants who might be able to avoid the full impact of the rent increases we have discussed: senior citizens. There is a senior-citizen rent exemption that is designed to avoid rent increases to older tenants, especially those on fixed incomes. If a senior citizen qualifies, he will not be required to pay most of the rent increases we have discussed, including the MBR increases.

In order to qualify for the exemption, a tenant must: (a) be at least sixty-two years old; (b) not be on welfare; (c) be the head of a household; (d) have a total annual disposable income of not more than $6,500; and (e) be subject to a rent increase that, if paid, would result in at least one third of the tenant's income going to rent.

If you think you might qualify for the exemption, write, call, or visit your district rent office (see Appendix A). Request the necessary form for the senior-citizen rent exemption.

If you have any difficulty completing the form, call the Mayor's Department for the Aging at 212-577-0800. They will provide you with the name of the nearest senior-citizen center with personnel trained to assist you in completing the form.

RENT INCREASES FOR NEW SERVICES

Under rent control, there are two types of rent increases permitted when a landlord provides new services. The first type requires consent by the tenant; the second does not.

• *Tenant's consent required* A landlord and tenant may enter into an agreement that results in an increased rent. For a landlord to be able to increase the rent as a result of the agreement, it must provide for a "substantial increase in dwelling space or a change in the services, furniture, furnishings or equipment provided in the housing accommodation."

For example: You and your landlord agree to the addition of a new service such as a separate freezer in the kitchen; your landlord may then apply for a rent increase. Before a landlord is permitted to increase your rent on the basis of increased service, furnishings, or dwelling space, he must secure approval from the Office of Rent Control. Do not pay a rent increase until the office notifies you of the exact amount of the rent increase.

The amount of increase allowed by the Office of Rent Control depends on the added service, furnishing, or dwelling space. In general, a landlord will be permitted to raise the monthly rent by one fortieth of the cost of the new service. There are, however, exceptions to this rule. You should contact the Office of Rent Control to determine the permitted rent increase for your particular case.

The rent increase will be permitted to stand only as long as the added service, furnishing, or dwelling space is actually maintained. For example, if your landlord installs an air-conditioner, with your consent, he is permitted to increase your rent. But if the machine breaks down or is removed, your rent should be reduced, because once the air-conditioner has been installed it becomes an essential service. You are entitled to it. So, if the service is reduced or eliminated, apply for a rent reduction on the grounds of decrease in essential services.

Rent increases may also be granted if there is a "subletting without written consent from the landlord or an increase in the number of adult occupants who are not members of the immediate family of the tenant." Under this rule, the landlord is allowed to seek a rent increase even though the total number of occupants of your apartment does not increase. In one case, a tenant lived with his wife and two children in a rent-controlled apartment. But then the family split up. When the wife and the two children left, the husband invited his three cousins to move in.

The landlord applied for and received a rent increase. The tenant protested, because there had been four occupants before his wife left and there were still only four occupants. But this reasoning did not hold up in court. The judge decided that the tenant's argument was "tenuous and untenable in the face of . . . the Rent Regulations." Rent increases are permitted where there has been an "increase in the number of adult occupants who are not members of the immediate family of the tenant." The term *immediate family,* the judge pointed out, includes only a "son, daughter, stepson, stepdaughter, father, mother, father-in-law, or mother-in-law." The tenant's three cousins did not fall within the definition of his immediate family. So, the rent increase was allowed to stand.

• *Tenant's consent not required* A landlord may apply to the Office of Rent Control for a rent increase under any of the following circumstances: (1) there has been a substantial rehabilitation of the building or the apartment that materially adds to the value of the property or appreciably prolongs its life—excluding ordinary repairs, maintenance, and replacements; (2) the landlord installs a major capital improvement (e.g., an air-pollution-control device); (3) the landlord is not receiving a minimum return on his investment in the building (grounds for the so-called hardship increase); (4) there has been an unavoidable increase in operating costs or labor costs.

In each of these circumstances, the landlord must convince the Office of Rent Control that he is entitled to a rent increase. Approval will be granted only if the landlord certifies that all essential services are being maintained.

ESSENTIAL SERVICES

Every rent-controlled tenant is entitled to receive "essential services" from his landlord. There is no comprehensive list of these services; the essential services to which you are entitled vary according to your particular circumstances. In general, you should be receiving the essential services that were supplied to your apartment and to the building on April 30, 1962.

This freeze-date (April 30, 1962) is important. Broadly, the purpose of rent control is to maintain the status quo. The law does not increase the number of services to which you are entitled; it merely assures you the right to continue receiving certain past services. These past services are determined as of April 30, 1962.

On that date, the current maximum rents on rent-controlled apartments were fixed. Today, your landlord is required to provide your apartment and the building with all the essential services that he provided on the freeze-date, April 30, 1962.

Some of the services being provided on the freeze-date were not, and are not, essential services. So, the problem is to define *essential service*. The closest that the rent-control regulations come to a definition is an exemplary list of services that are definitely considered essential: "repairs, decorating and maintenance, the furnishing of light, heat, hot and cold water, telephone, elevator service, kitchen, bath and laundry facilities and privileges, maid service, linen service, janitor service, and removal of furniture."

These examples clarify at least one point about essential services: they are not always *necessary* services. (How many tenants consider maid service essential?) So, a service is considered essential—even if it is not necessary—if it appears that a tenant might have considered the service important when he rented the apartment. Thus, "what is or is not essential in any particular case necessarily depends upon the facts and circumstances in that case. . . . In making a determination . . . the construction, size, type, location, leasing arrangements, facilities, utilities and services of the subject building are all relevant factors in deciding whether a particular service is or is not essential." In other words, what's essential on Park Avenue does not have to be considered essential on East Fordham Road.

"In the field of rent control certain criteria have been applied to determine what constitutes essential services. Among other things, the general usefulness of the service as to the everyday living or occupancy of the tenant is considered. The particular or unique use to which the tenant avails himself of a provided service is relevant, as is the question of whether the elimination of the service materially reduces the value of the demised premises. Finally, whether the service was actually contemplated or bargained for at the time of entering the premise or signing the lease is often determinative."

In one case the tenants protested their landlord's planned conversion of the lobby, which would have been substantially reduced in size. The state supreme court agreed with the tenants that "there is no doubt that such conversion would destroy the lobby. It would no longer be a spacious room but a passageway 9 feet deep and 43 feet wide. It is common knowledge that when a tenant rents an apartment in a fine residential community of our city he not only takes into consideration the size and number of rooms of his apartment but also the physical appearance of the building, the lobby and the locale."

The court decided that a large lobby was indeed an essential service. If the landlord reduced the size of the lobby, he would be reducing an essential service to the tenants. Thus, the landlord was prohibited from decreasing the size of the lobby.

Essential services are not always as grandiose as lobbies in luxury buildings. In one case, the metal poles supporting a clothesline were considered an essential service. The poles had rusted; the landlord had removed them but had not bothered to put up new poles. According to the Office of Rent Control, the tenants had been deprived of an essential service, so their rents were reduced.

Here are some varied examples of other reductions in essential services: conversion of elevators from manual to automatic; removal of switchboard service; removal of one elevator operator on duty at night; failure to maintain water pressure; removal of or failure to repair bell and buzzer systems connecting the lobby with individual apartments; lack of awnings and shades; broken door to a refrigerator compartment; rusty water; defective windows; lack of venetian blinds; removal of television-antenna privileges; and, in one case, removal of room service (at the Ritz Tower, an apartment-hotel).

This list indicates the wide range of services that might be considered essential in your apartment and building. What's more, the state's rent-control office has promulgated one useful guideline: "Experience has shown that where tenants are deprived of a service they deem essential, they do not usually suffer this deprivation without challenge." So, if you think you're being deprived of an important service—even if you're not sure that the service is essential—complain to your district rent office (see Appendix A for addresses). In one case, the tenants did not complain until eight years after the elimination of their roof garden; the failure to complain convinced a New York court that the garden was a nonessential service.

You should also bear in mind that the rent-control law does not give you an absolute right to continue to receive exactly the same services you have been receiving. The law says only that you have a right to essential services; it does not give you the right to say *how* those services will be delivered to you. This is what it all boils down to: If your landlord fires one of the porters in your building, you may argue that there has been a decrease in your essential services. However, if the landlord can prove that the building is just as clean as it was before the porter was fired, the Office of Rent Control is likely to find no decrease in essential services. After all, the service you were receiving was a clean building, not a porter.

Landlords must obtain approval from the Office of Rent Control before making any increase or decrease in essential services. If permission is granted, the office can increase or decrease the rents to reflect the change in services.

For example, if your landlord allows you to install air-conditioners in your apartment, the Office of Rent Control can allow him to raise your rent for the added service. Once that added service is provided, it becomes an essential service, which the landlord is not free to eliminate without suffering a reduction in rent.

In one case, a landlord eliminated the service of a laundry room and removed the lobby furniture. When the tenants complained to the Office of Rent Control, it decided that a laundry room and lobby furniture were essential services. The tenants' rents were reduced by two dollars per month (one dollar for the laundry room and one for the lobby furniture).

Finally, a landlord may reduce or eliminate an essential service if he secures permission from the Office of Rent Control and agrees to provide an *equivalent service*. For example, your landlord can seek permission to convert the elevators from manual to automatic, or to do away with doormen and lobby attendants (doormen, lobby attendants, and manually operated elevators are all essential services). While the Office of Rent Control might grant permission and order a rent reduction, a likelier result is that the landlord will be ordered to substitute another service for the one being phased out. Substitution is a possibility whenever essential services are eliminated, but it is most often used to make up for doormen, attendants, and elevator operators.

For example, let's take a look at *Katz 737 Corporation* v. *Weaver,* which involved a twenty-story luxury building on Park

Avenue. The building had two manually operated passenger elevators and one manually operated service elevator. There was also a lobby attendant on duty from 8:00 A.M. to 1:00 A.M. And from 1:00 A.M. to 8:00 A.M. there was a combination doorman–elevator operator for both passenger elevators. "Among the duties performed by the elevator man and lobby attendant, in addition to their normal functions of lobby protection, was attendance at the switchboard in the outer vestibule, announcing guests, [sorting] and delivery of mail, newspapers and packages . . . and assistance to tenants encumbered with luggage and packages or requiring other assistance."

The landlord requested permission to automate the two manually operated passenger elevators. The Office of Rent Control agreed to grant permission if the landlord would maintain an extra attendant in the lobby—in addition to the regular lobby attendant—from 8:00 A.M. to midnight, daily.

The landlord objected to this addition and went to court. The state supreme court decided that "[the Office of Rent Control] has power to impose appropriate conditions in consenting to the elimination of the elevator men as a result of the installation of self-service elevators. The duties of the extra lobby attendant, under the circumstances . . . are not merely a luxury service nor do they merely duplicate those of the doorman. On the contrary, the order requiring this attendant avoids a substantial diminution of the protection required to be furnished tenants and [the] absence [of an additional attendant] would deprive tenants of an essential service which is necessary for their security and protection. Whether, and to what extent, doorman service may be regarded as essential may vary according to the building and times. The record establishes that a building of the character, size, and location as here involved would not provide adequate protection with only an outside doorman. The maintenance of the man in the lobby in addition to an outside doorman to assist the tenants is essential.

"The maintenance of only one doorman, as here desired by the landlord, would result in the foisting upon a single doorman of, in addition to his own function, all the duties that were previously performed by the elevator operators. He would thus be required to also guard the lobby, screen visitors, operate the intercommunication system, deliver and [sort] mail and assist people of advanced age and infirm health." So, the landlord was permitted to convert the elevators but only on the condition that he substitute an extra lobby attendant.

If you feel you are being deprived of any essential services, apply for a rent reduction. Ask your district rent office for two copies of form A-34.2S (Tenant's Application for a Decrease in Rent). Complete the forms, providing as much detail as possible, and return them to your district rent office.

If your rent reduction is granted, you will be notified. Your rent will remain reduced until your landlord convinces the district rent office that the reduced service has been restored. However, before the rent is increased, you will be given the opportunity to present any facts that indicate that the service has not really been restored.

• *Painting rights under rent control* A tenant under rent control has the same basic right as all tenants to have a painting at least every three years (see page 169). However, the required three-year interval between paintings may be shortened. Painting is an "essential service" and therefore it must be regularly provided to rent-controlled tenants. The regularity depends on past practice. Rent control says your landlord must paint your apartment with the same frequency with which he painted it immediately prior to April 30, 1962. Whatever practice he was following then he must continue to follow now.

Many tenants have no idea how often their apartment was painted in 1962. Either they have forgotten or they moved in after April 30, 1962. In order to solve this problem, the courts have developed the so-called two-year presumption. This rule conveniently assumes that your apartment was painted every two years before 1962. The burden is on your landlord to prove that his policy was to paint at longer intervals.

In no case will your landlord be required to paint more often than once every two years. This is true regardless of his practices in 1962. For example, consider the following tenant's question: Prior to April 30, 1962, my landlord had a practice of painting the entire apartment every two years and the kitchen and bathroom every year. My apartment was last completely painted and decorated a year and a half ago. Can I make the landlord paint the kitchen and bathroom now? The official answer of the Office of Rent Control is no. The landlord is required to paint only every two years. If he fails to, apply for a rent reduction. Ask your district rent office for two copies of form A-34.2P (Tenant's Application for a Decrease in Rent Based on Failure to Paint); complete the forms and return both copies to your district rent office.

If your landlord refused to fulfill his painting obligation and you went ahead and painted the apartment yourself, can you still file for a rent reduction? The answer is yes. And if the district rent office agrees that your landlord failed in his obligation, it will order him to reimburse you for the expenses of painting.

However, if you paint your own apartment before a painting is required, your landlord will not be under any duty to reimburse you. But, when will your landlord be obliged to paint next? The answer is that "in computing the time period, the date when your landlord last painted the apartment determines whether or not he is in default of his obligation of maintaining the painting." Thus, the fact that you painted does not relieve the landlord of his customary obligation to paint.

Some landlords will try to make a tenant sign a piece of paper absolving the landlord of any liability if his painters damage property in the tenant's apartment. "You are under no obligation to sign such a paper. Should your landlord refuse to proceed with the painting . . . unless a release is executed, the District Rent Director will consider there has been a failure to provide the customary painting . . . service." And you should then file for a rent reduction.

Assuming that you arrange to have your apartment painted, what are your obligations? Do you have to move your furniture away from the walls and place it in the middle of each room? The official answer from the Office of Rent Control is: "While you do not have to remove heavy pieces of furniture, such as a piano or a very heavy combination radio-phonograph, your landlord's request that you place other pieces of furniture in the middle of the room is a reasonable one which you must comply with. It then becomes the obligation of your landlord to properly cover and protect your furniture while he is having the apartment painted." Also, if you have wall-to-wall carpeting, you are not obliged to roll it up before the painting; rather, your landlord is obliged to be careful.

If you do any wallpapering, you do so at your own risk. Your landlord is free to paint over the wallpaper or to insist that you remove it. The Office of Rent Control said: "Where the landlord previously either hung the wallpaper or paid for the wallpaper, it is his obligation to both remove the wallpaper and 'size' the walls if he now wishes to paint. If the tenant paid for the wallpaper and either paid for the hanging of the wallpaper or hung the wallpaper himself, the tenant will be required to remove same and size the walls." So a good policy would be to consult your landlord before you put up wallpaper. If he agrees to it, either have him pay for it or get his consent in writing. You should also ask him to put in writing that he will not paint over your wallpaper as long as you remain a tenant.

You are now ready for your painting. Suppose you have chosen a lovely pink for the bedroom, avocado for the kitchen, and dark red for the living room. The painters arrive bearing gallons of off-white. You have a choice: have a lovely off-white bedroom, off-white kitchen, and off-white living room, or send the painters packing. What are your rights?

If your landlord has previously painted the apartment in one color, that remains as his current obligation; he must repaint "the entire apartment in a neutral shade and in a workmanlike manner." If *you* added another color to your apartment, your landlord has no obligation to follow your precedent. However, if your landlord has in the past painted in your chosen color scheme, he must now repaint with the same colors.

Now, assume your landlord has agreed to paint and you have agreed upon the color. The painters show up Sunday afternoon during your daughter's sweet-sixteen party. What should you do? You could invite them to the party. But you don't have to. "Painting service should be provided by your landlord during normal working hours during the day and not on weekends and holidays. However, it would be permissible for you and your landlord to arrange for the performance of these services at any time that is otherwise agreeable."

Finally, your landlord has an obligation to do a workmanlike job. If you're not satisfied, file for a rent reduction.

CHAPTER 8

Rent Stabilization: Your Right to a Lease

YOUR RIGHT TO A RENEWAL LEASE

Every rent-stabilized tenant has the right to a lease, and when it expires, he has the right to a renewal lease. In this way, the rent-stabilization law guarantees a tenant's right to continued occupancy of his apartment.

When a tenant moves into a rent-stabilized apartment, he has the right to a lease—it is called a vacancy lease. How long this lease runs is left up to the landlord and tenant to negotiate. The tenant has no right to a vacancy lease of any specific length.

However, when the tenant renews his lease, section 60 of the Rent Stabilization Code takes over. This section provides strict rules that the landlord must follow. The sequence of events is important:

1. Not more than 150 and not less than 120 days prior to the end of the tenant's lease, the landlord must send a letter to the tenant offering to renew his lease.

2. Within 60 days of receiving the landlord's offer, the tenant must either elect to renew his lease or vacate his apartment at the end of his current lease.

Thus, at least 120 days before the end of your lease, the landlord must offer a renewal lease. The Rent Stabilization Code requires that the landlord offer you a one-, two-, or three-year lease renewal. The amount of rent increase permitted varies according to the length of the lease (see chapter 9). However, even if your landlord has decided to charge any rent increase after your current lease expires, you still have the right to a renewal lease.

You must notify your landlord within sixty days if you want to renew your lease. You have the right to choose a one-, two-, or three-year lease. Your landlord must accept your choice.

If you fail to notify your landlord within sixty days, you will, in all likelihood, lose your right to renew your lease. There have been a few cases in which a tenant was a little late in accepting the renewal-lease offer and the landlord refused to give the tenant the lease. Most courts when confronted with this situation allow the tenant a little leeway. For example, if the offer was accepted only five days late, you probably won't be in trouble. But don't take any chances. In at least one case, a tenant who sent in his acceptance after sixty days was up was evicted! We strongly suggest that you send in your acceptance well before sixty days is up, and that you use certified mail, return receipt requested. That way, you have proof that you accepted the landlord's offer within the required time period.

There are no magic words required to accept a renewal-lease offer. All you need write is that you want a renewal lease, and specify the length of the lease you want (one, two, or three years).

After the landlord receives your letter, he should send you a lease. The law has no particular time limit specified within which the lease must be sent to you. However, you should have the lease in hand at least before your current lease expires.

Your renewal lease must have the same terms and conditions as the expiring lease. This rule has been in effect since the original Rent Stabilization Law of 1969. Consequently, every rent-stabilized tenant should have the same terms and conditions in his present lease as he had in his first lease when his apartment became rent stabilized. After all, every renewal lease must have the same terms and conditions as the expiring lease, going all the way back to the first lease that the tenant signed under a rent stabilization.

Sometimes landlords try to change the terms or conditions in a renewal lease. These changes are void. So, if you had the right to sublet, it must be continued in the renewal lease. And if the old lease said nothing about pets, the new one can't prohibit them.

What's more, the renewal must not charge you extra for rights you are already enjoying. For example, if you have been permitted to keep a dog, you can't suddenly be charged twenty-five dollars a month for the privilege of continued permission during the renewal term.

Sometimes a landlord may try to delete clauses of peculiar value to an individual tenant. In one case, a tenant at 600 West 246th Street, Riverdale, had converted his kitchen broom closet into an eating area. His lease contained a clause in which the landlord waived any right to damages caused by the alteration. When the landlord left this waiver out of the renewal lease, the tenant complained to the Conciliation and Appeals Board. The board ordered the landlord to offer the tenant a renewal lease that included the waiver clause.

There are, however, some exceptions to this rule, which you should know about. A landlord is permitted to add what is known as a Rent Guidelines Rider. (A copy of a typical rider is in Appendix F.) A landlord may add this type of language to your lease even though it was not present in your expiring lease. Furthermore, if your landlord has filed plans to turn your building into a cooperative, he may add to your lease a clause allowing the termination of the lease on ninety days' notice.

Aside from these exceptions, your renewal lease must be on the same terms and conditions as your expiring lease. This requirement has posed some problems for landlords who use form leases. Sometimes they couldn't quite tell whether their renewal lease was identical with the expiring lease. Therefore, they developed a "saving clause." Instead of giving you a renewal lease containing the exact same terms, they give you a lease with the following clause (or something similar):

"In the event that there is any printed term or condition contained in the renewal lease presently being offered to you covering the premises which you presently occupy that in any way varies from your present lease, except for term and amount thereof, it is hereby understood and agreed that the printed terms and conditions as set forth in your present lease shall govern."

This clause simply states the law; your renewal lease must not be different from your expiring lease, but, if there is any difference, the terms of your expiring lease control. While at least one court found this type of clause objectionable, most currently agree that it is acceptable.

What should you do if your landlord offers you a renewal lease on terms different from those in your expiring lease (except for the permitted additions just mentioned)? As a practical matter you could sign the renewal lease anyway. Any terms that differed from those in your expiring lease are void and unenforceable. If you wanted, you could then file a complaint with the Conciliation and Appeals Board. They would order the landlord to give you a proper lease renewal. In other words, you take no risks by signing an improper renewal lease.

However, there may be a better course of action. It entails a little risk, but it may be worth it to you. Assume your landlord offers an improper lease renewal. For example, your current lease has a clause permitting you to sublet. The renewal lease your landlord sent you has no clause giving you permission to sublet. What happens if you refuse to sign the lease? Eventually, your landlord might try to evict you. However, you could beat him to the punch by filing a complaint with the Conciliation and Appeals Board, claiming that the landlord did not offer a proper lease renewal. If you do file the complaint, the board will eventually get to your case. If the lease renewal was improper, the landlord will be ordered to send you a proper renewal lease. Furthermore, the board will require that the renewal lease begin sixty days after you receive it. In other words, the lease cannot be retroactive.

You can save quite a lot of money this way: Let's assume your present lease is due to expire on June 1, 1979. The landlord properly offers to renew your lease. You accept a two-year renewal. The landlord sends you the renewal lease, and you discover that it is different from your expiring lease. And there is no "savings clause." You refuse to sign the lease, and you file a complaint with the Conciliation and Appeals Board.

Usually it will take a few months for the board to get around to your case. When they do, they will order the landlord to send you a proper renewal lease. The term of that lease cannot begin earlier than sixty days after you get the proper renewal lease. So, let's say the board decides your case on December 1, 1979. You get a proper renewal lease on December 15, 1979. That renewal lease cannot begin before February 15, 1980 (sixty days after you got it), and it must run for the full two years. During the period from June 1, 1979, to February 15, 1980, you should be paying only the amount of rent called for in your expiring lease; there can be no rent increase. Thus, you avoid almost eight months of rent increase, and you won't have another rent increase for almost two years and eight months from when your old lease expired!

In order to accomplish this feat, you must be very sure that the renewal lease offered to you is different from your expiring lease. We strongly suggest that you consult the Conciliation and Appeals Board, the Rent Stabilization Association, or a tenants' group. If you are absolutely convinced that you have been offered an improper renewal lease, *don't sign it.* File a complaint with the Conciliation and Appeals Board. Pay only the rent called for under your expiring lease. Then wait. Eventually the board will order your landlord to give you a proper lease renewal. And only sixty days after you got the lease do you begin paying a rent increase.

GROUNDS FOR NONRENEWAL

The Rent Stabilization Code lists five situations in which a landlord may properly refuse to offer you a renewal lease:

1. Your apartment is located in a building owned by a cooperative corporation or association, and the owner of your apartment wants to live in it.

2. The owner of your building or a member of his immediate family wants to live in your apartment. The term *immediate family* includes a husband, wife, son, daughter, stepson, stepdaughter, father, mother, father-in-law, or mother-in-law.

3. You refused to sign a proper renewal lease. In other words, if the landlord offers a proper renewal lease and you

don't sign it, he doesn't have to offer it again. The key word here is *proper*. As you read earlier, you don't have to sign an improper renewal lease.

4. The landlord wants to take your apartment off the rental market.

5. You are not occupying your apartment as your primary residence (see chapter 1).

If a landlord refuses to renew your lease for ground 1, 2, or 3, he must prove his right not to renew before a judge in court. The Conciliation and Appeals Board will not decide the merits of the case. So, if your landlord is relying on any of these three grounds for not renewing your lease, you should consider securing legal assistance.

However, for grounds 4 and 5 the landlord must satisfy the Conciliation and Appeals Board that he has met the requirements of the law. If the landlord refuses to renew your lease on either of these two grounds, we suggest you file a complaint with the board.

Frequently, when a landlord refuses to renew a lease it is because he plans to sell the building. This is not proper grounds for refusing to renew a lease. You are entitled to a renewal lease regardless of the landlord's sales plans.

In order to complain to the Conciliation and Appeals Board because your landlord refuses to renew your lease, contact the Rent Stabilization Association or the board (the addresses are in Appendix A) and ask for the necessary forms. Completing and filing the forms with the board should pose no problems.

CHAPTER 9

Rent Stabilization: Your Rent

Tenants who are subject to the rent-stabilization law, unlike those under rent control, have the right to a lease. The law strictly limits the amount of rent that may be charged in the first lease when an apartment becomes rent stabilized. Thereafter, a landlord is allowed to increase the rent whenever he signs a lease on the apartment. The amount of the increase is a fixed percentage of the previous rent.

Therefore, in order to calculate your proper rent you must know the amount of the proper first rent when the apartment became rent stabilized. This we call the "base rent." Then you will have to determine the number and amounts of all rent increases permitted since that time. The result will be the amount your landlord can legally charge you now.

THE BASE RENT

In order to determine your base rent you must know when your apartment became rent stabilized. (We suggest you read chapter 1 in order to fully understand when apartments became rent stabilized.) For purposes of determining base rent there are three basic categories of rent-stabilized apartments:

1. Apartments that were rent stabilized prior to July 1, 1971, and that were *not* destabilized because of a vacancy occurring

during the period of the vacancy decontrol law (July 1, 1971, through June 30, 1974). These are known as "continuously stabilized" apartments. The base rent is the rent actually paid on May 31, 1968. If your apartment belongs in this category, you have the right to inspect the lease that was in effect on May 31, 1968. In this way you can determine your base rent.

2. Apartments in which a vacancy occurred on or after July 1, 1971, but before July 1, 1974. These apartments were decontrolled or destabilized under the vacancy decontrol law. The base rent for these apartments is the rent that was actually paid on June 30, 1974. If you were not the tenant on June 30, 1974, your landlord must show you the lease that was in effect on that day and any subsequent leases.

3. Rent-controlled apartments that become vacant after June 30, 1974. These apartments will become rent stabilized if they are located in buildings that contain at least six apartments. The base rent for these apartments is the first rent paid by the first tenant who moves in after the apartment becomes vacant. If you were not the first tenant, you have the right to see the lease that was in effect for that tenant and any subsequent leases.

Now you should know your base rent. However, you may have come upon one of two problems. First, you may have found that your landlord was providing a concession to the tenant in occupancy on your base date. Second, there may have been a tax-escalator clause in the lease that was in effect on the base date.

• *Concessions* Sometimes there is a difference between the rent that was actually being paid on the base date and the rent specified in the lease then in effect. The difference arose probably because the landlord gave the tenant a concession. A concession is a form of rent discount. For example, a landlord might agree to give you three months' rent free out of a two-year lease. This concession induces you to sign the lease. You do not get the three months' free rent at one time; instead, it is prorated out over the entire twenty-four-month lease. The landlord reduces the monthly rent by an amount that, when multiplied by twenty-four, results in a saving of three months' rent. So, the rent actually being paid each month is less than the rent required by the lease.

Assuming that a tenant was receiving the benefit of a concession as of the base date, what is his base rent? Is it the amount specified in the lease then in effect, or is it the lesser amount he was actually paying? The answer is: the base rent is the rent that the tenant was actually required to pay on the base date, regardless of what the lease says.

The same principle applies to the so-called escalator clauses often found in leases. An escalator raises the rent at predetermined intervals during the term of a lease. For example, a lease might provide for a rental of $100 during the first year, $125 during the second year, and so forth. The base rent is the rent actually being paid on the base date, regardless of any later escalation.

• *Tax escalators* Some tenants pay a tax-escalator charge under a clause in their lease. Typically, a tax-escalator clause requires a tenant to pay a certain percentage of the real estate taxes paid by the landlord. Each year the amount of the taxes are determined, and the tenant pays his share.

We would like to explain the rules that apply to tax escalators. However, the guidelines issued by the Rent Guidelines Board are so garbled that we can't quite figure them out. Rather than guessing at what the board is trying to say, we suggest that anyone with a tax-escalator clause contact the Rent Stabilization Association or the Conciliation and Appeals Board (CAB) and request advice.

Most of you should now know your base rent. Some of you luckier tenants may even have the right to get your base rent reduced. Still others will have the right to get the rent reduced on the first lease you signed after you became rent stabilized. (Some of you will get both rights!) Basically, these rights belong to tenants who moved into apartments that had been rented during vacancy decontrol. These apartments frequently had high rents, since there was no limit, during vacancy decontrol, on what the landlord could charge.

There are three groups of tenants who may get their rent reduced:

1. Tenants whose apartments were rent controlled or rent stabilized prior to July 1, 1971, *and* were vacated on or between January 1, 1974, and June 30, 1974. Tenants in this group can

file a Fair Market Rent Adjustment Application. The procedure is discussed in the following pages.

2. Tenants who, after June 30, 1974, moved into an apartment in which the prior tenant was rent controlled. Tenants in this group may also file a Fair Market Rent Adjustment Application. (Again, the procedure is discussed in the following pages.)

3. Tenants who moved into apartments that had been decontrolled or destabilized during the vacancy decontrol law (July 1, 1971, through June 30, 1974). These tenants might have the right to have a limit placed on the amount that can be charged in the first lease that began after June 30, 1974. (This procedure is described on page 110.)

If you don't belong to any of these groups, you are ready to compute the rent increases that have been permitted above your base rent. The section Computing Rent Increases Over the Base Rent, which begins on page 111, will guide you through this process.

TENANT'S FAIR MARKET RENT APPEAL

The Rent Stabilization Code provides a procedure for adjusting the rent of certain rent-stabilized tenants. The procedure is available to the *first* tenants who: (1) move into apartments that were rent controlled or rent stabilized prior to July 1, 1971 (the beginning of the vacancy decontrol law), and were vacated at any time on or after January 1, 1974, but before July 1, 1974; or who (2) moved into apartments after June 30, 1974, in which the prior tenant was rent controlled. If you fit into either of these groups, you have the right to file a Fair Market Rent Adjustment Application with the CAB.

Before we look at what filing an appeal might accomplish, let's examine who has the right to appeal. Under the code, your landlord was required to notify you that you had the right to file an appeal. He had to have given you this notice on a form prepared by the CAB. If you were the first tenant to move into an apartment that was rent controlled before July 1, 1971, and that was vacated at any time on or after January 1, 1974, but before July 1, 1974, you should have received a DC-1 form. If the apartment was rent stabilized, instead of having been rent controlled, you should have received a DS-1 form. And if you moved into your apartment *after* June 30, 1974, and the prior tenant was rent controlled, you should have received a DC-2 form. In every case, the landlord was required to send you the form by certified mail.

Your landlord was required to send you the form within thirty days after you moved in. Obviously, most of you should have received your forms long ago if you moved into your apartment on or between January 1, 1974, and June 30, 1974. As a practical matter, though, many landlords never sent out these forms.

If you move into a formerly rent-controlled apartment anytime after June 30, 1974, you certainly have the right to receive a DC-2 form. This can happen at any time, since rent-controlled apartments are continuously being vacated and joining the ranks of the rent-stabilized apartments. However, once again, landlords are frequently forgetting their legal responsibility.

If you received the proper form, you were required to file an appeal within ninety days or lose your appeal right. However, if you never received the form, you have not given up any rights. You still have the right to file an appeal. Also, if a prior tenant had the right to appeal but was not served with the form, you still have the right. If you suspect that a prior tenant who should have received a form did not, file an appeal. The landlord will be forced to show his certified-mail receipt for having sent the letter and the form to the prior tenant. If he can't, you have the right to appeal.

Now that you know who has the right to appeal, what are you appealing about? The purpose of the appeal is to try to get your rent lowered. You see, if your rent is unreasonably high, the CAB has the authority to lower it. The board uses two standards to determine if a rent is unreasonably high. Explaining the standards is beyond the scope of this book. We suggest that if you have the right to file an appeal, you should file. Simply call the Rent Stabilization Association or the CAB (the addresses and phone numbers are in Appendix A). Ask for a Fair Market Rent Adjustment Application. Simply file the form with the CAB and wait. Eventually they will decide whether your rent is fair. You've got nothing to lose.

LIMITING THE BASE RENT

If the apartment you live in became vacant and was rerented during the vacancy decontrol law (July 1, 1971, through June 30, 1974), you may be paying a particularly high rent. A landlord was free to charge whatever rent he would get on leases beginning during the vacancy decontrol law. However, there is a procedure which may reduce these high rents. We call the procedure limiting the base rent.

The source of the limiting procedure is the Rent Guidelines Board. The board has issued rules limiting the rent that may be charged on an apartment rented during the vacancy decontrol law. To determine whether you qualify for the benefits of these rules, you must know: (1) whether the rules apply to your apartment; and (2) whether the rent on your apartment is so high that it violates the rules.

To determine whether the rules apply to your apartment, you must know when the first lease began on your apartment after June 30, 1974. You must also know whether this lease was a vacancy or renewal lease. (A vacancy lease is the first lease a tenant signs before moving into an apartment. All subsequent leases he signs are renewal leases.) You need this information because under the Rent Guidelines Board rules, the type of lease and when it was signed determine whether you qualify for the limiting procedure.

If you have been able to gather the information you need, you are ready to determine if you qualify for the limiting procedure. You qualify if the first lease signed on your apartment after June 30, 1974 either: (1) began on or after July 1, 1974, but before July 1, 1975, and was a renewal or vacancy lease; or (2) began on or after July 1, 1975, but before July 1, 1977, and was a renewal lease.

If you qualify for the limiting procedure, you should not assume that you are being overcharged. Qualification means only that your landlord should have utilized the limitation formula when he computed the maximum rent on the first lease of your apartment beginning after June 30, 1974. The limitation formula restricts the amount of rent that could have been charged. Whether you are being overcharged will depend upon whether the rent charged exceeded the maximum amount permitted by the formula.

Thus, every tenant who qualifies for the limiting procedure should compare his rent to the maximum permitted by the formula to determine if he is being overcharged. Unfortunately, this is not an easy process. The limitation formula is extremely complicated. Furthermore, the formula requires information about your apartment that you probably do not have. For example, you might need to know the rent on your apartment in 1971. However, no tenant who qualifies for the limitation formula was a tenant in his present apartment in 1971. Obviously, there is no reasonable method available for a tenant to determine on his own if he is being overcharged.

There is only one method in which we have confidence for accurately applying the limitation formula: complain to the Conciliation and Appeals Board. We realize that most of you will not feel comfortable about complaining to the board when all you really want is to have someone compute your proper rent. (Indeed, we have suggested to the board that the name of its complaint form be changed to Rent Computation Request.) However, as this book goes to press, complaining to the board is about the only way to determine your proper rent.

When you prepare your complaint to the Conciliation and Appeals Board it is perfectly okay to be honest and admit that you don't know if there is an overcharge but merely want to find out if there is one. The board will make all the necessary computations and let you know if you have been overcharged. If you have been overcharged, the board will order your landlord to refund any excess rent he has collected. The complaint procedure is explained on pages 123–124.

COMPUTING RENT INCREASES OVER THE BASE RENT

You should now know your base rent and the date on which it was fixed. Some of you also know the proper rent for your first lease beginning after June 30, 1974. The next step in computing your rent is adding any permissible rent increases to your base rent (or the rent in the first lease). Rent increases are permitted when a lease is signed on the apartment. The amount of the increase depends on three factors.

First of all, was the lease a vacancy lease or a renewal lease? A vacancy lease is the very first lease a tenant signs when he moves into an apartment. A renewal lease is one that extends a tenancy begun in the original, vacancy lease. There are different rates of increase for vacancy leases and renewal leases.

Second, when was the lease to begin? And third, what was the length of the lease? Both of these factors count, because there are different rates of increase depending on the length of a lease and when it began. Each year the Rent Guidelines Board publishes orders that state how large an increase will be permitted on leases beginning during that year. The size of the increases varies according to the state of the economy, the availability of housing, etc.

You have the right to examine all leases that were signed on your apartment after your base date. You will have to look at them in order to discover whether they were vacancy leases or renewal leases, when they were to begin, and how long they lasted. If your landlord refuses to let you inspect the past leases, complain to the Conciliation and Appeals Board.

Every lease signed after your base date must be compared in sequence with the orders of the Rent Guidelines Board. The comparison yields the proper rate on each new lease. With a little arithmetic, you can calculate exactly what your rent should be.

Remember when computing your rent that the percentage rent increases listed in the preceding orders are the *maximums*. If your landlord charged less than the maximum, the subsequent lease increase is based on a percentage of this lesser amount—i.e., what was actually charged, not what could have been charged.

Also, if a landlord charged more than the legal maximum, subsequent percentage rent increases are computed on the basis of what the legal maximum rent should have been, not what was actually charged.

Thus, the rule could be summarized as follows: When computing a rent increase on a lease, take the rent actually being paid under the expiring lease *or* the legal maximum rent under the expiring lease, *whichever is less*. Add the percentage in-

Orders of the Rent Guidelines Board

ORDER #1

Leases Beginning on or between June 1, 1968, and June 30, 1970

Vacancy Leases
(a) For two years: 15%
(b) For three years: 25%

Renewal Leases
(a) For one year: 10%
(b) For two years: 10%
(c) For three years: 15%

ORDER #2

Leases Beginning on or between July 1, 1970, and June 30, 1971

Vacancy Leases
(a) For one year: 14.5%
(b) For two years: 16.5%
(c) For three years: 19.5%

Renewal Leases
(a) For one year: 7%
(b) For two years: 9%
(c) For three years: 12%

ORDER #3

Leases Beginning on or between July 1, 1971, and June 30, 1972

Vacancy Leases (apartments vacant on June 30, 1971)
(a) For one year: 18%
(b) For two years: 20%
(c) For three years: 23%

Renewal Leases
(a) For one year: 8%
(b) For two years: 10%
(c) For three years: 13%

ORDER #4

Leases Beginning on or between July 1, 1972, and June 30, 1973

Renewal Leases
(a) For one year: 6.5%
(b) For two years: 8.5%
(c) For three years: 10.5%

ORDER #5

Leases Beginning on or between July 1, 1973, and June 30, 1974

Renewal Leases
(a) For one year: 6.5%
(b) For two years: 8.5%
(c) For three years: 10.5%

ORDER #6

Leases Beginning on or between July 1, 1974, and June 30, 1975

Vacancy Leases
(a) For one year: 8.5%
(b) For two years: 10.5%
(c) For three years: 12%

Renewal Leases
(a) For one year: 8.5%
(b) For two years: 10.5%
(c) For three years: 12%

ORDER #7

Leases Beginning on or between July 1, 1975, and June 30, 1976*

Vacancy Leases
(a) For one year: 12.5%
(b) For two years: 14.5%
(c) For three years: 17.5%

Renewal Leases
(a) For one year: 7.5%
(b) For two years: 9.5%
(c) For three years: 12.5%

ORDER #8

Leases Beginning on or between July 1, 1976, and June 30, 1977*

Vacancy Leases
(a) For one year: 11.5%
(b) For two years: 13%
(c) For three years: 16%

Renewal Leases
(a) For one year: 6.5%
(b) For two years: 8%
(c) For three years: 11%

ORDER #9

Leases Beginning on or between July 1, 1977, and June 30, 1978*

Vacancy Leases
(a) For one year: 11.5%
(b) For two years: 13.5%
(c) For three years: 16.5%

*If a tenant is receiving free electricity as part of his rent, the percentage should be increased by 3.5%.

Renewal Leases

(a) For one year: 6.5%
(b) For two years: 8.5%
(c) For three years: 11.5%

crease permitted by the appropriate Rent Guidelines Board Order to this rent to determine the maximum legal rent on the subsequent lease.

If there have been any fractional leases on your apartment—i.e., for terms not exactly one, two, or three years—use these rules: (1) a renewal lease for one year or less is considered a one-year lease; (2) a renewal lease for more than one year but less than two years is considered a two-year lease; (3) a renewal lease for more than two years is considered a three-year lease; (4) a vacancy lease for less than two years is considered a one-year lease; (5) a vacancy lease for more than two years but less than three years is considered a two-year lease; (6) a vacancy lease for more than three years is considered a three-year lease.

Here are some examples of how you might compute your rent:

Example of rent computation for continuously stabilized apartment: Continuously stabilized apartments have a base date of May 31, 1968. Thus, in order to compute your proper rent now, you must go back to the first lease signed after May 31, 1968, and work your way up to the present.

Let's try a relatively complicated case: The base rent for this tenant was $225.00—i.e., the tenant in occupancy on May 31, 1968, was actually paying $225.00 per month. Thereafter, the following leases were signed: (1) A new tenant moved in on a three-year vacancy lease beginning August 1, 1968, and ending July 31, 1971, at a rental of $237.00. (2) The same tenant renewed this lease for a two-year period beginning August 1, 1971, and ending July 31, 1973, at a rental of $260.70. (3) The same tenant signed another renewal lease, this time for one year, beginning August 1, 1973, and ending July 31, 1974, at a rental of $304.00. (4) The same tenant renewed his lease for another one-year period, from August 1, 1974, to July 31, 1975, at a rent of $325.00. (5) You moved in and signed a three-year vacancy lease beginning August 1, 1975, and ending July 31, 1978, at a rent of $400.00.

Now, you want to compute your proper rent. We start at the beginning. The base rent is $225.00. The first lease was a three-year vacancy lease beginning August 1, 1968. Rent Guidelines Board Order (RGBO) #1 covers this period and permits a 25% rent increase. The maximum rent permitted would be $281.25 ($225.00 plus a 25% increase). In this case, however, the landlord only charged $237.00. There is no overcharge so far.

The next lease was a two-year renewal lease beginning August 1, 1971. RGBO #3 covers this period and permits a 10% rent increase. The legal rent, then, is 10% over the rent actually charged or the legal maximum rent, whichever is less, under the expiring lease. In this case, the rent actually collected, $237.00, is the lower, so the maximum rent increase is 10% over $237.00, or $260.70. That is exactly what the landlord charged, so there is no overcharge.

Our next lease was another one-year renewal, this time beginning on August 1, 1973. The rent was $304.00. This lease is governed by RGBO #5. A one-year lease renewal is permitted a 6.5% rent increase over the rent actually paid or the legal maximum rent, whichever is less, under the expiring lease. In this case they were the same: $260.70. We increase $260.70 by 6.5% to get the maximum rent: $277.65. But the tenant was paying $304.00. *Overcharge!* The tenant who was overcharged, even though he is no longer in occupancy, could collect for the excess he paid over the legal maximum of $277.65.

The next lease was the same tenant renewing again for one year. The lease began on August 1, 1974, so it is governed by RGBO #6. A one-year lease renewal is permitted an 8.5% rent increase over the rent actually paid or the legal maximum rent, whichever is less, under the expiring lease.

In this case the legal maximum rent under the expiring lease was $277.65, less than the actual rent actually paid—$304.00. Therefore, allowing an 8.5% rent increase over $277.65, the legal maximum rent for this one-year renewal lease is computed at $301.25. However, the rent actually paid was $325.00. *Another overcharge!*

A new tenant (you, in this case) moved into this apartment on a three-year vacancy lease beginning August 1, 1975, at a rental of \$400.00. The legal maximum rent is computed by applying RGBO #7, which allows a 17.5% rent increase for a three-year vacancy lease. Increasing the maximum legal rent on the expiring lease (which is less than the rent actually paid) by 17.5% gives us the legal maximum rent for your three-year lease: \$353.97 (\$301.25 plus 17.5%). *You are being overcharged, since you are paying \$400.00!*

A useful technique for computing your proper rent when many leases are involved is to chart the leases and their permitted rent increases. For example, in the last case, you would have created a chart similar to the one shown on the opposite page. In the far left column you list the base date and any leases including the appropriate RGBO number. In the next column list the rent actually paid under the lease. In the far right column list the maximum legal rent. It's a convenient way to keep track of your computations.

Example of rent computation for previously rent-controlled or rent-stabilized apartment that became decontrolled or de-stabilized during vacancy decontrol: If you utilized any of the procedures for lowering your base rent described earlier in this chapter, you know your proper rent for your first lease after June 30, 1974. When that lease expires, simply use the appropriate RGBO number to compute your proper renewal-lease increase.

If you found that your rent on June 30, 1974, was not excessive (or if you didn't bother to make any computations), you know that your base rent is what you were paying on June 30, 1974. Simply take the first lease after that date, find the appropriate RGBO number, and compute the proper rent.

For example, assume the rent on your apartment was \$200 on June 30, 1974. The first lease after June 30, 1974, was when you moved in on August 1, 1976. Simply look at RGBO #8 and determine your proper rent increase. Now, if you signed a three-year vacancy lease, the landlord would be permitted to charge a 16% rent increase. Your maximum rent should be \$264.

Example of rent computation for tenants who move into previously rent-controlled apartments after June 30, 1974: If you were the first tenant to move in after the rent-controlled tenant

Rent Computation Chart

Base Rent $225.00	*Maximum Legal Rent*	*Actual Rent*
8/1/68–7/31/71 3-year vacancy lease RGBO #1	$281.25	$237.00
8/1/71–7/31/73 2-year renewal lease RGBO #3	$260.70	$260.70
8/1/73–7/31/74 1-year renewal RGBO #5	$277.65	$304.00 *Overcharge*
8/1/74–7/31/75 1-year renewal lease RGBO #6	$301.25	$325.00 *Overcharge*
8/1/75–7/31/78 3-year vacancy lease RGBO #7	$353.97	$400.00 *Overcharge*

moved out, you had the right to file a Fair Market Rent Appeal. If you did, the CAB will determine the rent. If you did not, the rent you paid becomes the base rent. Any future rent increases for new leases are governed by the appropriate RGBO number.

THE STABILIZER

The Rent Guidelines Board has recognized that the cost of running a building changes from year to year. But when a tenant signs a two- or three-year lease, his rent is fixed for more than one year. In an effort to create a system whereby rents could be adjusted each year regardless of the length of a lease, the board came up with the stabilizer. We will somewhat oversimplify the rules surrounding the stabilizer, because few people have been affected by its adjustments.

Basically, on July 1 of each year the Rent Guidelines Board may increase or decrease *all* leases by up to 1 percent. Even though you have a signed lease, the rent may go up or down slightly. There is, however, one catch: the rent may not go up unless there is a clause in your lease permitting such an increase if the Rent Guidelines Board so orders.

If the rent is ordered up or down, the change begins with the anniversary of your lease following the July 1 date on which the change was ordered—but only if the lease is not expiring on this anniversary. Therefore, for example, if the Rent Guidelines Board ordered a one-half percent rent reduction on July 1 of 1979, your rent should be reduced by one-half percent on the first anniversary of your lease after July 1, 1979. However, if your lease *expires* between July 1, 1979, and June 30, 1980, the change in the stabilizer has no effect on you.

The important point is that a tenant should remember to carefully check each July 1 to determine if his rent is due to go down at some time during that year. He should be concerned only if his lease does not expire during that year.

As this book goes to press, there has been only one situation in which rent was reduced by a reduction in the stabilizer. That occurred in RGBO #4. Thus, if you are a tenant in an apartment that was continuously stabilized (i.e., there was no vacancy during the vacancy decontrol law), you might have been entitled to a one-half-percent rent reduction.

Tenants who qualified for the rent reduction were those in apartments with leases that began on or after July 1, 1970, and before June 30, 1972. If a tenant had such a lease, and that lease did not expire on or between July 1, 1972, and June 30, 1973, he was entitled to a rent reduction. The rent should have been reduced one-half percent on the anniversary of the lease occurring on or between July 1, 1972, and June 30, 1973.

For example, assume you renewed your lease on January 1, 1972, for three years. On January 1, 1973, your rent should have been reduced by one-half percent.

If you were entitled to a reduction, contact your landlord and ask for a retroactive rent reduction. If he refuses (or doesn't know what you're talking about), complain to the Conciliation and Appeals Board (see pages 123–124). Bear in mind that even if you were not the tenant of the apartment when the stabilizer was reduced, your rent might be affected. Since all rent increases are based upon a percentage of the prior rent, if the rent back in 1974 was reduced, your present rent would be reduced.

SENIOR CITIZEN RENT EXEMPTION

There is one category of tenants who may be able to avoid the full impact of the rent increases we have discussed: senior citizens. There is a senior-citizen rent exemption that is designed to avoid rent increases to older tenants, especially those on fixed incomes. If a senior citizen qualifies, he will not be required to pay most of the rent increases we have discussed, including those charged when a renewal lease is signed.

In order to qualify for the exemption, a tenant must: (a) be at least sixty-two years old; (b) not be on welfare; (c) be the head of a household; (d) have a total annual disposable income of not more than $6,500; and (e) be subject to a rent increase that, if paid, would result in one third or more of the tenant's income going to rent.

If you think you might qualify for the exemption, write, call, or visit the Mayor's Council for the Aging. They will direct you to the nearest center where you can obtain the forms and the assistance required to prepare them. If you want to try completing the forms on your own, contact the Conciliation and Appeals Board (see Appendix A). The board has prepared a booklet that explains how the forms should be completed. If you give the board a call, they will send it to you.

BROKER'S FEES

Frequently, when a tenant rents an apartment he is required to pay a broker's fee. This fee, usually one or two months' rent, is paid to the broker who helped the tenant find the apartment. Sometimes a superintendent or the landlord himself will act as the broker and collect the fee.

These broker's fees may be in violation of the Rent Stabilization Code. The Conciliation and Appeals Board has decided that a landlord or his agent may not collect a broker's fee. Where the landlord himself collected the fee, there is no question but that the law has been violated. A complaint to the Conciliation and Appeals Board will result in an order to the landlord to return any fee he collected, in addition to the legal rent and security deposit.

However, where someone other than the landlord collected the fee, the board will look closely at that person. Was he acting on behalf of the landlord? Was he the landlord's agent? If the answer is yes, the board will order the fee returned to the tenant. However, if the person who received the fee has no relationship to the landlord, the fee will be permitted.

For example, in one instance, L. Lyons Hickey, Inc., a real estate management firm, collected a broker's fee from a tenant moving into 139 East Twenty-seventh Street in Manhattan. Hickey, in addition to being the broker, was the managing agent for the building. However, Hickey did not own the building.

The tenant complained, claiming the broker's fee was illegal. Hickey argued that the fee was legal, since he was not the owner of the building. The Concilation and Appeals Board decided there was an "interlocking" relationship between the landlord and Hickey: Hickey was the landlord's managing agent. The broker's fee was, therefore, illegal. The landlord was ordered to return it to the tenant.

The board seems to be saying that a broker's fee is illegal if it is paid to anyone acting on behalf of the landlord. However, the landlord must know that the fee is being collected. If, for example, a superintendent collects a fee without the landlord knowing it, he will not be ordered to return it. The super was acting on his own, not on behalf of the landlord. However, if the landlord knew what the super was doing, the board would order any payment made to the super returned to the tenant.

If you paid a fee to anyone in order to secure your apartment, determine the relationship between that person and the landlord. If there is any sort of interlocking relationship between the person who collected the fee and the landlord, ask the landlord to return the fee. If he won't, file a complaint with the Conciliation and Appeals Board. The procedure for filing a complaint is discussed in the next section.

COMPLAINING ABOUT RENT OVERCHARGES

If you feel that you have been overcharged by your landlord, we suggest that you contact him and try to resolve the matter directly with him. Remember, you are entitled to receive any rent that you have paid in excess of the maximum permitted by the Rent Stabilization Code.

If you have had some problems computing your rent, we suggest you contact either the Rent Stabilization Association or the Conciliation and Appeals Board and ask them to help you out. They should be able to tell you if you've been overcharged.

However, if you aren't satisfied with any of these solutions, don't hesitate to file a complaint with the Conciliation and Appeals Board. There is no charge, and the board will make all the necessary computations for you.

Filing a complaint of rent overcharge with the CAB is simple. Call the Rent Stabilization Association or the Conciliation and Appeals Board (the phone numbers are listed in Appendix A). Ask for copies of the form you need to file in order to complain about a rent overcharge.

You will need to complete two copies of the form and return them to the Conciliation and Appeals Board. Completing the form should be no problem. However, if you have a question, call the board.

After you send in the forms, your landlord will receive one copy. He will get a chance to respond. Thereafter, the board will try to resolve the dispute as to the rent. It may take some time for the board to get to your case. However, you won't lose any rights during the delay. If you have been overcharged, your landlord will be ordered to refund that overcharge since it first began.

RENT INCREASES FOR NEW SERVICES

Rent increases under rent stabilization parallel those under rent control. There are two broad categories of rent increases permitted under rent stabilization: those for which the consent of the tenant is required, and those for which no consent is required.

• *Tenant's consent required* If you and your landlord agree, *in writing,* to an increase in your dwelling space or the installation of new equipment, your rent may be increased. The amount of increase your landlord bargains for is strictly regulated by law. Whenever new equipment is installed with your approval, the monthly rent increase must not exceed one fortieth of the equipment's total cost (including installation).

There are two key requirements for a valid rent increase under rent stabilization. First, the new service or dwelling space must actually be an addition to what had previously existed. You should not pay extra for a service to which you are already entitled. If a landlord merely repairs an old service, he is not entitled to a rent increase. "The equipment must be 'new'; replacing defective or worn-out equipment does not entitle the owner to a charge for the replacement."

For example, Richard Rosenthal's apartment on East Sixty-second Street in Manhattan had two air-conditioners ever since 1968. The machines were installed through sleeves in the wall. One warm day, the machines gave up. So, the landlord bought two new machines and installed them in the windows. He covered up the sleeves in the wall left by the demised conditioners and added $17.74 per month to Richard's rent bill.

Richard objected and went to the Conciliation and Appeals Board. The board decided that Richard's rent could not be increased, because no *new* service was being provided. Changing air-conditioners from the wall to the windows was not a new service. Since the old air-conditioners had broken, the landlord was obliged to repair or replace them. A landlord will not be granted a rent increase for repairing an already existing service. Had he chosen to increase the cooling capacity of the air-conditioners (with the tenant's consent, of course), he might have qualified for a rent increase. But in this case the new machines were similar to the old ones. Any rent increase would have been impermissible.

The second requirement for a valid rent increase is written consent from the tenant. In one case, a tenant wanted a new bathtub in his apartment on Riverside Drive. He asked for one, and he got it. He also got a rent increase of five dollars per month. The tenant liked the bathtub but had mixed feelings about the rent increase. He went to the Conciliation and Appeals Board. The board provided a short and sweet decision: "No increase for new equipment shall be collectible during the term of the lease except upon the written consent of the tenant. In this case, the owner has not obtained the tenant's consent in writing." The rent was reduced by five dollars per month.

Usually, consent to a rent increase will take the form of a letter: "I consent to the installation of . . . at a monthly rent increase of $ . . ." Sometimes, however, the consent appears in the lease. For example, Henry Toledano's lease contained a clause that read, in part: "Upon introduction into the demised premises of any air conditioning unit" the rent on the apartment may be increased "for the term of the lease."

Indeed, the rent had been increased, before Toledano moved in. The previous tenant had installed three air-conditioners, for which he paid additional rental of fourteen dollars a month. When the tenant left, he took his air-conditioners with him. However, the landlord continued to charge Toledano an additional fourteen dollars.

Toledano chose to install only one air-conditioner. The landlord insisted upon charging the full fourteen dollars extra rent. When the Conciliation and Appeals Board was consulted, it decided that Toledano could not be charged more than one third of the fourteen dollars. Otherwise, he would have been paying for a service—namely, three air-conditioners—that he was not receiving.

There is an even more dangerous trap than the one that almost caught Henry Toledano. Your landlord might try to sneak your consent to a rent increase into your lease after you have already signed it. Impossible, you say? Consider the case of Mr. Grunner. He rented his apartment on April 1, 1971, for $289.51 a month. Two air-conditioners and the refrigerator had been damaged in a fire, but the landlord replaced these appliances before Mr. Grunner moved in. However, the landlord also added $15.00 to the rent bill for the new appliances. Mr. Grunner protested that no extra charge could be made, because he had never consented to a rent increase.

But the landlord was one step ahead of him. He pulled out the lease Mr. Grunner had signed, and, lo and behold, at the end of the lease was a clause inserted with a rubber stamp: "The tenant hereby consents to the installation of a new refrigerator and 2 air conditioners in the apartment." The rubber stamp clause also set $15.00 as the proper rent increase.

For Mr. Grunner this was too much. He knew that clause hadn't been there when he signed the lease. And he was not about to be forced to consent to something he didn't want. He complained to the Conciliation and Appeals Board.

The board examined the case and confirmed that the rubber-stamp clause had indeed been added after the signing of the lease. (Mr. Grunner had initialed all the other additional clauses, but there were no initials next to the stamped clause.) Since Mr. Grunner had not, in fact, consented to the rent increase, he could not be charged for it. Furthermore, because there were two air-conditioners and one refrigerator in the apartment when it was rented, the landlord was directed to supply these services at no extra charge.

Another basis for increasing a stabilized rent arises when a tenant adds new occupants to his apartment or sublets it. Usually, a lease restricts occupancy of the apartment to the tenant and his immediate family. So, if you want a friend to move in, your landlord could object. Or he might ask for a rent increase based upon the increased occupancy. If your landlord wants to raise your rent on this basis, he must seek approval from the Conciliation and Appeals Board. The board will decide if the increase is reasonable.

If your lease has a clause allowing you to sublet, the landlord may want a rent increase for the duration of any actual sublet. He is allowed to receive extra rent, but only if your lease specifically provides for the increase. Thus, if you sublet your apartment and your landlord asks for a rent increase, look at the lease. Is there a clause that provides for the landlord to increase rent on the apartment if the tenant sublets? If so, you must pay the increase. But if there is no such clause, you can exercise your right to sublet without paying increased rent.

How much extra may the landlord charge—assuming your lease allows a rent increase for subletting? The maximum amount of increase is strictly limited. It may not exceed the rent increase permitted for a renewal lease.

• *Tenant's consent not required* A landlord may apply on his own to the Conciliation and Appeals Board for a rent increase based on the grounds of hardship (i.e., he is losing money on the building) or on the grounds of a building-wide, major capital improvement. If the board approves an increase in either case, it will allocate the cost among the tenants. *You must be notified by the board of the rent increase*. And if the increase is based on a capital improvement, you have the right to inspect the specifications of the improvement (e.g., cost breakdown, blueprints).

The increased rent may be charged only if the landlord is maintaining all required services. If you feel your landlord is not fulfilling this obligation, complain to the Conciliation and Appeals Board. (The board's address is listed in Appendix A.)

A rent increase allowed by the board cannot be collected during the term of your current lease, unless your lease says otherwise. Therefore, check your lease if you are notified of a rent increase. Look for a clause that says, in effect, that the landlord may increase rent during the term of this lease if a rent increase is permitted under the rent-stabilization law. If you haven't got such a clause in your lease, check with the Conciliation and Appeals Board before you pay any rent increase.

CHAPTER 10

Rent Stabilization: Your Right to Services

The Rent Stabilization Code requires landlords to maintain all services being supplied to individual apartments and the building as a whole. In order to fulfill this requirement, the code created the concept of *required services.* You, as a rent-stabilized tenant, are entitled to receive all required services.

The code also recognized that tenants frequently pay money in addition to their rent for services associated with their apartments. For example, a tenant might pay for the right to use a swimming pool on the roof, or he might pay a monthly charge for permission to use an air-conditioner. The code recognizes that in order to control rents adequately it must also control the costs of these other services. For this purpose, it created the concept of *ancillary services.* These are defined as services for which a separate charge is made. You are entitled to receive all ancillary services, and the amount that may be charged for these services is limited by the code.

REQUIRED SERVICES

The primary purpose of the Rent Stabilization Code is to limit rent increases. However, this purpose would be seriously obstructed if landlords were left free to decrease the services that they provide. Indeed, any landlord stuck with a limitation on the rents that he may charge might be sorely tempted to decrease services and thereby increase profits. The solution to this problem is the concept of *required services*.

Every rent-stabilized apartment is entitled to receive all required services. These services are defined as "that space and those services which were furnished to the apartment" when the rent on the apartment became stabilized, the so-called freeze-date. Thus, a service will be required only if it was being provided on the freeze-date.

Different rent-stabilized apartments may have different dates. This is because apartments have become rent stabilized at different times. Also, the freeze-date may vary between building-wide services and individual apartment services. (The difference between the two types of service is simple: A building-wide service is provided to the entire building; an individual apartment service is provided just to your apartment.)

The first step in determining what services you are entitled to is determining your freeze-date. Here are the rules:

1. If your apartment became rent stabilized in 1969 under the Rent Stabilization Law of 1969 and was *not* decontrolled during the vacancy decontrol law (June 30, 1971, to June 30, 1974), it is what is known as a continuously controlled apartment. The freeze-date both for building-wide and for individual services is May 31, 1968.

2. If your apartment was rent stabilized in 1969 but became destabilized because of a vacancy during the period of the vacancy decontrol law, and became restabilized in 1974, your freeze-date for building-wide services is May 31, 1968; for individual apartment services it is May 29, 1974.

3. For all other apartments that became rent stabilized for the first time on July 1, 1974, including any apartments that become stabilized thereafter because a rent-controlled tenant moves out, the freeze-date both for building-wide and for individual services is May 29, 1974.

Once you have determined your freeze-date, you know that the services that were being provided on that date are *required services*. However, in addition, if a landlord has added any service since the freeze-date, that service also is considered a required service.

Before we examine some specific examples of required services, there are two rules you should know about. First, let's assume that on your freeze-date you had a dishwasher in your apartment and your landlord knew about it. However, your lease prohibited dishwashers. Is a dishwasher a required service? The answer is yes. The Conciliation and Appeals Board has ruled (and the courts have agreed) that it is the actual services that were provided on the freeze-date—not the ones in the lease provisions—that determine what is a required service.

The second rule is that a landlord who was providing a required service on the freeze-date free of charge is not allowed to institute a charge for the service. Say you were using an air-conditioner in your apartment free of charge on your freeze-date. An air-conditioner, as we shall see, is a required service. Now, your landlord comes along and demands ten dollars a month for permission to use the air-conditioner. This is illegal.

So, now you know that the *actual* services received on the freeze-date are required services, and you are entitled to all required services. But what kind of services are *required* services? Well, they differ from rent control's "essential services" in one important respect: Under rent stabilization, the required service need not be in any way essential, necessary, or even significant. The plain fact is that whatever services were provided on the freeze-date are still required. These services may run the gamut from adequate heat to a pool room in the basement. Required services include: "repairs, decorating and maintenance, the furnishing of light, heat, hot and cold water, telephone, elevator service, removal of refuse and janitorial services and ancillary services including but not limited to garage space and service, protective services and recreational facilities."

Several more-detailed examples follow. Bear in mind that these examples are by no means exhaustive. They are offered merely to give you an idea of how the CAB has dealt with various complaints of service decreases. If your particular problem is not discussed but you still feel that a required service is being decreased, file a complaint with the CAB.

• *Laundry room* A tenant moved into 444 East Fifty-second Street in Manhattan after the freeze-date. Another tenant told her that the laundry room was open in the evenings. But when she went down to wash her clothes, she discovered that the laundry room had closed at 5:00 P.M.

Since she never got home before 5:00 P.M., the change in schedule rendered the laundry room useless. She complained to the Conciliation and Appeals Board. The board decided that laundry facilities are a required service. The landlord was ordered to reopen the laundry room for the same hours in effect on the freeze-date.

In some cases, landlords who operate a laundry room seek to charge increases for the cost of using a machine. These increases may be subject to the limitation imposed by the rent-stabilization law. (A discussion of this question appears in the following section, Ancillary Services.)

• *Basement storage space* As of the freeze-date, there was a bicycle-storage room in the basement of 230 West Seventy-ninth Street in Manhattan. But it disappeared shortly thereafter. A bicycle-owning tenant was sufficiently disturbed to consult the Conciliation and Appeals Board.

The board decided: "The facts in this case show that the tenant has been storing his bicycles in the basement of the premises since 1965 in space specifically provided in the storage room for such purpose. The Board finds that storage space for the tenant's bicycles was a service furnished on the freeze-date and is, therefore, a 'required service' which the owner must continue to provide."

• *Swimming pool* The tenants of a building on Nostrand Avenue in Brooklyn noticed a decrease in the hours during which their pool was open. They went to the Conciliation and Appeals Board. The board ordered the landlord to keep the pool open during the same hours as it had been in the summer of the freeze-date.

• *Venetian blinds* Providing venetian blinds to tenants is a required service if blinds were being provided on the freeze-date. The landlord must replace any defective blinds when necessary. While replacement is a required service, reconditioning of venetian blinds is not. The CAB has ruled that the cleaning, retaping, and recording of venetian blinds need not be provided by the landlord.

• *Master-antenna service* With the advent of cable television service in many parts of New York City, many landlords have disconnected master antennas that were previously connected directly to each tenant's apartment. The problem is that cable television service costs money while a master antenna usually does not. The CAB has decided that if master-antenna service was provided on the freeze-date, it is a required service. For example, a typical order of the board might read: "The owner is directed to restore services to the required level by either providing a master TV antenna or by installing for the tenant, at the owner's cost and expense, an individual roof TV antenna."

• *Ventilating and cooling systems* Central air-conditioning that was provided on the freeze-date is a required service. Furthermore, the CAB has held that a landlord may not shorten the cooling season; he must maintain what was being provided on the freeze-date.

In addition, a landlord may not substitute a ventilating system for a cooling system. For example, in one case, the landlord had been supplying the freeze-date service of air-conditioned hallways. After the freeze-date he changed the air-conditioning into a simple ventilating system. He simply shut off the condenser coils in the system. A complaint to the CAB brought the following decision: "Based upon the uncontroverted facts in this case that the corridors were cooled on the freeze-date and based on the inspection report, the Board finds that the present system providing only a fan without a cooling system constitutes a diminution of services." The landlord had to turn the cooling system back on.

Sometimes the decrease in ventilation service constitutes an impermissible decrease in required services. For example, in CAB Opinion #5201 the landlord used to provide twenty-four-hour-a-day ventilator service to tenants' kitchens and bathrooms. After the freeze-date he cut down the service by turning off the ventilator between 7:00 P.M. and 11:00 A.M. You can guess what the CAB decided: turn that ventilator back on for twenty-four-hour-a-day service.

• *Garbage service* Under the air-pollution-control law, landlords are required to upgrade their incinerator service. Rather than comply, some landlords just close down the incinerator and have the garbage picked up. The garbage chute to the basement is closed down too. While the tenants may not care about the incinerator, they are inconvenienced if the garbage chute on their floor is closed.

For example, Mr. Pfister lived in Greenwich Village and had used his building's incinerator chute since before the freeze-date on his apartment (in this case, May 31, 1968). Then his landlord closed down the incinerator instead of upgrading it. So Mr. Pfister no longer had his chute. He complained to the J. M. Brown Management Company, his landlord. J. M. Brown responded by placing garbage cans on each floor. This solution alleviated carrying garbage to the basement each day. But soon the fire department declared the garbage cans a fire hazard. At first, Mr. Pfister resumed carrying the garbage downstairs each day. Finally, he went to the Conciliation and Appeals Board for help.

The board was not able to order the landlord to restore the incinerator because restoration would have violated the law. However, the board did order the landlord to substitute a service equivalent to the incinerator chute: "Discontinuance of incinerator service does not constitute a diminution of required services as long as the tenant does not have to leave his floor to dispose of his refuse. That is: an acceptable substitute for an incinerator would be collection service at the door at a reasonable hour, or the approved conversion of the incinerator chute to a refuse chute. . . . The provision of garbage cans in the basement for garbage disposal by the tenants does not constitute an adequate substitute service for incinerator service."

Even if tenants do not have to leave their own floors, there can still be a reduction in required services. In CAB Opinion #3430, the landlord upgraded the incinerator in the north wing of the building while discontinuing service in the south wing. As a result, one tenant in the south wing had to carry her refuse 254 feet—the length of an average city block—in order to use the north-wing incinerator. This inconvenience amounted to a dimunition in required services. The CAB ordered the landlord to supply an adequate substitute means for refuse disposal in the south wing.

• *Recreational facilities* Any service provided to tenants

for recreational purposes may be a required service. If there is a charge for the service, it is considered an ancillary service (we discuss this subject later in this chapter). However, if there is no charge, the service is considered required.

A recreational service might involve nothing more than a recreation room in the basement or on the roof. In one case, tenants had the use of a recreation room with a Ping Pong table, lounging sofa, and other amenities. In 1972 the landlord converted the room into his own private storage space. Some tenants whose freeze-date was May 31, 1968, complained to the Conciliation and Appeals Board. The board decided that "it is uncontroverted that on May 31, 1968, a recreation room was being provided by the . . . owner to the tenants. . . . The Board directs the owner to restore services to the required level by restoring the use of a recreation room."

In another case, the recreation area was not as simple as a room. The landlord of a building on Hoover Avenue in Briarwood sought to sell a portion of some land next to an apartment house he owned. The tenants, however, claimed that the area was used for recreational purposes. There used to be two swings, a sandbox, and benches. The swings were missing and the sandbox and benches were in need of repair.

The Conciliation and Appeals Board was asked to decide whether the landlord could sell the vacant land or whether it was a required service. The board found that on the freeze-date (May 31, 1968, in this case) the tenants had access to a 100-by-130-foot enclosed area that had benches, two swings, and a sandbox. The landlord's proposal to sell off more than two thirds of the area constituted a reduction in required services. While the landlord offered to convert the roof of the building to a recreation area, the board did not feel this was an equivalent service. On the contrary, they directed the landlord to repair the benches and put two swings and a sandbox back in the area!

In some cases a landlord was providing a required recreational service on the freeze-date and thereafter tried to institute a charge for the formerly free service. This is not permitted. A full discussion of this area is in the next section, Ancillary Services.

• *Lobby furniture* There used to be a chair in the lobby of

109-33 Seventy-first Road in Forest Hills. After May 31, 1968, the landlord removed the chair. An alert tenant whose freeze-date for building-wide services was May 31, 1968, noticed the loss (which was not very difficult, because the chair was the only piece of furniture in the lobby). He went to the CAB, complaining of a reduction in required services.

The landlord contended that the lone chair served no purpose whatsoever. But the board never even inquired into the chair's utility. As long as the chair had been furnished on the freeze-date, it had to remain as a required service. The landlord was ordered to find the chair, or its equivalent, and return it to the lobby.

While the elimination of lobby or hallway furniture is usually regarded as a reduction in required services, changes of a purely aesthetic nature are not. For example, changing the style from Spanish to modern is not, per se, a reduction in required service. In one case, a landlord decorated his lobby and removed wood paneling from the wall, claiming that with the new decorations he had added, wood paneling would look "horrendous." The CAB decided that the elimination of wood paneling was basically an aesthetic change and found no reduction of services.

Lobby and hallway furnishings include more than furniture. For example, carpeting, wallpaper, drapery, mirrors, lighting fixtures, artwork, piped-in music, etc., may all be required services. If any of these amenities are removed after the freeze-date, they must be replaced with amenities of similar quantity and quality. And, a landlord must not refuse to replace missing furnishings on the grounds that they served no useful purpose or were vandalized or stolen.

• *Appliances* Any appliances being supplied to an apartment on the freeze-date are required services. Also, any appliances that were required to be provided on the freeze-date are required services, regardless of whether they were actually provided.

For example, if the lease on an apartment on the freeze-date gave the occupant the right to install an air-conditioner at no charge, the present tenant still has this right, even if no air-conditioner has yet been installed.

If a landlord replaces an appliance that is a required service, the replacement must be of the same quality and size as the original appliance. In one case a tenant had an 11.8-cubic-foot refrigerator. The landlord replaced it with one that was only 9.5 cubic feet. The CAB decided that the decrease in size constituted an impermissible decrease in a required service. The landlord was ordered to install a refrigerator of at least 11.8 cubic feet.

Sometimes a landlord replaces an appliance that is a required service and seeks a rent increase for a new service. The CAB draws a careful distinction between mere maintenance of an appliance, for which there may not be a rent increase, and an increase in service, for which rent increases are permitted. Chapter 9 discusses this distinction in detail.

Frequently, lease provisions govern the use of appliances. As we pointed out earlier, a lease provision that prohibits the use of an appliance might not necessarily be valid. If a landlord was providing a service on the freeze-date, despite the fact that the lease in effect then did not require the service (nor, indeed, prohibit it), the service is, nonetheless, a required service. It is the services that you were receiving on the freeze-date that determine what is required—not what your lease says.

Sometimes, however, use of an appliance may be in violation of a local law. Though the service may be required, to allow it would cause the landlord to break the law. For example, many buildings in New York City are not wired adequately for room air-conditioners. When a violation is placed on the building by the Department of Public Works, the tenant is required to remove his air-conditioner unless the wiring of the building is upgraded. What are the tenant's rights?

For the answer, we need to compare two CAB opinions. In the first case, the lease on the freeze-date had prohibited the installation of air-conditioners without the owner's written consent; and tenants were expressly obliged to comply with all laws, ordinances, and governmental regulations. Despite these lease provisions, the landlord had, on the freeze-date, allowed tenants to install air-conditioners. This practice continued until the Department of Public Works issued a violation against the building for inadequate wiring. The landlord then ordered the tenants to remove their air-conditioners, unless they hired a licensed electrician to perform the rewiring necessary for legal operation of an air-conditioner.

Some of the tenants complained to the CAB of a diminution in required services, claiming that the landlord should upgrade the wiring at his *own* expense. The CAB rejected the complaint. While the owner's freeze-date practice of permitting air-conditioners—despite his own lease prohibitions—did create a required service, nevertheless, the tenant's continued right to install and maintain air-conditioners depended upon legal utilization of these appliances. (The freeze-date lease was explicit on the matter of obeying all pertinent laws and regulations.) By failing to object to the installation of air-conditioners, the owner did not assume any obligation to make legal use of the air-conditioners. Therefore, no diminution in required services occurred when the owner insisted that tenants either upgrade the wiring at their own expense or remove their air-conditioners.

A different result was reached in another CAB case. Here, unlike in the preceding case, no prohibition appeared in the freeze-date lease. Quite the contrary—the tenant's lease on the freeze-date expressly permitted the use of an air-conditioner up to three quarters of a ton in capacity. The lease also provided that the tenant must comply with all laws, rules, ordinances, and governmental regulations.

As in the previous case, the Department of Public Works found the wiring inadequate. And once again the tenants complained to the CAB. This time, however, the board decided that the landlord had to pay for upgrading the wiring in the building that was required to make the air-conditioners legal.

What accounts for the different results reached in these two cases? Apparently, the CAB concluded in the second case that the landlord has assumed the obligation to insure that use of air-conditioners (up to three quarters of a ton) would be legal. Indeed, the lease specifically permitted the use of air-conditioners, providing only a size limitation. Having once assumed the obligation, the landlord was required to do whatever was necessary to provide the service, including, in this case, upgrading the wiring. In the first case, however, the freeze-date lease specifically prohibited air-conditioners. The mere fact that the landlord had acquiesced in their installation was not sufficient to charge him with the duty to insure that the utilization of air-conditioners would be legal.

• *Building personnel* The personnel who staff a building must be maintained at the level existing on the freeze-date. That level is generally measured in terms of: (1) the number of personnel on staff at the building in various capacities (e.g., doormen, superintendents, handymen, porters, security guards, elevator operators, lobby attendants); (2) the nature and quality of the service provided by the various members of the building staff; (3) the total number of hours per week that each staff member devoted to his particular tasks.

The CAB has not taken the position that a reduction in the level of building-personnel service is, in every case, a reduction in a required service. Rather, the board has come up with a little fancy footwork called a "presumption of reduction." This means that if there is a decrease in building-personnel service, the board will presume that there has been a decrease in a required service. However, the landlord is given an opportunity to rebut this presumption. Thus, if he can show that the reduction in the number of staff members has not actually reduced the service that the tenants were receiving, the board will find no reduction in a required service.

Take a typical case involving a decrease in porter service. A tenant at 440 East Fifty-seventh Street complained to the CAB because the landlord had dismissed one of the building's two porters. One porter was doing a job formerly done by two. You might think this is clearly a reduction in a required service. Well, here's how the CAB saw the case. The language used by the board in this case has been repeated in numerous opinions: "In this case the owner denies that the reduction in porter staff, from two porters to one porter, has resulted in a reduction of maintenance services. Absent objective criteria, it is impossible to determine the comparison between the [freeze-date] and present-day levels of facilities, equipment, maintenance and all of the other items comprising services. Accordingly, this Board must apply uniform standards for determining such issues. Among these is the principle that a cut-back since [the freeze-date] in the number of employees exclusively engaged in the care and maintenance of the subject premises gives rise to a presumption that there has occurred a corresponding reduction in [freeze-date] services barred by the Law and Code. . . . This presumption casts the burden of proof on the owner to establish that there was in fact no reduction of services. . . . In this case, the owner rebutted the presumption based on actual conditions noted upon an unannounced inspection. Those areas of the building which are within the scope of a porter's responsibilities, including the cleaning of stairways, stairwells, hallways and other public areas of the building, were found to be clean." The CAB found no reduction of required services.

What the board seems to be saying is that a tenant is entitled to receive the required service of a clean stairway, hallway, etc. If the landlord can provide this service with one porter instead of two, that's his business. However, if the board inspects a building and finds that one porter is not adequate for the job, it will order the landlord to return a second porter to the staff.

This approach, which we feel is somewhat naïve, might work for porters, since it is possible to measure objectively the service being provided by porters. After all, halls are either clean or they are not. (How long they stay clean after the board has made its inspection is the factor that makes the board's position naïve.) However, when the reduction in service involves a superintendent, handyman, security guard, doorman, or lobby attendant, measuring adequate service is more difficult. And it is here that the board seems to get into some trouble. We will explain some cases to show you how the board deals with reduced building personnel in these areas. You should then be able to judge the chances of success if you file a complaint.

Superintendents and handymen seem to provide the biggest problem to the CAB when confronted with a claim of reduced building-service personnel. It is, after all, hard to measure the exact services being provided by a super or handyman. In the case of porters, you can inspect the hallways; but what do you inspect if the service of a handyman or superintendent is suspected to have decreased? Nonetheless, the board still applies the *presumption of reduction* concept.

For example, on the freeze-date a building had had the services of both a handyman and a resident superintendent. Thereafter, the superintendent was fired and the handyman moved into his apartment. The board "presumed" there was a reduction in a required service. But the landlord was given the opportunity to rebut that presumption. In this case, he did. Here's what the board said: "The dismissed employee had the general classification of 'Superintendent.' There is evidence however that he performed few functions, if any, in that classification. In any event, the job duties of the handyman then on staff [were] expanded to include whatever such duties were and none of the six tenants who testified at more than fifteen hours of hearings established any resulting diminution of real services." Thus, in this case, the board took fifteen hours of testimony to try to determine if there was any real decrease in service. The result of their efforts was to permit the landlord to decrease his building personnel without there being any reduction in a required service.

The board seems to be putting the burden on the tenants to show instances of decreased service as a result of the decrease in building personnel. Obviously, this can be a difficult burden if tenants are not well organized. This problem is discussed in greater detail in the last section of this chapter, where we discuss how to file a complaint with the CAB.

Where elevator-operator service is decreased through the use of automatic elevators, the CAB usually finds a decrease in service. Thus, in one case a tenant from 75 East End Avenue in Manhattan complained to the CAB because two of the building's three elevators, which had been manned on the freeze-date, were now operated automatically. The CAB responded by ordering the landlord to provide manned elevators during the same hours, and in the same numbers, as were provided on the freeze-date. This is generally how the CAB handles a verifiable complaint of decreased manned-elevator service.

However, there is at least one CAB opinion that shows that a decrease in manned-elevator service is not automatically a reduction in a required service. In CAB Opinion #5050, the landlord discontinued manned-elevator service from the hours of midnight to 8:00 A.M. The owner submitted consents from 92 percent of the tenants agreeing to this decrease in service. One of the tenants in the 8 percent who did not consent to the decrease filed a complaint. The board decided, in a one-sentence decision, that the facts did not show a decrease in service. Apparently, if 92 percent of the tenants consent to a decrease in service, it is no longer a required service. (We will comment on the case again later in this section.)

Doorman service is generally regarded as a required service. For example, a tenants' association at 222 East Seventeenth Street in Brooklyn noticed a reduction in doorman service. Doormen had once been on duty—as of the freeze-date—between the hours of 9:00 A.M. and 1:00 A.M. Then the landlord, Colemont Realty Corporation, reduced the service by half.

The tenants' association complained to the Conciliation and Appeals Board. The board decided "that on May 31, 1968, eighty hours of doorman service per week were provided for the . . . building, between the hours of 9:00 A.M. and 1:00 A.M. Therefore, the owner is directed to restore and maintain doorman service at this level."

In another case, the hours that the doormen were on duty was not contested, but the number of doormen on duty was. Max Azderban, who lived in Rego Park, remembered that on May 31, 1968, there were always two uniformed doormen on duty between 9:00 A.M. and midnight. By January 1971, Max noticed there was only one doorman on duty.

Max complained to the Conciliation and Appeals Board. The board ordered restoration of the two doormen. Whether two doormen were really necessary for the job was not even discussed. It was enough that the landlord had provided two doormen on the freeze-date.

In still another case, a landlord sought to reduce costs by reducing the hours of doorman service on all union holidays. The board had no problem in ordering the landlord to restore full holiday service as had been provided on the freeze-date.

Security-guard services are almost always considered a required service. For example, the Howard Carol Tenants Association complained to the CAB that there had been a decrease in security-guard service. They argued that on the freeze-date there had been a security guard with a dog at one of the buildings in the apartment complex, from 4:00 P.M. to 4:00 A.M., seven days a week, but that service had been decreased. In addition, a security guard for another portion of the complex had been discontinued entirely. The CAB was convinced that this service had been provided on the freeze-date and ordered the landlord to provide the same security service as had been provided on the freeze-date.

In another case, the landlord sought to substitute a different type of security service for that which had been provided on the freeze-date. After all, he argued, it's the service you receive that's important, not how you receive it. In this case, however, he tried to go too far. On the freeze-date the building had its own security guard with a guard dog. Thereafter, the landlord substituted a roving guard in an automobile to cover more than one building. The board found this to be a reduction in a required service. The building, on the freeze-date, had its own security guard. The landlord was ordered to rehire the security guard for the building.

• *Repairs* The Conciliation and Appeals Board has repeatedly decided that repairs are a required service. In general, a tenant is entitled to the same repair service he was receiving on his base date.

The range of repairs included is virtually unlimited. Anything from a broken doorknob to a falling ceiling is covered. If something in your apartment or the building (including the grounds surrounding the building and owned by the landlord) is not being properly maintained, the landlord is not supplying the required maintenance and repair service.

The main problem that does arise in repair cases is when an appliance is involved. Sometimes a landlord will claim either (1) that he has no obligation to repair the appliance; or (2) that a new appliance is needed and the tenant must pay for it; or (3) that the tenant caused the problem.

As to the first claim, the Conciliation and Appeals Board will presume that if a landlord is obliged to provide an appliance, he has the responsibility for maintaining it in good working condition. The burden is on the landlord to prove that on the base date the responsibility for repairs belonged to the tenant. If the landlord can't come forth with this proof, he will be required to repair the appliance.

A landlord can prove that the tenant has the obligation to make repairs on the appliance by showing a clause in the lease on the apartment that was in effect on the base date, which places the burden of repairs on the tenant. However, the language of the clause can be important. In one case, a tenant's dishwasher needed a new motor. The lease in effect on the base date required the tenant to pay for all "maintenance and repair" of the dishwasher. The Conciliation and Appeals Board decided that replacement of a motor was not ordinary maintenance and repair. It was, instead, an extraordinary repair, which was not covered by the lease. The landlord was ordered to pay for the new motor. However, had the lease clause placed on the tenant the burden of "replacement of all parts" as well as maintenance and repair, the outcome of the case probably would have been different.

The second claim landlords sometimes make in order to avoid making repairs is that the appliance needs to be replaced and the tenant must pay for it. This claim has no merit, as Jack Nagler found out. Jack had three air-conditioners in his apartment on his base date. When they broke down, the landlord tried to repair them. When that failed, he replaced them with badly worn units that did not work. Finally, the landlord offered to put new units in if Jack would pay seven dollars more per month per unit.

Jack refused, and complained to the Conciliation and Appeals Board. He argued that the landlord had the obligation to repair the air-conditioners and, if he couldn't repair them, then he should get new ones at no cost to the tenant. The board agreed, and ordered the landlord to replace the three units with new ones at no cost to Jack.

While in this case the landlord was ordered to supply new appliances, that is not the general rule. A landlord is permitted to supply a satisfactory used replacement (in Jack's case he couldn't find any). After all, you have no right to *new* appliances. Your right is only to a properly functioning appliance.

The third, and perhaps the most frequently heard, claim by landlords for not making repairs is that the tenant caused the damage that makes the repairs necessary. In these cases, the Conciliation and Appeals Board has taken a consistent position:

the landlord *must* make the repairs. If he then wants to sue the tenant for having necessitated the repairs, he can. But the landlord must make the repairs.

Sometimes landlords agree to make repairs but only if the tenant agrees to pay for all or part of the cost. Of course, if a tenant had the obligation to make repairs, then this would be permitted. However, there are a number of cases in which the landlord had the obligation to repair but, nonetheless, required the tenant to contribute all or part of the cost.

For example, Anna Lemkow complained to her landlord about loose tiles in her parquet floor. The landlord sent a repairman who fixed the problem. The repairman gave Anna a bill for $122 for the repairs. Anna did not pay the bill. She claimed the landlord should pay. The landlord claimed that a few loose parquet tiles were not a serious problem, and anyway, Anna had agreed to pay for the work.

The Conciliation and Appeals Board decided that the landlord must pay the bill. Anna could not be charged for a service she was entitled to receive free. The board implied that even if Anna had agreed to pay for the repairs, that agreement would be void.

Indeed, any agreement by a rent-stabilized tenant to pay for a repair that the landlord is required to provide free of charge is void. If you have paid for a repair that was a required service, you might want to complain to the Conciliation and Appeals Board and try to get your money back.

• *Painting* As a rent-stabilized tenant, you have the same general right as all tenants, namely, to have your apartment painted at least every three years. But this interval may be shortened, just as it can be under rent control. You see, painting is a required service. Therefore, your landlord must paint your apartment with the same frequency with which he painted it immediately prior to your base date. For example, if your landlord was painting your apartment every two years prior to May 31, 1968, you now have the right to a painting every two years.

When you move into a rent-stabilized apartment, you may have your apartment painted right away or wait until the next painting is due. The landlord bears the full cost of this painting. However, when you renew your lease and the apartment is repainted, you might have to pay for part of the painting. The law provides: "In the event of a lease renewal for a term of less than three years, the tenant may be required to bear a pro rata part of the actual painting cost provided however, that such charge shall be proportionately refundable to the tenant in the event the same tenant further renews."

Take a close look at this rule. If you renew your lease for a full three-year term, you need pay nothing for the painting. The rule requires payment only on lease renewals of less than three years. If you sign a lease renewal for one year, you must bear two thirds of the painting cost. If you sign a two-year renewal lease, you must pay for one third of the painting cost.

Now, assume you have paid for part of the painting. And then you renew your lease again. You are entitled to have some or all of the money you paid returned to you. If the second renewal of your lease, when added to your first lease renewal, results in a total lease renewal of three or more years, all the money you paid for painting must be returned to you. For example, your first lease renewal might have been for one year. So you paid for two thirds of the painting cost. Then you renewed the lease again, this time for two years. The first renewal, one year, plus the second renewal, two years, result in a total lease renewal of three years. You are entitled to a return of the entire two thirds of the painting cost you paid.

In some cases a second lease renewal does not result in a total lease renewal of three or more years. In such cases you are entitled to a pro rata return of the money you have paid. For example, your first lease renewal was for one year. You paid two thirds of the painting cost. You then renewed your lease for one more year. You are entitled to a return of half of the amount you paid for painting. If you renew the lease again, for at least one year, you will be entitled to the other half of the money you paid. Because you will have had a total of three years of renewals, you should pay nothing.

Assuming your landlord has agreed to paint, you may already have taken out your color wheel. Before your choice gets too bizarre, consider the case of Nathan Ginsberg. Nathan lived in Flushing. Thirteen years ago his apartment was last painted. The bedroom was blue and the living room and foyer were yellow.

Then, for the first time in thirteen years, the landlord's painters appeared at Nathan's door. Nathan showed them the colors in his bedroom, living room, and foyer. The painters showed Nathan eight gallons of flat white. Nathan showed the painters the door. And then he complained to the Conciliation and Appeals Board. The board decided that Nathan had a right to a painting "utilizing standard colors to be selected by the tenant." Nathan was entitled to receive the same service he had been receiving on his base date. His apartment had been painted in colors at that time. Therefore, Nathan was entitled to a colorful apartment now if he wanted it.

Some tenants have clauses in their leases that place the burden and expense of painting the apartment on the tenant. In its most recent cases on the subject, the Conciliation and Appeals Board has ruled that *any* waiver of the right to painting in a lease is void. For example, Bernard Schiff moved into a rent-controlled apartment on November 1, 1972. The landlord had never painted the apartment when it was rent controlled. He didn't paint it when Bernard moved in.

After the apartment became rent stabilized in 1974, Bernard asked for a painting. When the landlord refused, Bernard complained to the Conciliation and Appeals Board. The board decided that despite the fact that the landlord had never painted, under the Rent Stabilization Code he was required to paint. Furthermore, any agreement in the lease to the contrary was void. The landlord was ordered to paint Bernard's apartment at no cost!

This is a rather extraordinary ruling, since tenants in Bernard's position have never received painting as a service. Indeed, there are some earlier board decisions that appear to be in conflict with cases such as Bernard's. However, the most recent decisions by the board clearly show that a tenant cannot be made to give up his right to a painting, regardless of the practice of the landlord on the base date. If you have been paying for the cost of painting your apartment, you may want to ask your landlord to take over the expense. If he refuses, complain to the Conciliation and Appeals Board.

If a landlord refuses to paint when required, a tenant has a choice. He can either complain to the Conciliation and Appeals Board or he can paint the apartment himself and then complain.

Arnold Goldman chose the latter course. He spent $453 painting his apartment. He then filed a complaint with the board when the landlord refused to reimburse him for the expense. When Arnold painted his apartment, three years had already elapsed since the preceding painting. At the time he painted his apartment, he signed a two-year renewal lease.

The board ordered the landlord to pay Arnold two thirds of $453, the amount Arnold spent to paint the apartment. The board reasoned that Arnold had signed only a two-year renewal. Therefore, in order to have a painting, he should deposit one third of the cost with the landlord. However, since Arnold had already been forced to pay for one full painting, the board simply subtracted the one third he would have had to pay the landlord from the full amount the landlord owed Arnold. That way, Arnold was entitled to two thirds of the full cost of a painting.

All this convoluted reasoning makes sense if you think about it long enough. What it really all boils down to is that if a tenant is entitled to have his apartment painted and the landlord refuses, the tenant may do the painting and bill the landlord. The board will order the landlord to reimburse the tenant. However, if, when he paints, the tenant has not signed a full three-year lease, the rules for prorating the cost of a painting will apply.

ANCILLARY SERVICES

In the preceding section on required services we pointed out that a landlord is not permitted to charge for any required service if, on your freeze-date, he was providing the service at no charge. However, if he was charging for the service on the freeze-date, the service is known as an ancillary service. The landlord may continue to charge for the service. However, the amount he charges is governed by the limits imposed by the Rent Stabilization Code.

Since ancillary services are also required services, a landlord may not reduce the service he was providing on the freeze-date. However, the freeze-date for ancillary services is slightly different from that for the required services discussed previously. The only change is that if your apartment was rent stabilized in

1971 and was then decontrolled due to a vacancy during the vacancy decontrol law (June 30, 1971, through May 31, 1974), then your freeze-date for *both* building-wide and individual apartment services is May 31, 1968. For other cases the freeze-date remains the same as for required services.

The Rent Stabilization Code defines an ancillary service as "including but not limited to garage space and service, protective services and recreational facilities. . . ." However, as we will see, the CAB will consider almost any service an ancillary service as long as the requirements of the code are met.

The most important requirement is that there must be common ownership of the service between the landlord and the operator of the service. For example, if on your freeze-date an *independent contractor* was operating the garage in your building, garage service is *not* an ancillary service. There is no common ownership.

It is sometimes difficult, however, to determine whether a particular service is actually owned by your landlord. For example, you may receive a bill for the rent from the XYZ Corporation and a bill for your garage from the ABC Corporation. Quite possibly, your landlord owns both corporations. If he does, the garage service is an ancillary service.

The reason for this rule is that the charge made for an ancillary service is strictly limited by rent stabilization, because the cost of the service is considered part of your rent. The cost can be increased only under the same rules that apply to your rent. Clearly, it would be impractical to impose service-charge-increase limits on an independent contractor.

Occasionally the cost of a service falls under rent stabilization even though the service is not owned by the landlord. In one case, a landlord allowed his tenants to use the facilities of an independently owned beach club at a one-half discount. The landlord paid the other half. This practice was followed on the freeze-date. But, at a later date, the landlord declined to pay his half.

The tenants went to the Conciliation and Appeals Board. The board recognized that the landlord did not own the beach club. So, the price of admission could not be controlled. However, the landlord's practice of paying half the beach-club cost was a required service. Although he had no say over the charges made by the beach club, he was still required to provide the same services that he had provided on the freeze-date. Thus, the board ordered the landlord to resume paying half the cost on behalf of his tenants.

While any service supplied to a tenant in conjunction with his apartment and operated by the landlord may be an ancillary service, most complaints about such services relate to one of three categories: garage service, recreational services, and appliances.

• *Garage service* Many tenants lease garage space from their landlords. If the cost is part of their leases, they should simply consider the service as part of their rent. For example, if your rent is $300 a month and your garage space is $50 a month, treat your rent as $350 per month. When you determine your proper rent in chapter 9, rent increases on your garage space are governed by exactly the same rules that govern the rent on your apartment. You also have the right to a renewal of your garage-space lease, which is discussed in chapter 8.

If you have a separate lease for garage space, view it as a separate apartment lease. The same rules for lease increases (chapter 9) and lease renewals (chapter 8) apply to a lease for garage space.

Not only are the rents on a garage lease limited, but the landlord is not permitted to decrease the service he provides. After all, an ancillary service is a required service. For example, in one case, Henry Schwartz complained to his landlord, the Padar Realty Company, about a decrease in the number of garage attendants. The landlord admitted reducing the service but argued that he was operating the garage as a "separate entity" and, therefore, it should not be subject to the Rent Stabilization Code.

The board did not buy the landlord's argument. There was common ownership of both the building and the garage (Pandar owned both). There was no disputing the fact that on the freeze-date (in this case, May 29, 1974), there were three more garage attendants. The board ordered the landlord to bring service up to par by rehiring three garage attendants.

• *Recreational facilities* In the preceding section we discussed recreational facilities as a required service. If the landlord charged for the use of the facility on your freeze-date, then the required service is also an ancillary service. You should treat the cost of the service as part of your rent. Only rent increases permitted under the rent-stabilization law may be collected for the cost of recreational facilities.

• *Appliances* In chapter 9 we explained the circumstances under which a landlord may charge extra for giving a tenant permission to use an appliance. Once the tenant installs the appliance and pays the extra charge, that appliance then becomes an ancillary service. In effect, it becomes part of the rent. For example, assume the use of air-conditioners in your apartment is not a required service. You want air-conditioners, so you ask your landlord for permission to install them. He says you can but it will cost thirty-five dollars a month. You agree. Once you install the air-conditioners, they become ancillary services. Your landlord may not increase the thirty-five-dollar charge except under the same conditions as the law permits your rent to be increased.

Sometimes, the appliance for which you are being charged is not in your apartment. In one case an alert tenant complained when the landlord increased the charges in the basement laundry room. The size of the loads was reduced and the costs increased. On the freeze-date, twenty-five cents bought an eight-pound wash and ten cents got you fifteen minutes of dryer time. After the freeze-date it cost fifty cents for a twelve-pound wash and ten cents for only ten minutes of drying time.

The CAB treated this case as seriously as it treats all its cases. After analyzing who owned the machines and when, the board concluded that the cost of the washing and drying *was* an ancillary service. The problem was that increasing the costs at the same rate that rents increase would result in a charge of, for example, 12.3¢ for a ten-pound wash. The board determined that there were no coin boxes that took pennies (must less .3¢). The remedy was to make the landlord promise not to increase his charges for the next two years.

COMPLAINING ABOUT REDUCED SERVICES

If you feel your landlord has reduced or eliminated a required or ancillary service, contact him. Tell him why you feel that he has violated the Rent Stabilization Code. If he does nothing, file a complaint with the Conciliation and Appeals Board.

There are two forms available for making a complaint. One is to be used for individual apartment complaints. The other is used for building-wide complaints. In order to get copies of whichever form you need, simply call the CAB or the Rent Stabilization Association at the numbers listed in Appendix A.

Preparing the form should be simple. However, there are a few words of advice. When making your complaint, be sure to be prepared to show what service was being provided on your freeze-date. Only then will you be able to show that there has been a decrease in service. But don't worry if you can't prove *exactly* what service was being provided. Do the best you can. The board will make its own investigation. For example, if you complain about a decrease in building personnel, the board will order the landlord to send in copies of his payroll for the freeze-date. From those payrolls, you will be able to see exactly what service you were receiving.

If the problem you are complaining about is building-wide, get your building organized before you make the complaint. When a complaint of decreased building-wide service is made, the board is usually interested in the views of all the rent-stabilized tenants in the building. After all, if you are the only tenant complaining, the board just might reason that the service involved can't be very important.

In most cases, the CAB is likely to reach a rational decision. However, we feel compelled to criticize the direction the board is heading in. In particular, we regret the board's insistence upon placing the burden on tenants to gather the necessary information to "prove" that elimination of building personnel does constitute a "real" decrease in service. The board itself promulgated the rule that a reduction in building personnel creates the presumption of a decrease in a required service, which the landlord must rebut. To then turn to the tenants and ask them to prove the decrease violates the board's own rule. Tenants, unlike landlords, are not in the business of monitoring building services. To place the burden of proof on tenants is unfair. We hope that the board will come forth in the future with a rule that it finds it can follow.

We also believe that the board should stop placing the collective will of a building above the rights of an individual tenant. In one case we discussed earlier, the board allowed a reduction in service because 92 percent of the tenants went along with it. The reduced service was the elimination of midnight-to-8:00 A.M. manned-elevator service. We don't know why the 8 percent didn't go along with the rest. Maybe they were nurses who came home late at night and valued the security of a manned elevator at that late hour. Whatever the reason, the board should remember that a tenant has a contract with the landlord, not with the other tenants. The Rent Stabilization Code protects the rights of individual tenants, not the collective will of a portion of a building.

CHAPTER 11

Passing On a Good Apartment

A good rent-controlled or rent-stabilized apartment is a major capital asset. It is passed down from father to son like a sacred family heirloom. And with good reason. The rents on continuously controlled apartments are generally lower than those prevailing in the open market.

However, the ranks of the rent-controlled tenants have been decreasing since 1971, when the vacancy decontrol law went into effect. Under the law, and still today, any rent-controlled apartment that is vacated loses the protection of the rent-control law (see chapter 1). Since 1974, most decontrolled apartments become rent stabilized upon decontrol. However, in making the switch, the rents increase substantially. And, more important, the landlord is free to rerent the vacated apartment to anyone he wants to.

The rent on a rent-stabilized apartment that becomes vacant also may increase, though the amount of the increase is limited. However, after the apartment is vacated, the landlord is free to rent to anyone he pleases.

In order to pass on your apartment to someone of your choosing, you must not allow the apartment to become vacant. Therefore, all the "pass on" techniques discussed below have one goal: to give someone else the right to live in your apartment without the apartment becoming vacant.

PASSING ON A RENT CONTROLLED APARTMENT

Passing on your rent-controlled apartment to a relative is quite simple if the relative is your son, daughter, stepson, stepdaughter, father, mother, father-in-law, mother-in-law, grandfather, grandmother, stepfather, or stepmother. All these people are members of your immediate family and are entitled to live with you under most leases. Once they move in, they become legal occupants of your apartment. When you leave, they remain legal occupants. They must not be removed, because they are rent-controlled tenants.

For example, William and Martha Morris lived in the same rent-controlled apartment for twenty years. Their daughter Clara and her three children lived with them. William and Martha decided to leave, but Clara and the children remained. The landlord had other plans. He sought to evict Clara and the children because they were not his tenants.

The judge refused to issue an eviction order: "Clara Morris and her children were part of the family unit of the tenants and as such were entitled to possession, use and occupancy of the apartment. The fact that William and Martha moved from the apartment, leaving the remainder of the family unit in possession, did not render those remaining less entitled to such possession, use and occupancy." Clara and her children were entitled to remain in the apartment as rent-controlled tenants.

The rule allowing a rent-controlled apartment to stay in the family runs into some trouble if the family relationship breaks up. Following a divorce, ex-husband and ex-wife are no longer related. If they have a lease, the only person entitled to remain in the apartment is the one who signed the lease. Usually, it seems, this is the husband. What can be done, then, if the former wife wants to remain in the apartment? The answer is for the husband to leave and the former wife to remain and pay the rent. Unless the landlord is aware of the divorce, he surely will accept rent from the former wife. Once he has cashed the rent checks, the former wife becomes the legal tenant. The case of *BBC Holding Corporation* v. *Coster* explains why.

BBC owned a Manhattan apartment building where Mr. and Mrs. Coster were tenants. The Costers got divorced and Mr.

Coster moved out. Mrs. Coster stayed on and paid the rent, which was accepted by BBC. Mrs. Coster then remarried, and her new husband moved in with her. Perhaps, because of the change in name, BBC refused to accept the rent and tried to evict the newlyweds.

But the court would not allow an eviction. When Mrs. Coster's rent checks were cashed, her illegal occupancy became legal. After Mrs. Coster remarried, her new husband became part of her immediate family and was entitled to live with her. The newlyweds were entitled to remain in the apartment. There had been no vacancy.

A rent-controlled apartment can be passed on to friends as well as relatives. To accomplish this transfer, you rely on one basic rule: A nonrelative legally occupying your apartment with you on the day when you leave is entitled to continue in occupancy as a rent-controlled tenant. One way to set this rule in motion is to take on a cotenant in your apartment before you move out. If your landlord recognizes your friend as a legal cotenant, he may remain in your apartment even after you vacate. There is no vacancy and he remains in a rent-controlled apartment. The rule upon which this technique is based was explained by the New York State Supreme Court: "Where an occupant of an apartment remains in occupancy *after* the tenant removes, no . . . eviction [will be allowed] if after such removal, [the landlord] acquiesced in the continued occupancy. Such acquiescence can be established by the landlord accepting rent from such occupant, after knowledge of the tenant's removal."

For example, a friend moves into your rent-controlled apartment shortly before you plan to leave. After you leave, he starts to pay the rent. If the landlord, or the superintendent, knows of the change in occupancy but nevertheless accepts rent from your friend, you have effectively passed on your apartment. The landlord could have evicted your friend. However, by accepting rent from him, the opportunity was lost. Your friend became the legal tenant, and the apartment remains his rent-controlled prize.

Before you seek to pass on your rent-controlled apartment by getting a cotenant, a word of caution is in order. The courts are not stupid. They will not sanction blatant attempts to fool the landlord into allowing a pass on. For example, in the case of *In re Veltri,* a tenant asked his landlord if a friend, Ms. Daniels, could act as a caretaker of his apartment while he was away. The landlord said it was okay. Two years later the caretaker was still in the apartment. The landlord had had enough. But the caretaker claimed that she was now a cotenant and could remain in the apartment. The court would not buy the argument: "The tenant simply cannot have it both ways. He cannot claim that Ms. Daniels is a caretaker in order to avoid her eviction, and then claim she is a tenant in order to avoid decontrol." This tenant pushed the passing-on principle one step too far. Caretakers are not tenants. He called his cotenant a caretaker, and she was stuck with that status.

Another technique of passing on an apartment is available for a rent-controlled tenant who has no lease. If he can sublet his apartment for an indefinite period, he has effectively passed on his apartment. The subtenant will have the right to remain in the apartment indefinitely under the protection of rent control.

Of course, getting permission from your landlord for the sublet can be difficult. However, if you sublet your apartment for an indefinite term, and your landlord fails to object, he might be forced to allow the sublet. (This principle is described in greater detail in chapter 6.) And a number of courts have held that where a landlord received a rent increase for permitting a sublet, the subtenant becomes a rent-controlled tenant with the right to remain in the apartment.

Finally, there is one pass-on technique that you can't plan for: dying. Under the rent-control law, upon the death of a tenant of a rent-controlled apartment, the "surviving spouse of the deceased tenant or some other member of the deceased tenant's family who has been living with the tenant" has the right to remain in the apartment as a rent-controlled tenant.

Notice that the law does *not* limit the right to the deceased tenant's "immediate family." Rather, the law speaks of "other members" of the family. One court has cited *Webster's Third New International Dictionary* to conclude that a nephew had the right to remain in the apartment of his deceased uncle. (Remember, a nephew is not a member of the tenant's "immediate family.'') The conclusion is that if a tenant of a rent-controlled apartment dies, any other family member related by blood or by marriage should be entitled to remain in the apartment as a rent-controlled tenant.

PASSING ON A RENT STABILIZED APARTMENT

Your right to remain in a rent-stabilized apartment arises from the landlord's obligation to offer you renewal leases (see chapter 8). In order to pass on your apartment, therefore, you must create *in someone else* the right to demand a renewal lease. If that person can renew your lease, there will be no vacancy after you leave, so the apartment won't be decontrolled.

Who has a right to a renewal lease? The law provides that any person in ''lawful occupancy'' on the day the lease expires has the right to demand a renewal lease. Who is a lawful tenant at the end of a lease? A member of the tenant's immediate family is—his husband, wife, son, daughter, stepson, stepdaughter, father, mother, father-in-law, mother-in-law, and, according to one court case, a son- or daughter-in-law living with a resident son or daughter. The Conciliation and Appeals Board has decided that ''where changes in occupancy of one dwelling unit are limited to members of the same immediate family and there is continuous occupancy by at least one member of the same immediate family, the tenants are to be considered renewal tenants.''

For example, say you live in a rent-stabilized apartment and your son returns from college and moves in with you for a few months. Then you decide to move into a smaller apartment, but your son would like to take over your place. Will your son have the right to demand a renewal lease? The answer is yes. Your son was a lawful occupant of the apartment on the day your lease ended. He therefore has the right to demand a renewal of the lease, and in his own name. The result would be the same if any other member of your immediate family was living with you when the lease expired. Thus, passing on your apartment to a family member is quite simple.

The rule regarding families also applies when a family unit is enlarged by marriage. For example, Bonnie Green and Linda Saul lived together at 22 East Sixty-third Street in Manhattan. Linda moved out when Bonnie married Henry Druckerman. Henry moved in with Bonnie. This move was legal, because when Henry married Bonnie, he became part of her immediate family and was entitled to live in her apartment.

The lease then expired. The landlord claimed there was a vacancy. The Conciliation and Appeals Board said no. Bonnie was a lawful tenant under the original lease and still resided in the apartment. The addition of Henry was legal, since he was part of Bonnie's family. The lease had to be renewed because no vacancy had occurred. Bonnie and Henry remained as rent-stabilized tenants.

But suppose a divorce, rather than a marriage, calls for passing on a rent-stabilized apartment. Can this feat be accomplished? Yes. If both husband and wife have signed the lease, there is no problem; either can remain in the apartment as a rent-stabilized tenant. However, if only the husband signed the lease, and the former wife wants to remain, there could be a problem. Since the former wife is no longer related to the person who signed the lease, what right has she to keep the apartment? The answer lies in CAB Opinion #512. The board decided that a separated wife is a lawful tenant, and, if she lives in the apartment on the day the lease expires, she has the right to renew the lease.

Another method of passing on a rent-stabilized apartment is by adding on a roommate. You have already seen how putting a family member in legal occupancy before the lease expires gives the family member the right to demand a renewal lease. The same rule applies if a nonrelative is added as a roommate. (Remember the basic rule: Any legal occupant of an apartment on the last day of the lease has the right to demand and receive a renewal lease. There is no vacancy and the apartment remains rent stabilized.)

Assume you have a rent-stabilized apartment and invite a friend to live with you. The landlord accepts your roommate as a cotenant, and you both pay rent. At the end of the lease you leave. Your roommate has the right to renew the lease, and the apartment stays stabilized.

If you think your landlord will never approve an additional roommate, you'll have to try out the waiver rule. Under this rule, if a landlord accepts rent from an unauthorized roommate, he is presumed to have approved of the roommate, regardless of his real intentions. Having given his consent, he is forced to accept the roommate as a legitimate cotenant.

For example, Sharon Fitelson and Sheila Amos lived together at 165 Christopher Street in Greenwich Village. Sheila moved out and was replaced by Emmalyn Johnson. A few months later Sharon moved out and was replaced by Janet Goertz. The new occupants, Emmalyn and Janet, paid their rent directly to the landlord, who cashed their checks.

The lease expired and the landlord, Cosmo Realty, contended that there was a vacancy. Cosmo notified Emmalyn and Janet that the lease would not be renewed. The women went to the Conciliation and Appeals Board with canceled checks in hand. Cosmo Realty also appeared, and argued that "at no time was the name Emmalyn Johnson contained in the lease; that the occupants of the apartment are not the people who rented [the apartment] but are squatters; and that the owner has no intention of renting to them and, if necessary, will go to court to evict them as squatters."

The board was not impressed with Cosmo's argument. It decided that "it is uncontroverted that Emmalyn Johnson and Janet Goertz took occupancy of the subject apartment during the term of the original tenant's lease. It is also uncontroverted that the owner accepted their rent checks. . . . The Board finds that the present occupants [Emmalyn and Janet] were in possession of the subject apartment with the consent of the owner prior to the expiration of the lease with the original tenants and, having been accepted as tenants by the owner, are entitled to a renewal lease." Thus, though the two women entered without the landlord's explicit consent, the fact that he accepted rent amounted to consent. The women were, therefore, legal occupants on the last day of the original lease and were entitled to a renewal lease. There had been no vacancy and, hence, no destabilization of the rent-stabilized apartment.

Sometimes the landlord's consent can't be directly implied—as it was in the case of Cosmo Realty. Nevertheless, his consent can be indirectly implied. Indirect consent usually travels to a tenant by way of one of the landlord's employees or agents. The agent's consent is presumed to indicate his boss's consent.

For example, three cotenants, Hunter, Lunt, and Bieger, lived together at 380 Riverside Drive. During their two-year lease they left one by one and were replaced by Launder, Ruhl, and Manix. When the lease expired, not one of the original three cotenants remained in the apartment. However, the new tenants had registered with the superintendent when they moved in. Under the law, the superintendent's knowledge of the new tenants was imputed to the landlord. Since nothing was done to evict the new tenants, the law presumed that the change in occupancy had been approved by the landlord. Therefore, the three new tenants had a right to demand renewal of their lease; and the apartment remained rent stabilized.

The final method of passing on a rent-stabilized apartment employs the relationship of tenant and subtenant. Assume you sublet your apartment to a friend for the remainder of your lease. When the lease expires, your subtenant will have the right to renew the lease. There will be no vacancy and he will, therefore, remain a rent-stabilized tenant.

How does this extraordinary result come about? Remember, the person who has the right to renew a lease is the person in lawful occupancy on the day the lease expires. If you sublet your apartment for the entire remaining portion of your lease, your subtenant will be the legal occupant on the last day of the lease. He will therefore have the right to renew the lease and remain under rent stabilization.

For example, say you have a lease that expires on June 1, 1978. A clause in the lease permits you to sublet your apartment with the landlord's permission. You receive permission and sublet your apartment until June 1, 1978. The subtenant is in legal occupancy on the day the lease expires. He has the right to demand and receive a renewal lease. There is no vacancy.

Remember that in order to pass on your apartment to a subtenant, you must make a sublease that runs until the last day of your lease. Should the sublease expire earlier, the transfer will not work. For example, Steve Jensen had a lease on a rent-stabilized apartment from April 1, 1968, until March 31, 1971.

In November 1968, Jensen sublet his apartment to Esther Schwartz. The sublease ran from November 1, 1968, until March 30, 1971, one day less than Jensen's own lease term. The sublease expired, and Esther sought a renewal. The landlord refused, and the case went before the Conciliation and Appeals Board.

The board decided that Esther had no right to a renewal. "[The law] defines a renewal lease as any extension of the tenant's lawful occupancy of a dwelling unit after the completion of his lease term. As the sublease will expire on March 30, 1971, one day before the expiration of the prime lease [between Jensen and the landlord], the subtenant will not be in lawful possession of the dwelling unit on the expiration date of [Jensen's] lease." Thus, on the last day of the lease, the critical day, Esther was an illegal occupant. Her sublease had run out the day before. She was not entitled to renew the lease.

As long as the sublease lasts until the end of the original lease, the subtenant should get a renewal, even if his subtenancy was never explicitly approved by the landlord. Implied approval is sufficient. For example, Jeffry Lewis and Robert Golden were subtenants at 240 East Seventy-sixth Street in Manhattan. They had sublet an apartment from the Joneses, who, they thought, had received permission from the landlord. Jeffry and Robert paid their rent directly to the landlord.

The sublease expired on the same day as the lease the Joneses had with the landlord. Jeffry and Robert sought a renewal lease. But the landlord claimed there was a vacancy. The case came before the Conciliation and Appeals Board. The board found that since the sublease expired on the same day as the lease between the Joneses and the landlord, the subtenants had the right to demand a renewal.

The landlord argued that there had never been an approved sublet. The board responded that "consent of the owner may be inferred from the fact that the present tenants paid rent directly to the owner." Thus, although Jeffry and Robert had no actual permission to sublet, the acceptance of rent by the landlord implied his permission. He could not now argue that the subtenancy had been illegal.

Each of these pass-along techniques will work only if there is no evidence of bad faith on the tenant's part. By this we mean that the Conciliation and Appeals Board will not blindly follow the rules we have discussed if there is evidence that the landlord was deceived. For example, you bring a roommate into your apartment in violation of your lease. When your landlord objects, you tell him that your friend is staying only a short time while looking for another apartment. If you later claim that the friend is now a cotenant entitled to a lease renewal, you will probably be in trouble. The CAB is likely to point to your statement that your friend was only staying a short time. You will have what the law calls "dirty hands." The CAB won't clean them for you.

PART III

Maintenance and Repairs

CHAPTER 12

The Right to Good Upkeep

HEAT, TRASH, PAINTING, AND THE SUPER

New York City's Housing Maintenance Code requires landlords to supply adequate heat, hot water, and sanitation. These requirements apply to all tenants who live in a multiple dwelling. (Basically, a multiple dwelling is a building with three or more separate apartments.) You are entitled to the basic decencies set forth in the code regardless of whether your apartment is rent controlled, uncontrolled, rent stabilized, or cooperative.

The essential requirements of the code can be summarized as follows:

• *Heat* As a general rule, all buildings must be equipped with a central heating system. (Individual heating units may be provided in limited circumstances with city approval.) Centrally supplied heat has to be maintained at the proper levels. From October 1 through May 31, your apartment should be kept at the following temperatures:

1. Between the hours of 6:00 A.M. and 10:00 P.M., a temperature of at least 68° F., whenever the outside temperature falls below 55° F.

2. Between the hours of 10:00 P.M. and 6:00 A.M., a temperature of at least 55° F., whenever the outside temperature falls below 40° F.

• *Water and plumbing* Your landlord must properly maintain the plumbing and sewer drainage system in your building. He has to provide your apartment with adequate appliances—e.g., toilets, sinks—for receiving, distributing, and draining water during all hours. And these appliances must be kept in good repair.

• *Hot water* In general, all buildings should be equipped with a central source of hot water. (Individual gas or electric water heaters may be provided in limited circumstances with city approval.) Centrally supplied hot water must be maintained at all times between the hours of 6:00 A.M. and midnight at a constant minimum temperature of 120° F.

• *Waste collection* Your building must be supplied with enough trash cans to hold the waste accumulated during a seventy-two-hour period. In general, the cans should be kept leakproof, made of metal, and equipped with tight-fitting covers. A trash can must not weigh more than a hundred pounds when filled. The metal cans have to be covered at all times and disinfected regularly. They may be stored inside your building in an accessible place until the time for collection. Then they should be placed in front of your building and, after collection, promptly returned to their storage space.

• *Sanitation* Unless you live in a rooming house, you have to keep your apartment clean and sanitary. To that extent, the landlord is not your maid. He is, however, a servant to the rest of your building. The public parts of the building must be maintained in a clean and sanitary condition. (Public parts include any hall, lobby, stairway, storage area, or space used in common by the tenants or members of the public.) Your landlord is also responsible for the building's exterior. He has to keep the roof, yard, courts, and other open spaces clean and free from filth, garbage, or other offensive material.

• *Snow* Within four hours after snow stops falling, snow and ice are supposed to be removed from the sidewalk in front of your building by the landlord. (Not included in the allotted four-hour period are the hours between 9:00 P.M. and 7:00 A.M.)

• *Cockroaches and rats* The landlord must keep your building free from rodents and infestation by cockroaches (not to mention flies, lice, silverfish, beetles, bedbugs, ants, termites, bees, wasps, spiders, and centipedes). If there is infestation, continuous eradication methods must be applied, such as fumigation.

• *Painting and wallpapering* The Housing Maintenance Code requires landlords to paint apartments at least once every three years. A landloard and tenant may, however, agree that a painting is not needed for an additional two years. The regular three-year interval may be shortened if your apartment is rent controlled (see page 96) or rent stabilized (see page 145).

If wallpaper is your thing, you probably won't find a very cooperative landlord. There is no law that requires a landlord to paper the walls. Should you decide to paper the walls on your own, be prepared to pay for wallpaper removal when you vacate. Of course, if the wallpaper is installed by the landlord or with his consent, you won't be obligated to remove it.

Before you wallpaper, note the requirements of the Housing Maintenance Code: "Neither the owner nor a tenant of a dwelling unit shall place wallpaper or wall covering upon a wall or ceiling in the public or tenant-occupied parts of a dwelling unless existing wallpaper or wall covering is first removed and such wall or ceiling is cleaned and repaired. However, if wallpaper or wall covering is in good condition, free from vermin and a coat of acceptable paint or sizing is applied, one additional layer of wallpaper or wall covering may be applied."

• *Janitorial service* Every multiple dwelling is entitled to adequate janitorial services. The code defines janitorial services to include: "cleaning and maintenance . . . the making of minor repairs; the furnishing of heat and hot water, where supplied from a central source; the removal of garbage, refuse, ashes, and wastes from the premises; and the removal of snow, ice, dirt, and other matter from the sidewalk and gutter." The landlord may perform these services himself or hire someone else.

If the multiple dwelling has at least nine apartments, janitorial services must be provided in one of three ways:

1. The landlord may perform janitorial services himself, *if he resides in the building*.

2. The landlord may hire janitorial services to be performed on a twenty-four-hour basis.

3. The landlord may hire a janitor (popularly known as a "super") specifically for the building. If the landlord does not reside in the building, the super must; or, at least, the super

must live within one block or two hundred feet from the building—whichever distance is greater. If two or three multiple dwellings are connected or adjoining, the super who services them can reside in one of the buildings. However, he cannot service more than sixty-five apartments on his own. Whether or not your super is a resident, he must be able to perform janitorial services in a competent manner.

Suppose that neither your landlord nor your super resides in the building. How do you know who your super is? The landlord must post a legible sign, conspicuously displayed, containing the super's name, address (including apartment number), and telephone number. If there is a change in supers, a new sign must be posted in your building within five days after the change.

Beyond the bare requirements of the Housing Maintenance Code, the rent-control and rent-stabilization laws may dictate that a building be staffed by a wide array of personnel other than a super—e.g., doormen, porters, elevator operators. (The rights of rent-controlled and rent-stabilized tenants in this regard are discussed in chapters 7 and 10.)

LANDLORD'S DUTY TO REPAIR

"Thou shalt repair." Both the Housing Maintenance Code and the Multiple Dwelling Law carve this commandment into your landlord's forehead. He is obliged to keep your building and apartment in "good repair." This legal duty is imposed upon the landlord of every multiple dwelling (remember, that's a building with at least three apartments) regardless of whether apartments in the building happen to be rent controlled, rent stabilized, or uncontrolled. (If you are a co-op tenant, your landlord is the cooperative corporation, and it has the duty to make repairs.)

The landlord's duty to repair covers all the public parts of your building—e.g., halls, stairs, lobby, basement, roof, elevators—as well as the structural, electrical, and plumbing systems. And the duty goes further: it continues right into your apartment. The law requires the landlord to keep "every part" of the building in "good repair"; and your apartment is part of the building. So, if your radiator's leaking, or your plaster's crumbling, or your door's jammed, or your window's broken, or your drain's clogged, etc., the landlord must fix it.

This rule applies even if you're the one who broke something. The fact that you may be at fault does not relieve the landlord of his duty. Of course, you can get into trouble if you deliberately, or through gross neglect, break something. You could be fined for violating the Housing Maintenance Code; or you might be sued by the landlord for the damage that you've caused. But even under these conditions, the duty to repair sticks with the landlord. It does not shift to you. The code is crystal clear on this point.

THE WARRANTY OF HABITABILITY LAW

On August 1, 1975, Governor Hugh Carey signed into law a landmark tenant-protection bill, called the warranty of habitability law. (It is contained in section 235–b of the state's Real Property Law.) The new law borrows concepts from the law of consumer warranties and applies them to housing. The warranty of habitability law attempts to assure decently maintained apartments for all tenants, whether they are rent controlled, rent stabilized, or uncontrolled.

How does the law operate? In effect, by reading into every lease (whether written or oral) certain warranties that the landlord is deemed to make to the tenant. Under this law, the landlord warrants that the apartment and all public areas of the building "are fit for human habitation and for the uses reasonably intended by the parties and that the occupants of such premises shall not be subjected to any conditions which would be dangerous, hazardous or detrimental to their life, health or safety." Any agreement by a tenant (say, in a lease) to waive or modify his rights under the new law is void.

What is the meaning of the warranty? That depends entirely upon how New York courts develop and apply the concept of *habitability,* which lies at the heart of the law. Obviously, if habitability meant nothing more than that your landlord couldn't graze sheep in the lobby, the new law wouldn't be worth much. But there is already every evidence that habitability will be interpreted to include most of the services, and even the amenities, essential to comfortable apartment living.

This interpretation of habitability recognizes the justifiable expectations that tenants have when they rent an apartment. In the words of one federal judge: "When American city dwellers, both rich and poor, seek 'shelter' today, they seek a well-known package of goods and services—a package which includes not merely walls and ceilings, but also adequate heat, light and ventilation, serviceable plumbing facilities, secure windows and doors, proper sanitation, and proper maintenance." If the landlord fails to deliver upon this package of goods and services that the tenant bargained for, the warranty of habitability has been breached.

Over the past few years, New York courts have found a breach of warranty in a wide range of circumstances. Some of these decisions were predictable, because they arose in situations where the habitability of an apartment had clearly been diminished: for example, a tenant's ceiling leaked badly; or there was no heat or hot water; or a tenant's toilet stopped working; or the walls of an apartment were covered with dangerous lead-based paint. In each of these cases, the decrease in habitable conditions wasn't hard to identify.

However, New York courts have gone beyond bare essentials in applying the concept of habitability. Thus, courts have found a breach of warranty when landlords failed to eliminate offensive odors from pets or to quiet down rowdy, noisemaking neighbors. In one case, the failure to repair a stove for seventeen days breached the warranty; in another, there was a breach when the tenant was deprived of a working air-conditioner for two summer months. So, you can see how versatile the habitability concept can be. If judges continue to expand the concept, the law may grow into one of the best safeguards for New York tenants.

Assuming a landlord does breach the warranty or habitability, what recourse does a tenenat have? The law does not specify, because the legislators intended to leave open a wide array of remedies. As Governor Carey commented when signing the bill,

"It will be the courts' function to fashion remedies appropriate to the facts of each case."

In practice, the most common remedy has been for tenants to withhold their rent; when the landlord sues for nonpayment, the tenant raises the breach of warranty as a defense. The well-settled legal theory here is that the tenant's duty to pay rent is dependent upon the landlord's duty to maintain habitability. If the landlord doesn't do his duty, then the tenant should also be relieved. (This technique of using the warranty of habitability is discussed in chapter 14.)

It's also possible to sue your landlord for damages if he breaches the warranty. In other words, you take the offensive, rather than withholding rent and going on the defensive. (This particular strategy is discussed in chapter 16.)

CHAPTER 13

How to Demand Good Upkeep

Demanding and getting good upkeep from your landlord often involves a process of escalation. It begins with a polite request and it may go all the way to withholding rent, or even to a full-fledged building-wide rent strike. In this chapter we'll look at some of the milder steps in the process, beginning with the complaint to your landlord. If he is unresponsive, contact an important city agency, the Office of Code Enforcement. Should this step prove unsatisfactory, you can resort to a tenant-initiated action in New York City Housing Court. Finally, we'll look at a self-help remedy: you do your own repairs and then try to recover your expenses from the landlord.

COMPLAINTS TO YOUR LANDLORD

Whenever you need repairs or maintenance, your first step should be to notify the landlord. Always do this, even if you have had bad luck with the landlord in the past. The reason for giving the landlord notice is not just to get him to act. You are also protecting yourself from a later charge that you let some condition get out of hand and deteriorate to the point where serious damage resulted. Remember, you may be held responsible for damage caused by your gross neglect.

To be on the safe side, you should notify the landlord in writing. Even if you have spoken to him (or the super), you ought to confirm the conversation in a letter. For example:

Mary Tenant
Apartment 1E
1051 Main Avenue
New York, N.Y. 10028
(home telephone)
(work telephone)
(date of mailing)

John Landlord
Management Office
900 West 44th Street
New York, N.Y. 10036

Dear Mr. Landlord:

I just want to confirm the conversation we had today on the telephone. As I told you, the ceiling in my living room needs repair. The plaster around the steam pipe is cracked and it is starting to sag. I am afraid it may begin to fall, causing damage and possible harm.

As I said on the phone, I am relying on you to make the needed repairs. Thank you for saying you would do so. I will expect the repairman you promised to send up next Friday.

Sincerely,
Mary Tenant

This letter is sufficient. It contains the important ingredients: (1) the tenant's name, apartment number, and address; (2) telephone number(s) and the date of mailing; (3) a detailed description of the condition needing repair or maintenance; (4) an indication that the tenant is relying on the landlord to do his duty; and, where appropriate, (5) a confirmation of the fact that the landlord has promised to have the work done at a fixed time.

If you want to keep your own file on the landlord, make a copy of the letter for yourself. You should send the letter via certified mail, return receipt requested. This way, you will have proof that the letter was mailed on a certain date and that it was received by the landlord. Both facts could be important later on—if the landlord fails to do his duty and you have to take more drastic measures.

THE OFFICE OF CODE ENFORCEMENT

If the landlord is unresponsive to your complaints, try to get some help from the city's Office of Code Enforcement (OCE). This office fields all complaints about repair, maintenance, heat, and hot water in multiple dwellings (i.e., buildings with at least three separate apartments). The OCE will handle your complaint regardless of whether your apartment is rent controlled, rent stabilized, uncontrolled, or cooperative.

The OCE has one main office and five borough offices. While you can visit your local office, complaints should be made to the Central Complaint Bureau (CCB), which is part of the OCE. (See Appendix A for the addresses and phone numbers of the OCE and the CCB.)

While the CCB used to operate seven days a week, twenty-four hours a day, financial cutbacks have forced curtailment in service. During the so-called heating season (October 1 through May 31), the CCB generally operates seven days a week, from 8:00 A.M. to 8:00 P.M.—although twenty-four-hour service may be reinstituted if the necessary funds are made available. Outside of the heating season, the CCB currently operates Monday through Friday, from 9:00 A.M. to 5:00 P.M.

Normally, complaints to the CCB should be made by phone. Immediately after calling, you can if you wish send a confirming letter via certified mail, return receipt requested. This is not necessary; but if you later wish to take your landlord to court for housing violations, a copy of your confirming letter and the proof-of-mailing receipt will help to establish the date on which you originally complained to the CCB.

When you complain, be brief and be specific. Identify yourself; give the address of your building; if you can, supply the name and phone number of the landlord or person who manages the building. Describe precisely the condition that bothers you—don't make vague complaints, like the apartment is "in disrepair." Instead, pinpoint the problems—"a leak under the kitchen sink," or "a crack in the bedroom ceiling." This way, if there is an inspection, the inspector will know exactly what condition he's supposed to check out.

All incoming complaints are initially classified by the CCB into one of three categories. These categories determine the degree of priority with which the complaint will be processed. In ascending order of urgency, the three categories are designated by the letters *N*, *G*, and *E*. The *N*s are noninspection-generating complaints, which do not automatically get inspected by the OCE. For example, if you call up and complain that your apartment hasn't been painted in more than three years, your complaint will be initially classified *N*. Next up the ladder are the *G*s, the inspection-generating complaints, which will be inspected by the OCE. For example, if you complain about a run-of-the-mill leak, it will probably be classified *G*, and an inspector will be dispatched from your OCE borough office.

At the top of the ladder are the true emergency complaints. They get classified *E* and are inspected on a priority basis—sometimes the same day they come in. As might be expected, real disaster stories will be classified *E*. Typical *E* conditions include: no hot or cold water; no heating fuel; defective, inoperative, or missing boiler; defective or inoperative oil burner; leaking oil tank; no gas; obstructed toilet; nonflushing toilet; cascading water leak; dangerously broken plumbing; gas-pipe leak; loose or bulging plaster in imminent danger of collapse; no lights in the public halls; stairs and flooring in public halls broken and defective, impeding safe use as a means of egress; fire escape defective and unsafe; electricity not being provided to the entire building; electrical defects creating a fire hazard; roof leaking or open to the elements; broken and missing windows and skylights that permit the elements to enter (this condition is classified *E* only during the heating season); rat infestation. Also included in the *E* category are any other hazardous defects that create an unsafe condition, such as defective flooring and beams.

If your complaint demands immediate attention, by all means impress upon the CCB the urgency of the situation. But don't blow things up out of all proportion just to be mistakenly classified top priority (*E*). Thus, if the water is dripping under your sink, don't mislead the CCB into thinking that you've got a cascading water leak.

Depending upon how a complaint has been initially classified, it will be processed differently by the CCB. In the case of both *N*s and *G*s, the landlord will be sent a Notice of Complaint form, which describes the complaint and tells the landlord to make the necessary repair immediately. Simultaneously, the tenant will be sent an Acknowledgment of Complaint form, which duplicates the data recorded on the Notice of Complaint.

As a matter of routine, the *G*s are scheduled for inspection by the appropriate OCE borough office. (During the heating season, however, usually only heat complaints and emergencies are inspected.) An *N* will not ordinarily be inspected, unless the landlord fails to make repairs within thirty days after the tenant's complaint was made. If such is the case, the tenant should sign the Acknowledgment of Complaint form that he received and send it back to the CCB; then an inspection will be scheduled (subject, again, to the exigencies of the heating season).

All this paperwork is bypassed in the case of *E*s. The CCB will telephone an *E* into the appropriate OCE borough office, often within a few hours of when complaint was received. At the borough office, the chief inspector decides whether the complaint warrants immediate inspection, which may be scheduled for the very same day.

Unfortunately, you won't get any advance notice of when an inspector may visit your building; it's virtually impossible for the OCE borough office to predict when an inspector will arrive. If you're not home when the inspector calls, and your complaint dealt with public parts of the building, he will try to gain access from the super or one of the other tenants. When an inspection cannot be conducted, the inspector will leave a card advising you of the date and time for a return visit. The card will specify a phone number to call if another date would be more convenient for you. If you wish, call this number to let the OCE know that some other tenant will be holding the key to your apartment when the inspector returns. (The time to make such arrangements is, ironically, after the inspector can't get in the first time around—not before the first attempt at inspection.)

Once an inspection is conducted, it's up to the inspector to determine whether housing code violations exist in your apartment or building. If there is no violation, or if it has been corrected, the inspector will so report, and the tenant will be notified of this finding by postcard. The tenant is similarly notified of violations that the inspector determines do exist.

Under the city's Housing Maintenance Code, housing violations are divided into three categories—"A," "B," and "C"—and the inspector decides which category covers each violation that he finds. (Don't confuse these classifications with the ones used by the CCB to process incoming complaints.) Classification "A" covers nonhazardous violations such as: lack of a proper toilet seat; dirty walls in the hallways; lack of painting; no lighting in the laundry room; no peephole in the tenant's apartment door; no mirrors in a self-service elevator; lack of a sign indicating the name, address, and phone number of any nonresident janitor; failure to provide the tenant with a rent bill or receipt.

Classification "B" covers hazardous violations such as: lack of sufficient metal cans and covers to hold the building's garbage; inadequate lighting (less than sixty watts) in the halls; presence of vermin.

Classification "C" covers immediately hazardous violations such as: defective gas appliance that's emitting carbon monoxide; presence of rodents; broken-down central-heating system; obstructed toilet.

Certain violations could be classified "A," "B," or "C," in the judgment of the inspector, depending on the degree of severity as determined by the inspector. Take broken plaster—if there's just a crack, it'll probably be classified "A"; but, if the plaster is sagging or falling, it may be classified "B" or even "C." The same is true of almost all violations requiring general repair work or removal of rubbish. Inadequate heat or hot water will be classified either "B" or "C" depending on the seriousness of the situation.

After the inspector reports the violations that he's found, an official Notice of Violation is sent to the landlord. The notice describes the violations, lists their classifications, and specifies the date by which violations must be corrected. In the case of nonhazardous violations ("A"), the landlord will be given ninety days (from the date of mailing of the notice) in which to make corrections. With hazardous violations ("B"), the time for corrections is only thirty days (from the date of mailing of the notice). If a violation is immediately hazardous ("C"), the notice will be served personally to the landlord, and he will then have twenty-four hours in which to correct the condition.

The notice also tells the landlord that he may be subject to civil penalties if he doesn't correct the violations. Under the Housing Maintenance Code, these penalties increase with the severity of the violation and, sometimes, the length of time it has persisted. Each nonhazardous violation that is not corrected by the deadline set in the Notice of Violation can result in a penalty of from ten to fifty dollars. Each hazardous violation can cost the landlord from twenty-five to one hundred dollars, plus ten dollars per day for each day that the violation exists beyond the OCE deadline. In the case of an immediately hazardous violation, the landlord may be subject to a twenty-five-dollar-per-day penalty for each day after the OCE deadline.

A landlord who receives a Notice of Violation is required to *certify* to the OCE that he has corrected the violations. Certification must be made in writing, under oath, no later than fourteen days after the OCE deadline set for correcting the violations. If the work was performed by the landlord himself, or by his employees (e.g., the super), then the workman in question must also certify in writing, under oath, that he did do the work.

The Housing Maintenance Code prescribes stiff penalties for false certification, and they may be imposed in addition to the penalties for failing to correct violations on time. For willfully making a false certification the landlord may be subject to a civil penalty of from $50 to $250 for each violation that was falsely certified. Besides this penalty, a landlord who falsely certifies may be guilty of a misdemeanor, punishable by a fine of up to $1,000 and/or one year imprisonment.

A copy of the certification will be mailed by the OCE to the complaining tenant within twelve days after it has been received. The tenant will have the opportunity to contest the landlord's certification on a special form designed for that purpose. On that form, the tenant will be instructed to indicate all violations that the landlord has certified as having been corrected but which the tenant claims have not been corrected. In effect, the tenant will be claiming false certification by the landlord. It is of the utmost importance that the tenant execute and return the form to the OCE immediately. (The form itself requests return within five days.) Later court action by the tenant depends on his prompt return of the form.

The OCE will generally give priority to a reinspection of violations on which the tenant has claimed false certification. This reinspection must be accomplished within seventy days after the date on which the landlord's certification was received. (Therefore, the tenant should return his claim of false certification immediately, so that the OCE will have enough time to reinspect.)

Suppose the tenant makes no claim of false certification. The OCE may conduct a reinspection anyway as a routine check; if there is a reinspection, it must be performed within seventy days after receipt of the landlord's certification. Assuming that the reinspection is conducted, and that it reveals that the violations have indeed been corrected, the violations will be removed from the OCE's computerized records. But when a reinspection turns up violations that have not, in fact, been corrected, the landlord will be charged with false certification.

The OCE may not always be able to conduct routine reinspections within the seventy-day period; other, more pressing problems, like heat complaints, might prevent such reinspection. If this happens, then after the seventy days are up, the violations that were certified as corrected, and that were not objected to by the tenant, will be deemed to have been corrected and they will be removed from the OCE's computerized records.

What happens if the landlord never makes any certification at all on the violations? The OCE will not ordinarily reinspect in such a situation. However, the computer in which all violations are stored is programmed to expect certification by a certain date. When no certification comes, the computer goes, "Tilt! We got a winner here." And the landlord can then be taken to court by the city. Unfortunately, there are a lot of winners—more than the city's present legal manpower can handle. So, you may have to take the landlord to court on your own.

Resorting to the CCB and OCE might in itself put enough

pressure on your landlord to get the maintenance and repairs that you need. If so, fine. But there are some obstacles that may forestall such a happy ending. For example, what if no inspector ever shows up? Or, if he does, what if you miss him? What happens when no violation is placed upon a condition that you believe needs attention? What if the landlord certifies falsely that violations have been corrected but the OCE doesn't reinspect? Finally, what if the landlord never even certifies? Don't lose hope. In all these situations, you have a legal remedy—you can drag your landlord into New York City Housing Court (see pages 185–192).

• *Heat complaints* Heat complaints deserve special attention because they are handled a bit differently by the CCB and OCE. (The same holds true for hot-water complaints; generally speaking, during the winter, if the heat's out, the hot water is also out, because usually the same system provides both.) The heat requirements of the Housing Maintenance Code are in effect from October 1 through May 31. During the peak of this so-called heating season, heat complaints take priority over every other complaint except emergencies. In a crisis, all OCE inspectors will be doing heat checks, and sometimes even supervisory personnel are sent out on heat inspections.

Heat complaints are processed manually when they come into the CCB. After you call in a heat complaint, the CCB will attempt to telephone your landlord that very day—as opposed to sending out a Notice of Complaint form, as with run-of-the-mill complaints. The landlord will be told to correct the condition that's depriving you of heat. Within twenty-four hours the CCB will call you back to see if the heat has been restored. If it has, your complaint will be canceled. Many heat complaints are satisfactorily closed through this call-back system.

But suppose the heat is still out when the CCB calls you back. Then your complaint will be forwarded to the appropriate borough office of the OCE, where an inspection will be scheduled. If you're not reached on the call back, an inspection will still be scheduled. The CCB will not take the landlord's word that the condition has been corrected.

Even with such expedited processing of complaints, there is

an inevitable and often frustrating lag between the time when you complain and the time of the actual inspection. Under the best of circumstances, it will ordinarily take three days before an inspector can respond to your complaint. For example: You call the CCB on Monday about no heat. Twenty-four hours later they call you back and discover there's still no heat. So, they notify your OCE borough office. At the borough office, however, the inspectors are not sitting around like Western Union messengers waiting to deliver candy; they're probably out checking other heat complaints. By the time an inspector can be dispatched to cover your building, it will be Wednesday, at least; and when the bitter-cold weather comes, it may be Thursday or Friday before an inspector can get to you. By which time, of course, you may have heat again! So, no violation will be found. (Roughly, only 10 percent of all heat inspections result in violations being reported.)

To further frustrate matters, if the inspector is unable to gain access to your building, he will *not* leave a card requesting a reinspection date (as is done in the case of run-of-the-mill complaints). Instead, he will leave a card that tells you to make another complaint. Why is this? First of all, there would be no guarantee that the inspector could keep any reinspection date that he might designate. Second, the daytime temperature on the reinspection date may rise above fifty-five degrees, in which case the heat requirements no longer apply.

There is one possible avenue of self-help for tenants—especially those who belong to a well-organized tenants' group in their building. Everyone in the group installs a reliable indoor-outdoor thermometer in his apartment. Daily logs are kept, comparing the temperature outdoors with the temperature indoors. The evidence of lack of heat is then used in a court action aimed at having a judge find violations against the landlord. By initiating their own legal proceeding, the tenants attempt to circumvent the difficulty in getting a heat violation placed by the OCE. (Such tenant-initiated actions are discussed on pages 185–192.)

• *Emergency repair program* The OCE runs the Emergency Repair Program (ERP), which corrects emergency conditions that a landlord won't fix. The ERP attempts to serve tenants in any multiple dwelling, regardless of whether their apartments are rent controlled, rent stabilized, or uncontrolled.

A wide range of conditions may qualify for emergency repairs. Actually, a list of these conditions has already been given in the earlier discussion of the CCB's operations. There, it was explained how incoming complaints about certain conditions are classified *E* by CCB personnel and processed with top priority. The conditions listed there are the very ones which, if verified by an inspector, can precipitate emergency repairs by the city. This is not to say that only complaints initially processed as *E*s will trigger emergency repairs. An emergency condition may be uncovered on a routine inspection of a "G" or "N" complaint.

Whenever an inspector discovers a condition calling for emergency repair, he telephones in to a central emergency-control number at the OCE. For example, an inspector might report that the building he's visiting is without heat because it has no fuel; he will explain that the building has a three-thousand-gallon tank which needs number 4 fuel oil. This information will be recorded on a special report form, one copy of which will be sent that day to the landlord. Along with the copy is a form letter telling the landlord that he must call the OCE within twenty-four hours or else a private contractor will perform the necessary work—in this case, supply number 4 fuel. If the landlord doesn't call back as requested, then a private contractor will be hired to do the job.

Because of obvious paperwork delays, not to mention further delays incurred when the city has to deal with private contractors, the ERP's response to your particular problem will probably be slower than you might have wished (after all, you're living with an emergency). Inevitable delays are further aggravated during the heating season by the sheer volume of crisis situations to which the OCE, in general, and the ERP in particular, must respond. We've already seen how it takes several days for the OCE to inspect a heat complaint. Add to this time several more days necessary to certify a building for oil delivery or boiler repairs. Then there's the time it takes for a private contractor to undertake and finish the work.

In 1974 the ERP's activities were severely curtailed because of the city's fiscal crisis. The ERP responded only to heat and heat-related emergencies (e.g., boiler breakdowns, defective burners, no fuel, inadequate water supply to the boiler). In October 1976, however, the city did obtain increased funding, and the ERP resumed emergency repairs on such conditions as defective roofing, electrical malfunctions, rubbish accumulation, inadequate fire exits, and dangerously broken plaster.

Whenever the ERP does perform work—either through its own city repair crew or through private contractors—the city files a lien against the landlord's building. If the landlord doesn't pay the city, then ERP charges will be tacked onto his tax bill, or the city may try to collect rent directly from the tenants to cover ERP expenditures for their building.

GETTING REPAIRS THROUGH HOUSING COURT

Suppose you encounter some of the hang-ups hinted at, in the preceding section, when you complain to the Office of Code Enforcement (OCE). There is a judicial remedy that you may invoke on your own in New York City Housing Court. Commonly referred to as a tenant-initiated action, it's available to all tenants, regardless of whether their apartments are rent controlled, rent stabilized, uncontrolled, or even cooperative.

Basically, what is the tenant-initiated action designed to accomplish? First of all, it gets you into court quickly—within a week, normally. Second, your landlord is summoned into court by formal court order (Order to Show Cause). Third, you and the landlord confront each other in a judicial setting, where the force of law, rather than idle threats, may be invoked. Fourth, a judge (actually hearing officer of the housing court) will determine the validity of your complaints and what the landlord must do about them.

It's not necessary for you to have a lawyer in a tenant-initiated action. The filing fee to bring the action is only fifteen dollars. And the action can be fairly effective in getting you some, if not all, of the repairs that you need. While you will have to do a little legal paperwork, it's not all that complicated.

If you undertake a tenant-initiated action, plenty of help will be available along the way. One good source is a court clerk, who will tell you how to fill out the court papers and have them served on the proper parties. There's an even better source of assistance located in lower Manhattan:

Tenant Education Unit
125 Church Street (6th floor)
New York, N.Y. 10007
Tel.: 212-566-6253

This unit is part of the city's Housing and Development Administration (HDA). It is staffed by counselors who advise tenants on all aspects of bringing tenant-initiated actions. (The unit is also eager to train tenant-group leaders regarding tenant-initiated actions, so that the leaders can, in turn, pass the information on to their group members.)

When can you bring a tenant-initiated action? Basically, one of three sets of circumstances must exist. (These circumstances will be familiar to you if you've already read about complaints to the OCE in the preceding section of this chapter.)

1. *No violation found by the inspector* You can bring a tenant-initiated action against your landlord, if, within thirty days after you complained to the OCE about a housing condition, no violation has yet been placed in response to your complaint. You can now see why it was suggested in the preceding section that all complaints to the Central Complaint Bureau (CCB) be either in a letter or be confirmed in a letter, sent via certified mail, return receipt requested. That way, you will have written proof of the date on which your complaint was made. Thirty days thereafter, if no violation has resulted from your complaint, you can turn to the housing court for relief.

2. *No reinspection after a false certification* You will recall from the preceding section that a landlord must certify that he has corrected any violations placed by the OCE. You then have an opportunity to promptly deny the truth of this certification. If, following your denial, and within seventy days after receiving the landlord's certification, the OCE does not reinspect the disputed violations, you proceed to housing court.

3. *No certification by the landlord* Suppose the landlord not

only fails to correct violations within the time limit set in a Notice of Violation, but also fails to file any certification with the OCE. Then you proceed to housing court, as long as thirty days have passed after the date set for correction of the violations.

Assuming you're in one of the three situations just outlined, how do you get into housing court? At the risk of sounding facetious, the first thing you must do is find the court. Housing court is actually part of the New York City Civil Court (indeed, housing court is formally known as the "housing part" of civil court). There are five locations of the civil court—one in each borough—and housing court is held in each one (see Appendix B).

Go to the court in your borough. Locate one of the housing-court clerks. (In the Bronx, find the "pro se clerk.") Ask for the forms that a tenant needs to bring a tenant-initiated housing-part action against his landlord. There are three forms that you will need: Order to Show Cause; Affidavit; and Affidavit of Service. (These forms are reproduced on pages 188–190.)

At first glance, the forms are a bit intimidating, but the clerk or HDA's Tenant Education Unit will help you fill them out. You're going to have to serve a copy of the Order to Show Cause and the Affidavit on both the landlord and the HDA. (Technically speaking, HDA is a party to the action that you're instituting, although, as a practical matter, HDA almost never appears at or participates in a tenant-initiated action.) The clerk or the Tenant Education Unit will explain how to serve the forms. It's usually done simply by mailing the forms to your landlord and to HDA, via certified mail, return receipt requested.

The court clerk will instruct you on where to go in the court building to pay the fifteen-dollar filing fee. You'll get an index number identifying your action, your Order to Show Cause will be signed by a judge, and you'll be given a date for appearing in court. The clerk will also explain to you that after you have served the Order to Show Cause and the Affidavit, you must complete two copies of the Affidavit of Service and file them with the court clerk.

On the date set for your appearance, when you show up at the court you will be directed by the clerk to a hearing room, where

5M-1123069(77) 346
43-2130

CIVIL COURT OF THE CITY OF NEW YORK
COUNTY OF
HOUSING PART

Petitioner —against— Respondent and H. D. A.	**ORDER TO SHOW CAUSE** **Index No.** **Street and Number** **Of Premises:**

PRESENT: Hon. , judge

On reading the affidavit of
sworn to the day of , 19 , and good cause having been shown it is:

ORDERED that the respondent herein is directed to appear before the Court and show cause at a motion term of the Housing Part of the Civil Court of the City of New York, to be held at the Courthouse thereof, No. , County of , City and State of New York, on the day of , 19 at o'clock in the noon of that day or as soon thereafter as the parties or counsel can be heard, why an order should not be made directing the owner to correct the violation, and upon failure to do so within the time set for certifying the correction of such violation pursuant to D26-51.01 (c) of the Administrative Code of the City of New York, for an order directing the HDA to enter.a judgment against the respondent for the penalties stated in Section D26-51.01 (a) of the Administrative Code

ORDERED that this order and the papers on which it is granted shall be served upon the owner and also upon the Department of Rent and Housing Maintenance, either personally or by certified mail, return receipt requested, on or before the day of , 19

If the owner is registered with the Department, such mailing may be made to that address.

Mailing to the Department of Rent and Housing Maintenance shall be made to the Housing Litigation Bureau at 125 Church Street, New York, N. Y. 10007.

Signed this day of , 19 ,
New York City

Judge of the Civil Court of the City of New York, County of

CIVIL COURT OF THE CITY OF NEW YORK
COUNTY OF
HOUSING PART

Petitioner

—against—

Respondent and

H.D.A.

Affidavit

Index No.

STATE OF NEW YORK,
CITY OF NEW YORK,
COUNTY OF

, being duly sworn, says:

(STRIKE OUT WHICHEVER PARAGRAPH IS INAPPLICABLE)

1. I am the petitioner and a tenant in premises No.
County of , City of New York.

2. The respondent is the owner or its registered agent of the aforesaid premises.

3. The owner violated the following sections of the Multiple Dwelling Law, or the Administrative Code or the Health Code, and I requested the Department to issue a notice of such violation upon the owner as follows:

Item	Section	Violation Description	Date Requested

4A. The Department has failed to issue such notice of violation and that more than thirty (30) days have elapsed since such request.

OR

4B. The landlord has falsely certified correction of the violations and the Department has failed to re-inspect the premises after notification by petitioner.

OR

4C. The Department issued such notice of violation upon the owner as requested, and more than thirty days have elapsed from the date said violation was to be corrected, but the owner has failed to correct such violation, and has failed to file a certification of correction with respect to such violation.

5. No prior application has been made for the relief herein requested or for any similar relief.

WHEREFORE, application is hereby made for an order directing the owner to correct the violation, and upon the failure to do so within the time set for certifying the correction of such violation pursuant to D26-51.01(c) of the Administrative Code, for an order directing the HDA to enter the judgment against the respondent for the penalties stated in Section D26-51.01(a) of the Administrative Code.

(Signature, with name printed underneath)

Sworn to before me this

day of , 19

5M-1123069(77) 346
43-2132

5M-1123069(77) 346
43-2131

CIVIL COURT OF THE CITY OF NEW YORK
COUNTY OF

HOUSING PART

Petitioner

—against—

Respondent
and

H. D. A.

Index No.:
AFFIDAVIT OF SERVICE

STATE OF NEW YORK
COUNTY OF } ss.:

being duly sworn deposes and says: That I am over the age of eighteen years of age and at That on , 197 , at approximately (A.M.) (P.M.) I served a copy of the annexed Order to Show Cause and Affidavit upon , the respondent-owner, by:

(1) Delivering a true copy to him personally at the following address: Said person can be described as (give sex, skin color, hair color, approximate age, weight and height, and any other identifying features):

OR (2) Delivering a true copy to his registered managing agent at the following address: Said person can be described as (give sex, skin color, approximate age, weight and height, and any other identifying features):

OR (3) Mailing a true copy, properly sealed and enclosed in a post-paid wrapper, by certified mail, return receipt requested, number , in a post office of the United States Government located at N. Y., addressed to the respondent owner (or his registered managing agent) at the address registered with the Office of Code Enforcement.

That on , 197 , at approximately served a copy of the annexed Order to Show Cause and Affidavit upon the Department of Rent and Housing Maintenance by:

(1) Delivering a true copy to , a person in the Department of Rent and Housing Maintenance, Housing Litigation Bureau, 125 Church Street, New York, N. Y. 10007.

(2) Mailing a true copy, properly sealed and enclosed in a post-paid wrapper, by certified mail, return receipt requested, number , in a post office of the United States Government located at , N. Y. addressed to the Department of Rent and Housing Maintenance, Housing Litigation Bureau, 125 Church St., New York, N. Y. 10007.

(Type or print name underneath)

Sworn to before me
this day of , 197

your case will be heard by a hearing officer of the housing court (equivalent to a judge). The proceeding is very informal—as informal as small claims court, if not more so. You and the landlord and the hearing officer sit around a table and talk. You don't need a lawyer, because the hearing officer will generally look out for your interests. In one sense, you're actually better off appearing on your own. Without a lawyer to poke holes in the air and make fine points of law, the issue will remain focused on your need for repairs, rather than becoming sidetracked on some legalistic detour. "Look, Judge," you'll basically be saying, "all I know is, my bedroom wall is crumbling—for the rent I'm paying, I think I deserve repairs!" To fix the wall, or not to fix the wall: that is the issue.

You don't need to bring any expert witnesses with you to establish the existence of a defective condition, although you could bring your next-door neighbor if you wish. It's usually enough for you simply to state the nature of your complaint. If the landlord disputes your claim, the hearing officer will probably order an inspection before he makes his decision.

The bottom line in any tenant-initiated action is, of course: Will you get relief? Your chances are fairly good of getting some things—though not all—fixed in your apartment, depending on their cost to the landlord. After all, the landlord is probably incurring legal fees because of your tenant-initiated action. So, it's likely to be cheaper for him to try to do something rather than let matters drag on before the hearing officer. What's apt to happen if you complain, say, about ten things in your apartment, is that the hearing officer will not let matters rest until maybe six or seven items have been corrected by the landlord.

There is also the possibility that civil penalties may be assessed against the landlord. (You will recall the graduated scale of penalties discussed in the preceding section.) As a practical matter, however, penalties are not usually imposed in tenant-initiated actions. This is, in part, due to the fact that HDA, which is technically a party to every tenant-initiated action, and which would ordinarily enforce any judgment for penalties, does not generally participate in tenant actions.

Perhaps the most troublesome thing that can happen in a

tenant-initiated action is a default by the landlord: he doesn't show up at all. Then, the hearing officer may advise the tenant to withhold rent; and if the landlord sues for nonpayment, the same hearing officer will retain jurisdiction over the case. Conceivably, the hearing officer might even direct the tenant to make his own repairs and deduct their cost from the rent.

Generally speaking, the tenant-initiated action is a fairly effective way of pressuring a landlord into making repairs in an apartment. Some tenants bypass such an action, however, preferring instead to withhold their rent and then defend a nonpayment action on the grounds of inadequate repairs. Impatience over bringing a tenant-initiated action, while understandable, may be shortsighted. For one thing, there is usually nothing—not even withholding rent—faster than a tenant-initiated action when it comes to getting into court. (Technically, that's because the tenant-initiated action is brought on by a fast-acting Order to Show Cause.) This speed factor is especially true if you happen to have paid your rent, say, within the last week. Then you'll have to wait three more weeks before you can even withhold rent, and a few more weeks before the landlord brings a nonpayment action.

What's more, in a tenant-initiated action, you're on the offensive, pressing a single issue—to repair or not to repair. When the landlord brings a nonpayment action against you, you're on the defensive. Your defense of lack of repairs gets clouded by another key issue—namely: Did you pay your rent?

DO IT YOURSELF AND CHARGE THE LANDLORD

If your landlord won't make repairs, and city agencies can't seem to help either, you might just decide to do it yourself. So, you hire a repairman, who solves your problem but gives you a new one: his bill. You pay bitterly, wondering why you should get burned when it was the landlord's responsibility to begin with.

The answer is to force the landlord to reimburse you. Rent-stabilized tenants can attempt to do this by filing a complaint with the Conciliation and Appeals Board (CAB). Under the rent-stabilization law, tenants are entitled to receive all required services, *including maintenance and repairs*. If a landlord fails to perform necessary maintenance and repairs, the tenant can legitimately complain to the CAB about an unwarranted reduction in required services (see chapter 10).

Over the years, many rent-stabilized tenants who encountered such reductions decided to help themselves. They hired repairmen to fix all sorts of equipment that the landlord was obliged to supply and maintain—e.g., locks, air-conditioners, radiators. In some instances, tenants even replaced worn-out items that the landlord had neglected to recondition. Having incurred the expense, these tenants then complained to the CAB about reduced services and demanded reimbursement. Generally speaking, the CAB has responded by ordering the landlord to reimburse a tenant, who pays for repairs that should have been supplied by the landlord.

Here are a few examples of reimbursement ordered by the CAB:

• *Air-conditioner* A Queens landlord failed to fix one of two air-conditioners supplied with the tenant's apartment. To keep cool, the tenant rented a small air-conditioner for ten dollars per month. The CAB ordered the landlord to reimburse the tenant for all of his rental fees.

The landlord of 1600 Caton Avenue in Brooklyn refused to repair an air-conditioner supplied with the tenant's apartment, and told the tenant that she would have to buy her own. This she did, for $189.93. Upon a complaint to the CAB, the landlord was ordered to pay the tenant $189.93, whereupon the landlord became the proud owner of a new air-conditioner.

• *Dishwasher* Werner Renberg lived at 525 East Eighty-second Street in Manhattan. His lease required him to maintain and repair the dishwasher supplied with his apartment. When the motor in the seven-year-old machine broke down, the landlord refused to replace it, claiming that was the tenant's responsibility. Werner installed a new motor for $86.33 and complained to the CAB about a diminution in services. The CAB ruled that the tenant's obligation under the lease was limited to ordinary repairs; replacement of the motor was an extraordinary repair, for which the landlord remained responsible. So the landlord was ordered to pay Werner $86.33.

• *Doorknob* On the morning of November 4, 1974, Max

Miller was leaving his apartment at 2285 Ocean Avenue in Brooklyn to go to work. Unfortunately, the doorknob broke off in his hand, preventing him from closing the door without being locked in. Max immediately notified the super. Three times he complained to the landlord. Yet, two days passed without any repairs, while Max lost time from work waiting for the super. Finally, Max hired a locksmith, who fixed the doorknob for $55.28. Max complained about a reduction in services, and the CAB ordered the landlord to pay him $55.28.

• *Electricity* On June 19, 1975, there was an electrical failure in apartment 5L at 123-25 Eighty-second Avenue in Kew Gardens. The tenant, K. E. Coupland, complained repeatedly of no lights or power in her living room, kitchen, and foyer. By July 9, when the landlord had not responded, Ms. Coupland hired an electrician, who restored service at a cost of $45.00. Ms. Coupland then filed a complaint for reduction of services, and the CAB ordered the landlord to pay Ms. Coupland $45.00.

• *Lock* When Edward Gallipoli moved into apartment 2E at 99-44 Sixty-seventh Road in Forest Hills, the lock on the apartment door was broken. He had to pay the super $10.00 to install a new lock. Edward complained about a reduction in services, and the CAB ordered his landlord to reimburse him for the expense.

• *Radiator* In 1975 the CAB ordered a Brooklyn landlord to reimburse a tenant $4.20, which she had spent for two new radiator valves; the landlord had neglected to replace the old, defective valves.

• *Toilet* For three months the landlord at 61-20 Grand Central Parkway in Forest Hills neglected to replace a tenant's broken toilet seat, despite numerous complaints. Finally, the tenant bought a new seat and then filed a complaint of reduction in services. The CAB ordered the landlord to pay the tenant $16.04, which she had spent on the toilet seat.

• *Window* On January 4, 1974, Lisa Lutomski complained to her landlord about a broken windowpane in her apartment at 227 East Eighty-ninth Street in Manhattan. When three cold days passed without repairs, Lisa hired a glazier, who replaced the pane for $19.26. Upon a complaint for reduction in services, the CAB ordered the landlord to pay Lisa $19.26.

For rent-stabilized tenants, complaining to the CAB involves very little risk. Even if the CAB should decide that there has been no reduction in required services, the tenant is merely out the cost of his self-made repairs. Tenants who are not rent stabilized, however, may have to run considerably greater risks, with less prospect of success, if they try to make their own repairs at the landlord's expense. One way to do this is to deduct the amount of the repairs from your next rent check. Before doing so, a lawyer should be consulted, because withholding part of the rent is likely to precipitate a nonpayment lawsuit by the landlord. The chances of winning such a lawsuit are uncertain; judges can respond quite differently to repair-and-deduct tactics, depending largely on the circumstances.

In one such case, *Jackson* v. *Rivera,* the tenant's toilet stopped working. She hired her own repairman, after the landlord had refused to do the job. The bill came to twenty-two dollars, which she paid and then deducted from her rent. The landlord promptly sought to evict her for nonpayment of rent.

In Manhattan civil court, Judge Leonard Sandler ruled that the tenant had a right to act as she had. According to Judge Sandler, a tenant may make his own repairs and deduct their reasonable cost from the rent when three conditions exist: (1) There is an emergency that seriously affects the habitability of the apartment. (2) The landlord has refused to make the repairs. (3) It would be unreasonable to let the emergency continue while the city tries to crank its bureaucracy into action. Judge Sandler found that all these factors existed in the case before him. So, the tenant was able to defend herself successfully against eviction, and the landlord got stuck with the repair expenses.

If deducting repair expenses from your rent seems too risky, there's another, more affirmative strategy that you can adopt. Instead of setting yourself up for a nonpayment action, go on the offensive and sue your landlord. Drag him into New York City Small Claims Court and seek to recover the money you spent on repairs. (You can sue for up to a thousand dollars. Cases in which tenants have won their expenses back from the landlord are discussed in chapter 16.)

PART IV

Court Actions

CHAPTER 14

Your Right to Withhold Rent

In chapter 13, you saw several ways to demand proper maintenance and repairs: complaining to your landlord or the Office of Code Enforcement; bringing a tenant-initiated action in housing court; even doing the repairs yourself and then trying to recover your expenses from the landlord. What happens, though, if you've tried everything and your landlord still won't budge? The answer might be: change tactics. Instead of chasing after the landlord, make him come to you. You have the best possible bait for attracting a stubborn landlord: your rent. So why not stop paying it?

It's a gutsy play—not paying rent—and the wise tenant will talk to a lawyer first, because the landlord really has to respond. He can, of course, do nothing—in which case, you'll be living rent-free. Or he might give in to the pressure and make the repairs—in which case you'll pay up what you owe. Or else—and here's where that lawyer is essential—the landlord will sue you. Perhaps he'll sue you for the money that you owe, or maybe he'll try to evict you for nonpayment of rent.

If you and your lawyer have planned well, you will be able to defend yourself successfully. (Essentially, your defense is that the landlord failed to perform his legal duty to provide maintenance and repairs; so you should be relieved of your duty to pay rent.) A successful defense will bring you important benefits—you can wind up getting repairs, or paying your rent into court, or living at a reduced rental. An unsuccessful defense will not leave you out in the street. You can always pay the rent you owe *before* a warrant of eviction is issued by the judge. Paying up prevents your eviction (see page 235).

There are three basic ways to defend yourself successfully. You would be wise to discuss them with your lawyer before you start withholding rent.

THE 755 ACTION

The first way to defend yourself is through what lawyers call a 755 action. (Section 755 of the state's Real Property Actions and Proceedings Law authorizes this particular legal action.) It is based on the existence of either housing code violations or dangerous living conditions that the landlord has failed to correct. His failure to do his duty relieves you of your obligation to pay rent—this is the argument you will make in court. If it succeeds, you will win a double victory. First, the landlord's lawsuit against you will be put on ice. (The judge will "stay" the proceedings.) So, the threat of eviction or a money judgment against you is frozen stiff.

Second, you will be allowed to stage what amounts to a one-man rent strike. The judge will order you to pay your rent into court—rather than to the landlord. Whatever rent is due when the order is given goes to court. Future rent will also be paid into court, for as long as the judge's order remains in effect. (Failure to deposit rent with the court clerk within five days after it's due can result in the stay being vacated by the judge.)

The court is now your bank, so to speak. To get at your rent deposits, the landlord must first challenge the judge's order. A challenge requires the landlord to prove that he has made the necessary repairs. Of course, you may be able to prove that the landlord is lying, or that, despite what he says, new violations and disrepair have replaced the old conditions. In such a situation, the judge can turn down the landlord's attempt to get at your money. So the message to your landlord is clear: Make repairs or forget about the rent.

Sounds pretty good, doesn't it? You may, however, see one

catch. What if you go on paying rent into court and no repairs are ever made? Perhaps your landlord has just given up on the building. Maybe he figures it's cheaper to lose your rent than to pay for repairs. Or, quite possibly, he can't pay for the repairs without your rent money, which is locked up in court.

Whatever the reason is, you don't have to sit around helplessly. Remember, you entered court with one aim—to get some repairs. The fact that you left court on a one-man rent strike doesn't help much, because you are actually still shelling out your rent money, even though it's going into court. So you are going to have to return to court and ask the judge for your money's worth.

Fortunately, the judge has the power to help you out. He can release some or all of your rent deposits to pay bills for building maintenance and repairs. For example, the judge can authorize payments for fuel, electricity, gas, janitorial services, or the labor of and materials for repairmen. Most likely, your lawyer will want to get the judge's approval before any repair work is actually begun. After the judge okays the proposed repairs (and their estimated cost) the work can go ahead, and payment from your rent will follow.

As you can see, you will be using the court system to funnel your rent money where you think it is most needed. You owe it to yourself to watch out for conditions that may be grounds for withholding your rent and starting the legal wheels rolling. Essentially, there are two sets of conditions to look for. First there are housing law violations, which have been recorded against your building. (You can discover whether your building has violations by visiting your local division of the Office of Code Enforcement and requesting a search of the records on your building (see Appendix A for the addresses). There is a ten-dollar fee for the search and report.

The violations must be serious—maybe bad enough to force you out of your apartment, although that degree of severity isn't necessary. Violations are considered serious if they endanger life, health, or safety—or even if there is only a likelihood that danger might arise in the future.

The violations can exist in a tenant's apartment or in the building's public parts, used by all the tenants. In a 1973 case the tenant's apartment was infested with roaches, because of a near-total lack of extermination services. The back door to the apartment was nailed up and the lock on the front door didn't work (the doorknob kept falling off too). There were some severe leaks, and dirty water constantly backed up in the kitchen sink. With such violations, a 755 stay was ordered by the judge.

Violations in the public parts of two Lower East Side buildings led to 755 stays. At 309 East Houston Street the hallways were laden with thick layers of dust and dirt that had accumulated over the years. And at 427 East Sixth Street, thirty-four violations, including: a broken lock on the vestibule door, defective handrails on the stairways, missing bulbs in the halls, doors that weren't fireproof, and the need for painting in the halls.

Even if there are no violations recorded against your building, you can still have grounds for withholding rent and getting a 755 stay. *Any condition that is likely to become dangerous to life, health, or safety* is grounds for withholding rent and later defending yourself in court; the condition need not be one that has been recorded as a violation by the Office of Code Enforcement.

If the landlord sues you for withholding rent, you will have to defend yourself by proving that conditions are likely to become dangerous to life, health, or safety. Therefore, it is wise to be sure of your proof before you stop paying rent. The question is: What kinds of conditions can you prove are dangerous? There is no flat answer. Of course, your lawyer will be in a position to advise you about the conditions you are afraid of.

In one 1971 case, *Morbeth Realty Corporation* v. *Rosenshine,* a tenant proved that eight dangerous conditions existed in her apartment: (1) Water leaked from a pipe connected to the toilet whenever the toilet was used. (2) The toilet was not connected to the wall and needed to be reset. (3) Water leaked from the holes around the bathroom light fixture, so, when the upstairs tenant used the shower, water caused the bulb to burst. (4) The lightswitch in the kitchen needed repair. (5) There were roaches in the kitchen. (6) The doorknob of the closet needed to be replaced. (7) The apartment needed plastering and painting. (8) The window frames were broken, several glass panes were broken, and defective insulation permitted cold air to come in from outside. Faced with this proof, the judge had little trouble deciding that the conditions endangered life, health, and safety.

Many different conditions have been proved dangerous in court. They range from rat holes to a leaky penthouse skylight. There is simply no formula that dictates which conditions are dangerous and which are not. Instead, everything depends on the forcefulness of your proof. Strong proof of a potential danger to life, health, or safety can make your case.

Suppose there are a few cracks running across your ceiling. Without more, this condition would not be considered an actual danger and might not even seem to be a potential danger. But what if you can offer stronger proof in court? Say, evidence that the ceiling is actually starting to sag, or the plaster is falling apart. Now you have presented concrete facts on which to base your conclusion that the ceiling is likely to become dangerous.

It is worth mentioning one possible pitfall in your defense against the landlord. He might try to prove that the conditions you complain about were caused by your negligence or destructiveness. If he's able to prove this, your defense will fail. You cannot withhold your rent and then defend yourself in court on the basis of disrepair that you carelessly or deliberately caused. Your lawyer can advise you best on whether or not you're to blame.

If you embark upon a 755 action, there's a chance you may half win and half lose. Picture this scene: You withhold rent because of dangerous conditions. The landlord tries to evict you for nonpayment. You defend yourself successfully in court. Months go by while you pay rent into court. Still the landlord makes no repairs. Conditions go from bad to worse. Finally, in desperation, you move out when conditions are unbearable.

Question: Who gets the money—all that rent money that you've been depositing in court for months? Answer: You get the money; the landlord isn't entitled to any of it, unless he's made some substantial effort toward restoring better living conditions. New York judges are reluctant to allow a landlord to just sit back, do nothing, wait for the tenant to move away, and then swoop into court and pick up all the deposited rent money. However, if the landlord has at least tried to fix things up, then the rent deposit may be apportioned between him and the long-suffering tenant—say, on a fifty-fifty basis.

RENT IMPAIRING VIOLATIONS

The second way to defend yourself in a nonpayment action is based on the existence of a rent-impairing violation. (This defense is authorized by section 302-a of the state's Mutiple Dwelling Law.) The defense is available to any tenant who lives in a multiple dwelling (a building that contains at least three apartments), regardless of whether his apartment is rent controlled, rent stabilized, or uncontrolled.

Broadly speaking, the term *rent-impairing violation* encompasses fire hazards and other serious threats to life, health, or safety. The task of defining specific rent-impairing violations and locating them belongs to the Office of Code Enforcement. Currently, the office lists seventy-six violations as rent-impairing (see Appendix G).

When rent-impairing violations are found by a code enforcement inspector, they are officially recorded and the landlord is notified. He has a duty to correct the violations. If he does, they will be canceled from the records of the Office of Code Enforcement. But months may go by without correction, despite the accumulation of civil penalties.

After such a delay, you may want to act on your own. And you can—six months after your landlord was notified about a rent-impairing violation. By that time, if the recorded violation has not been canceled, you can stop paying rent.

There is absolutely no requirement that the violation be in your own apartment. You can stop paying rent even if the violation is in some public part of the building (used by all the tenants)—like the halls or stairs. Or the violation may be in an area under the landlord's control—like the heating or plumbing system. When the rent-impairing violation affects the building rather than a particular apartment, any tenant in the building can stop paying rent after the six-month period.

For example, suppose there is a rent-impairing violation recorded against your building's fire escape. Say the apparatus is not securely bolted to the brick wall. Such a violation affects the entire building—not just one apartment. So, after the six-month period, any tenant could stop paying rent. The law does not limit the number of tenants that can stop paying rent; nor does the law require any minimum number of tenants (as in a rent strike) before rent payment can be stopped. Therefore, you could stop paying rent on your own, or act with your neighbor, or join the entire building.

On the other hand, suppose the rent-impairing violation is confined to one apartment. Then, only that tenant can act after the six-month period. The other tenants cannot use the violation as an excuse to stop paying rent.

If this whole strategy interests you, find out whether there are any rent-impairing violations recorded against your building or your apartment. You can do this by visiting your local division of the Office of Code Enforcement. (The addresses are listed in Appendix A.) At the office, fill out a form requesting a report on any violations against your building. (A ten-dollar fee is charged for the report.) The official records will be searched, and you will then be sent a computer printout listing whatever violations there are. A star next to a violation means the violation is rent-impairing. (To be doubly sure, you can check the printout against the list of rent-impairing violations in Appendix G.)

The printout will indicate the date on which the violation was recorded. This date should also be the date on which notification was sent to your landlord. Once you know the date of notification, you can tell whether six months have passed, allowing you to stop paying rent. (Sometimes there is a delay in notification after the violation is recorded. A lawyer can discover such a delay by subpoenaing records from the Office of Code Enforcement.)

If you stop paying rent after the six-month period, you will probably need a lawyer, because the landlord is apt to sue you for the money or try to evict you for nonpayment of rent. In either case, you have a defense—namely, the rent-impairing violation. Your defense boils down to this: The landlord lost his right to your rent because he did not correct the violation within six months after notification.

When you raise this defense you have to deposit in court the amount of rent claimed by your landlord. (So it's a good idea to save up your rent after you stop paying it.) This deposit will be held by the court clerk, awaiting the outcome of the case. In the meantime, the deposit has an important legal effect: It destroys the landlord's right to end your lease because of nonpayment of rent.

After you offer your defense, the landlord may resort to four possible answers: (1) He can try to prove the violation never really existed, despite the official record at the Office of Code Enforcement. (2) He can try to prove he has actually corrected the violation, even though the official records do not yet show this fact. (3) He can try to prove that you caused the violation—or your family did, or your guests, or even some other tenant's family or guests. (4) He can try to prove that you refused him entry when he wanted to fix the violation.

If the landlord offers one of these answers, the battlelines will have been drawn. Remember, he originally sued you; then you defended on the grounds of a rent-impairing violation; and he tried to answer your defense. The legal question is: Who has proved his case—you or the landlord? If the landlord prevails, he wins the rent money you deposited with the court. (He can also recover up to one hundred dollars in court costs from you, should the judge decide that you were acting in bad faith when you raised the defense of rent-impairing violations.)

On the other hand, if you win, you get your rent deposit back, so you will have lived rent-free from the time you stopped paying rent. What's more important, you will continue to live rent-free from the date of your victory until the violation is removed from your apartment. The court's finding of a rent-impairing violation leads to a complete abatement of your rent.

If the rent-impairing violation found by the court exists in some public part of the building—or in an area under the landlord's control—then the rent abatement affects every tenant in the building. As long as the violation remains uncorrected, the landlord will be prohibited from collecting rent from *any* tenant.

THE WARRANTY OF HABITABILITY

The third way to defend yourself in a nonpayment action is based upon the state's new warranty of habitability law. In chapter 12, we learned how this law requires the landlord to maintain your apartment and building in habitable condition. A binding warranty to this effect is read into your lease. If your landlord breaches the warranty of habitability, one remedy you can resort to is withholding the payment of rent. Your obligation to pay rent depends on whether the landlord honors his warranty. If he fails to do so, then you don't have to go on paying rent. As one New York court recently put it: "Tenants are not required to pay for services they did not receive."

In response to the withholding of rent, a landlord will, of course, bring a nonpayment action. The tenant then raises breach of warranty as a defense and seeks a total or partial abatement of rent (depending on the degree to which basic habitability has been decreased). Or the tenant may counterclaim, seeking to have a specific sum deducted from the rent claimed by the landlord (again, based on the decrease in habitability).

In translating a breach of warranty into dollars and cents, a judge is not supposed to rely on mere guesswork. He should, instead, use some rational system of measurement. One such system is computation of the reduction in rental value that an apartment has undergone because of a breach of warranty. The test here can be stated in general terms: What is the difference in rental value between an apartment that is supplied with all the services to which a tenant is entitled and the same apartment without all those services? When applying this test, courts have often calculated the percentage of apartment space rendered unusable by the breach in warranty. By multiplying this percentage by the rent claimed by the landlord, the court arrives at the amount of the tenant's damages. This amount may then be deducted from the rent, in the form of a rent abatement.

In *Bassett* v. *Gluck,* a tenant was unable to use his bedroom because of a foul odor of cat urine emanating from the apartment next door. The tenant had complained to the landlord, who had promised to alleviate the smell but had failed. When the tenant withheld rent, the landlord sued for nonpayment. The court held that the foul odor, which the landlord hadn't corrected, breached the warranty of habitability. So, the tenant was entitled to a rent abatement. Since the unusable bedroom amounted to one sixth of the tenant's six-and-a-half-room apartment, the tenant had to pay only five sixths of the rent due.

In *New York Eldorado, Inc.,* v. *Balsam,* approximately 40 percent of the tenant's apartment was affected by water leakage. However, the adverse effects occurred only sporadically, usually after heavy rainstorms. No specific property damage was claimed by the tenant. Given these facts, the court calculated that the rental value of the apartment had diminished 10 percent. So, the tenant was granted a 10 percent abatement.

In two other nonpayment actions where a breach of warranty was found, rent abatements of 20 percent were calculated on the basis of numerous housing code violations that had impaired basic habitability: for example, leaks, broken plaster, garbage accumulation, roaches, inadequate hallway lighting, broken windows, and a defective front-door lock. An even more extreme case resulted in a total abatement of rent for a five-month period, because the tenant had been forced to live in a "chamber of horrors." She had no heat, hot water, gas, exterminator service, or janitorial service—not to mention that the toilet didn't flush and the walls were badly broken and soggy from many leaks.

Suppose a breach of warranty occurs because tenants are deprived of certain building-wide services—for example, use of a laundry room, or doormen guarding the entrance. How can a court compute the amount of damages suffered by an individual tenant? Obviously, it's difficult to prove a reduction in value for individual apartments. Conceivably, if the tenants pitch in and perform building services themselves, they can prove how much their time and inconvenience is worth. Or if tenants suffer any direct monetary loss—say, the expense of having to send clothing to an outside laundry—that particular item may be a partial measure of the tenants' damages.

If no evidence of this nature is available, however, New York courts may try to calculate the extent to which the landlord has been unjustly enriched by the cutback in services; after all, he has saved on salaries and expenses, while the tenants went on paying for services that they no longer received. The question is: What percentage of the landlord's savings is a tenant entitled to in the form of a rent abatement? The answer depends upon two basic figures: (1) the total savings to the landlord resulting from the cutback; and (2) the percentage of the building's monthly rent roll represented by an individual tenant's monthly rent. If a court multiplies the percentage figure by the total savings, it will arrive at a logical rent abatement for breach of warranty.

This formula was employed following the 1976 strike by the building employees' union (local 32-B). For seventeen days in May 1976, New York City tenants were victimized by lack of essential building services. For example, the tenants at 171 West Seventy-ninth Street in Manhattan were deprived of the following services during the strike: use of the laundry room; security doormen; mail and parcel delivery; garbage pickup; cleaning of the halls and lobby. Two tenants, Anthony Doknovitch and Domenica Lupu, withheld their rent. In the nonpayment action that followed, *Goldner* v. *Doknovitch,* Judge John Milano decided that the seventeen-day deprivation of services constituted a breach of warranty.

But how much were Doknovitch and Lupu entitled to by way of a rent abatement? Well, the monthly rent roll at 171 West Seventy-ninth was $22,512.58, and Doknovitch and Lupu were paying monthly rents of $317.55 and $318.49, respectively; therefore, the portion of the rent roll that they contributed each month was .0141%. As a result of the seventeen-day strike, the landlord realized a savings of $1,594.94 on the salaries of the strikers. Multiplying $1,594.94 by .0141%, Judge Milano awarded Doknovitch and Lupu rent abatements of $22.49 each.

A similar case arose because of the strike conditions at Park West Village on Central Park West in Manhattan. Without maintenance personnel, the buildings became badly littered with garbage, attracting vermin and flies and causing a stench. Twenty tenants withheld rent. At the nonpayment action that resulted, there was a finding that the tenants had clearly been deprived of services for which they were paying rent. However, no elaborate computation was made regarding rent roll percentages or savings realized by the landlord. Instead, the court simply concluded, on the basis of the conditions during the strike, that the loss sustained by the tenants amounted to approximately 10 percent of their rent. So each tenant was entitled to a 10 percent rate abatement.

The warranty of habitability law specifically provides that "in determining the amount of damages sustained by a tenant as a result of a breach of warranty . . . the court need not require any expert testimony." So, the tenant's own testimony, or that of his neighbors, can provide ample basis for placing a price tag on the deprivation suffered by the tenant. In two recent cases (one in 1976, the other in 1977), tenants testified that they had been deprived of the use of working air-conditioners that were supplied with their apartments. Both courts found a breach of warranty and allowed a hundred-dollar monthly rent deduction during the period of deprivation. (In the 1976 case, an additional ten-dollar monthly deduction was allowed for the five and a half months during which the tenant's gas stove wasn't working properly.)

Sometimes the tenant's testimony does not provide an adequate basis for the assessment of damages. In *Schwartz* v. *Jiminez,* the tenant merely testified that he would have offered only $150.00 per month for his $273.40 apartment if he had known about the lack of services. The court concluded that this testimony "was at best highly speculative and subjective, nor did it or could it possibly reflect an unfettered judgment as a nonclaimant in a free market situation at the very time of his entry into the apartment. . . . If the tenant had attempted to sublet his apartment to various individuals out of possession and in an arm's length situation, then testimony as to what they offered would have been some proof of the market value of the apartment, absent certain maintenance and services." Because of inadequate proof, the tenant was entitled to only nominal damages—namely, one buck.

One good way to come up with adequate proof is to resort to some form of the repair-and-deduct technique (see page 192). In other words, when you are deprived of repairs or services, supply them yourself and deduct the expense from your rent; when the inevitable nonpayment action comes, raise breach of warranty as your defense and claim your expense as the true measure of your damages.

An enterprising tenant transformed repair-and-deduct into eat-and-deduct in a 1976 case, *Hilary Gardens* v. *Dutcher*. The tenant, a late-night television producer for NBC, lived in a new luxury building. Because of the unusual hours of her work, she had most of her meals at home. One day her gas stove broke down, and despite numerous complaints, the landlord took seventeen days to fix it. During that period, the tenant was forced to eat all her meals in restaurants. She calculated that the cost of her restaurant meals, as against purchasing food and cooking her own meals, was in excess of $10 per day. So, she withheld her expenses from her monthly rent—$400—and in the nonpayment suit that followed, she counterclaimed against the landlord.

The court ruled that the lack of a working stove for seventeen days constituted a breach of the warranty of habitability. The tenant had amply proven the measure of her damages: namely, $10 per day for seventeen days. So the tenant was allowed a $170 deduction from the rent claimed by the landlord.

Obviously repair-and-deduct (or eat-and-deduct, for that matter) is not much good if you can't afford to supply yourself with the services you've been deprived of. Furthermore, if you should lose in a subsequent nonpayment action, you'll not only owe back rent, you'll be out-of-pocket for the expense you incurred. Repair-and-deduct does, however, go a long way toward solving the proof-of-loss problem encountered in some warranty of habitability cases.

You would be well advised to consult a lawyer if you're seriously interested in trying repair-and-deduct. Small claims court is also a possibility if you want to risk repair-and-deduct, but don't want to pay for a lawyer. In one recent small claims case, tenants successfully sued their landlord to recover the fees they had paid on rental air-conditioners when their building's central air-conditioning broke down (discussed on page 231).

Despite all the formulas that judges have devised for computing damages, some serious problems still remain in certain situations involving breach of warranty. One big problem area has been cases involving lack of heat or hot water. Courts thus far have been unwilling to speculate on how much the rental value of an apartment is reduced when there is no heat for several days or even weeks.

Whenever judges who find a breach of warranty hesitate to assess damages because mathematical precision in unattainable, the efficacy of the warranty law is undermined. Realizing this, our state legislators may eventually amend the law so as to provide judges with guidelines for calculating damages. Until this occurs, tenants should make every effort to provide as much hard evidence as possible, so that the measure of their damages (and, hence, any rent abatement) can be calculated.

CHAPTER 15

The Rent Strike

In chapter 14 you learned several ways to turn the tables on your landlord—by withholding rent and then raising a good defense in court. There is yet another tactic for squeezing maintenance and repairs out of your landlord. It is best suited to organized tenants who want to go on the attack as a group. They have the power to band together and call a rent strike. When properly staged, a rent strike does not require taking the law into your own hands, because the law is there already. Since 1965 New York has had a rent-strike law on the books. It authorizes what lawyers call an article 7–A proceeding (the rent-strike law is contained in article 7–A of the state's Real Property Actions and Procedure Law).

In a nutshell, the rent-strike law allows a group of tenants to pay their rent to a court-appointed administrator rather than to the landlord. The purpose is to provide funds for maintenance and repairs that the landlord has not made. Since he won't do his duty, the administrator does it for him under judicial supervision.

The rent-strike law covers New York City multiple dwellings that contain at least six apartments. These apartment buildings may be in Manhattan's "gilded ghetto" or in the real-life ghettos. The rent-strike law plays no economic favorites. It is not just a poor-man's law; rich people can use it too. As a civil-court judge once quipped: "The law in its majestic equality should protect the opulent, as well as the indigent, tenant from the indifferent attitude of an unfriendly landlord.''

This equal coverage was not immediately recognized when the rent-strike law was passed in 1965. The state legislature seemed to have been concerned chiefly with slums. However, the notion that only slums had conditions dangerous to life, health, or safety vanished quickly. Three weeks after the law went into effect (on July 17, 1965), a rent-strike case—*Himmel* v. *Chase Manhattan Bank*—arose over a high-rise on Manhattan's fashionable East Side. The building, 511 East Eightieth Street, had been completed about November 1963. It was to be a fine and elegant fourteen-story residence for 124 tenants seeking above-average comfort.

From the day the doors opened, however, the tenants had various complaints: (1) The central air-conditioning system appeared not to be of sufficient capacity to air-condition the building adequately, with the result that the system fell into disrepair regularly. (2) The water supply in the building appeared to be contaminated with a heavy sediment as a result of a corrosion condition within the hot water system in the building. (3) The incinerator shaft in the building appeared to have insufficient insulation—it created an undue amount of heat, smoke, fumes, and odors, which seeped into the public incinerator rooms and into the adjoining apartments. (4) The plumbing fixtures drained either very poorly or not at all. (5) The ventilators did not operate properly. (6) The elevators in the building were frequently out of order. (7) The laundry equipment in the basement was regularly out of order. (8) Many tenants complained of an infestation of rodents throughout the building. (9) The security system was inadequate and resulted in a substantial number of instances of burglary, vandalism, and loitering.

The tenants formed a committee, and seventy members petitioned the court for appointment of an administrator. The landlord argued that the new rent-strike law was unenforceable because of the difficulty that judges would have in determining exactly which conditions endangered tenants and, thereby, established the need for an administrator. ''Some question may be raised as to what are conditions dangerous to life, health, or safety,'' the judge admitted. ''Each case will depend on its own facts." Then, turning to the facts at hand, the judge observed: "There was some testimony by a tenant having a form of respiratory ailment and to whom air-conditioning was a health factor. The constant breakdown of elevators in high-rise . . . dwellings can obviously become both a health and safety factor. Inadequate heat, hot or cold water are health factors." So, contrary to the landlord's claim, the judge easily detected conditions dangerous to life, health, and safety.

The rent-strike law itself lists some conditions that may be grounds for a rent strike: lack of hot, or running water, or light, or electricity, or inadequate sewage-disposal facilities. Infestation by rodents is also singled out. These conditions do not have to occur at the same time before tenants can call a rent strike. Any one of these conditions is enough. However, the condition must have existed for at least five days.

This list of conditions is not exclusive. There may be many other hardships that would support a rent strike. The state legislators knew this. So, after their specific list, they declared that "any other condition dangerous to life, health or safety" might also be grounds for a rent strike. (Once again, any such condition must have existed for at least five days.)

The real guts of the rent-strike law lies in the key phrase "any other condition dangerous to life, health or safety." This sweeping language is not specifically defined by the law. That task is left up to judges as each case arises. (So, in the case of the East Eightieth Street high-rise, the judge found that defective air-conditioning could be dangerous to health, and elevator breakdowns could endanger both health and safety.)

In general, dangerous conditions tend to present an emergency. They are much more serious than run-of-the-mill inconveniences. However, there is absolutely no requirement in the rent-strike law that the conditions be official violations actually recorded by the city. This key fact distinguishes the rent strike from other tactics discussed in chapter 14, which sometimes require violations recorded by the Office of Code Enforcement.

Once in court, rent strikers must convince the judge that conditions in their building are dangerous. The judge is apt to be persuaded by a wide range of factors. For example, a crime wave was decisive in a 1972 Bronx case, *Tynan* v. *Willowdale Commerical Corporation*. The building under strike was at 2240 Grand Avenue. The strike was touched off by a broken bell and buzzer system, connected to each apartment from the entrance door. The system had been out of order for much longer than the necessary five-day period. (Indeed, the strikers charged twenty years had passed without repair; the landlord said there had been "only" three years of disrepair.)

"What is there about a nonfunctioning bell and buzzer system," asked Judge Joseph Sullivan of the Bronx civil court, "that makes it 'dangerous to life, health or safety' or akin to any of the other [rent strike] conditions such as lack of heat, running water, light, electricity . . . ?

"For the answer one need look no further than to the headlines in our newspapers chronicling with chilling impact the daily acts of crime and violence which have set the climate of fear in which we live."

Another key characteristic of a dangerous condition is that it does not have to exist building-wide. The rent-strike law states that the condition may exist in the building "or in any part thereof."

Assuming that dangerous conditions do exist, a building must be actively organized in preparation for a rent strike. You will need the support of at least one third of the tenants occupying your building. It takes that many before you're set to go to New York City Civil Court.

Your lawyer will then petition for a judgment directing that rents be paid to a court-appointed administrator. This petition will be served on your landlord. It will also be posted conspicuously in your building, notifying your fellow tenants who have not joined in the strike. They learn that, if you win, they will also be ordered to pay their rent to the administrator. So, a strike that starts with a bare one third of the tenants can wind up bringing down the whole house—on the landlord's head.

The landlord has three possible defenses. (1) He can try to prove that the dangerous conditions don't exist, or that they've been fixed. (2) He can try to prove that the conditions were caused by the tenants, their families, or their guests. (3) He can try to prove that any tenant refused entry to a repairman trying to fix the dangerous conditions.

If you win, the prize is repair of the dangerous conditions. The prize may be awarded in one or two ways. First, the judge may order that all rents be deposited with a court-appointed administrator. This judgment will be served even on the nonstrikers in your building. Thereafter they, like you and the original rent strikers, will pay rent to the administrator during the strike. Under the judge's direction, the administrator can buy materials, hire labor, and pay for services necessary to eliminate the dangerous conditions. Whatever money is left over when the work is done goes to your landlord.

There is a second way you may win your case. Before the judge appoints an administrator, your landlord may apply to do the work himself. He will have to demonstrate the ability to undertake the work promptly. He must also deposit security money in court to assure his performance. It's then up to the judge to decide whether your landlord should be given a chance.

Suppose the judge says yes and sets a deadline for the completion of the work. Then you will keep paying rent to your landlord. But you won't sit idly by. You'll make sure that the repairs are progressing. If your landlord is not proceeding diligently, you can get relief. Even before the work deadline arrives, you have a right to ask the judge to appoint an administrator.

Should an administrator be appointed to take over, he will use the security money left in court by your landlord. You will continue paying rent to the landlord. But, if the security money won't cover the job, the judge will order rents to be paid to the administrator. Either way, your money or the landlord's will be used to eliminate the dangerous conditions.

So the rent strike can be a powerful tool. It is available to all tenants, whether they are rent controlled, rent stabilized, or uncontrolled (as long as they live in buildings that contain at least six apartments). According to one 1970 case, co-op tenants cannot take advantage of the rent-strike law. During the rent strike, your landlord has no legal claim to the rent money that you are paying to the administrator. The fact that you've paid the administrator is a good defense in any nonpayment action the landlord might initiate against you. These safeguards are dictated by the rent-strike law; any provision in your lease to the contrary is void and unenforceable. For that matter, any lease provision that restricts your right to participate in a legal rent strike is void.

CHAPTER 16

How to Sue Your Landlord for Damages

A surprising number of tenants believe that landlords can't be sued; some sort of legal immunity is thought to cloak the owner of an apartment building. Where this misapprehension originated is not clear, although canny landlords have probably contributed to it. At any rate, the notion that landlords can't be sued is utterly false.

In the first two sections of this chapter we'll consider suing a landlord for negligence. Such a lawsuit is appropriate when the landlord's carelessness causes you personal injury or property damage or leads to a crime being committed against you. The third section looks at suits based on the state's new warranty of habitability statute. Finally, we'll see how to sue your landlord for up to a thousand dollars in New York City Small Claims Court—without the need of a lawyer!

THE NEGLIGENT LANDLORD

Crumbling plaster, creaking floorboards, burned-out hall lights, leaky pipes—all those nagging little defects that your landlord neglects to repair can add up to more than mere inconvenience. That crumbling plaster might one day fall, crushing your priceless jade vase; the floorboards could collapse beneath your feet; you might fall down the stairs in the unlit hallway; and those pipes could burst, flooding your entire wardrobe. Thus, your landlord's failure to provide proper maintenance and repairs can cause you property damage or personal injury. You can sue the landlord and recover your losses, if they were his fault.

Under the *law of negligence,* a landlord can be held liable for the consequences of his carelessness. In a nutshell, the law of negligence requires that the following five factors exist before a landlord can be held liable to a tenant: (1) The landlord must have had a legal duty to perform maintenance or make repairs on some given condition. (2) The landlord must have known, or in the exercise of reasonable care should have known, that the condition in question needed maintenance or repair. (3) Neglecting his legal duty, the landlord either performed no maintenance or repair work, or did the work in a careless manner. (This particular factor constitutes the so-called act of negligence.) (4) The tenant suffered personal injury or property damage as a direct result of the landlord's negligence. (5) This injury or damage was a reasonably foreseeable result of the landlord's negligence. (By the way, don't be hoodwinked by language in your lease that seems to insulate your landlord from liability for negligence; as explained in chapter 2, such a lease provision is unenforceable.)

The first factor is usually satisfied by the landlord's general legal obligation to perform maintenance and repairs. The best way to make sure that the second factor is fulfilled is to contact the landlord directly. In a sample letter (see page 175), Mary Tenant complained to John Landlord that her ceiling was cracked and sagging. While the letter was primarily a request for repairs, it also served as fair warning that damage might result if repairs were not made.

Even if a landlord doesn't actually know about some deteriorating condition, the law may still treat him as if he did know. For example, the condition may be one that the landlord would have discovered had he regularly checked up on his building in a businesslike manner. Or, perhaps, the condition was brought to the super's attention; since the super is the landlord's agent, whatever the super knows, the landlord is presumed to know.

Once your landlord is on notice of a defective condition, the ball is in his court. If he fails to act soon enough, or if his response is careless, he can be held responsible for consequences that are reasonably foreseeable. Your landlord is not required to be a prophet, who guards against accidents that no one could have realistically foreseen. However, he may be held liable, even though the exact nature of the damage could not have been precisely foreseen; it is sufficient that the general threat was reasonably foreseeable.

So much for abstract principles; let's get down to cases. In *Acosta* v. *Irdank Realty Corporation,* some tenants on the Lower East Side won a $4,320 judgment against their landlord because he failed to repair the dangerous lead-based paint that was peeling off their walls. The tenants lived with their infant daughter, Yvette, on East Eighth Street. Yvette got lead poisoning after eating some of the paint chips that peeled off the walls, and she had to be treated at Bellevue Hospital for over two months.

For at least three months prior to the hospitalization, the landlord knew about the condition of the walls in the apartment. Yet, he did nothing, despite his clear legal duty to make repairs. Was it reasonably foreseeable that Yvette would get lead poisoning? Yes, said Judge Emilio Nunez: "That small children go around the house picking up everything within their reach and placing it in their mouths and attempting to eat it is well known. They often have a craving to put in their mouths and eat most unusual things. It would not be unreasonable, therefore, to foresee that Yvette would pick up pieces of plaster and paint if they were lying around and eat them. It is well known that paint contains lead which may cause lead poisoning to anyone ingesting it. . . .

"The hazard which the broken walls presented should have been reasonably foreseeable to the landlord. Given the broken walls and plaster, the lead content in the paint . . . the child in the apartment, the known propensities of children and the results that followed, I find that Yvette became ill with lead poisoning as a direct result of the landlord's negligence in failing to keep the premises . . . in proper repair." Judge Nunez awarded Yvette's parents a total of $4,320 ($2,500 to compensate for the injury, plus $1,820 to cover the hospital bill).

Two other personal-injury cases are worth looking at. In one, the tenant kept having trouble with her shower. It had an annoying habit of suddenly becoming extremely hot while running. Sometimes steam would actually be released. The tenant complained to the super, but no repairs were made, despite the landlord's clear duty. Eventually, the tenant was badly scalded. She sued the landlord on the grounds of negligence and won a $3,500 judgment.

In the second case, the tenant had a leak in his bedroom ceiling. The landlord had assured him that the ceiling would be fixed. So, the tenant had been lulled into a false sense of security by the time he went to bed one cold winter's night. During the night, water from the roof leaked into the tenant's bed. The next morning he awoke with a chill, which rapidly developed into the grippe and required a doctor's attention. The tenant sued his landlord for negligence and won a $110 judgment to cover his medical costs.

If your furnishings or personal belongings are damaged because of the landlord's negligence, you can sue him to recover your property losses. Consider the victory won by two tenants at 175 West Seventy-ninth Street in Manhattan. One of them, Mr. Lobell, lived directly beneath the other, Mr. Mendelsohn. Lobell noticed some wet plaster in his closet and showed it to the super. Nothing was done by either the super or the landlord to discover the cause of the wetness. Three weeks later, the cause became apparent—a water pipe had burst inside one of Mendelsohn's walls, just above Lobell's closet. As a result, both apartments were flooded.

Corrosion had caused a slow leak in the pipe (hence, the wet plaster in Lobell's closet). The landlord had a duty to uncover that leak after learning about the wet plaster. He should have opened up the wall and followed the trickling water up to the source in Mendelsohn's apartment. The landlord's failure to do this and to repair the leaking pipe was negligent. Since his negligence caused damage to the tenants, they recovered their losses from him in court.

You can now see why it is so important to notify your landlord as soon as you feel you need repairs. Given your notification—and the landlord's duty—he must act or pay the price. A lawyer will be able to advise you on the prospects for a lawsuit against your landlord. You should also be aware, however, that New York City Small Claims Court is available if you want to act without a lawyer.

MUGGINGS AND BURGLARIES

If you're ever victimized by a criminal in your apartment building, your first reaction will most likely be to call the police (that is, as soon as you regain consciousness). Then, if you happen to have insurance—say, against theft—you'll contact your agent. What you'll probably never even think of doing is suing your landlord. That can be a grave oversight. After all, consider how the criminal managed to get into your building. Was it because the front-door lock doesn't work, and the landlord has neglected to fix it? Or perhaps the landlord refused to fire that doorman of yours, who's always sleeping at his post. Loosely speaking, your landlord's carelessness may have made him a partner in crime with the intruder. In such a situation, your landlord may be held personally liable to you for the losses or harm that you've suffered.

The landlord's potential liability comes from the law of negligence. Earlier in this chapter, we learned that negligence is the legal theory under which a landlord may be held liable for the consequences of his carelessness. There must, of course, be a causal connection between that carelessness and the harm that results to you.

For years, New York courts ruled that there was no such causal connection in cases where a criminal intruder took advantage of a landlord's negligence. The criminal's infliction of harm upon a tenant was generally regarded as an intervening cause—one that insulated the landlord from any liability, even though his carelessness may have facilitated the criminal's entry into the building. Judges were reluctant to impose liability upon an admittedly negligent landlord, because they concluded that he could not have reasonably foreseen that his negligence would lead to the commission of a crime.

For example, in the 1971 case *Smith* v. *ABC Realty Company,* a female tenant lived on the top floor of a five-story, East

Village walk-up. The building, located in a high-crime area, was a hangout for drug addicts. A fire escape from the roof to the ground passed right by the tenant's window. One day a piece of glass was removed from this window by an unknown intruder. The tenant made numerous demands upon the super to repair the window, but he did nothing, and neither did the landlord. Two weeks later, at five o'clock one summer morning, an intruder reached through the hole in the window, unlocked the window, entered, and at knifepoint raped the tenant.

The tenant sued the landlord for his negligent failure to repair the window. In New York City Civil Court, the tenant won a ten-thousand-dollar judgment. The court found that the landlord's negligent failure to repair the window was the legal cause of the criminal intrusion. According to the judge, a reasonable person in the landlord's position should have anticipated that an opening in the window by the fire escape would be an invitation to criminal entry. On appeal, however, this well-reasoned opinion was reversed. The appellate term of the state supreme court found no clear chain of events connecting the landlord's negligence with the crime; what's more, the crime was thought not to be a reasonably foreseeable result of the landlord's negligence.

New York courts have had less difficulty finding a causal connection in situations where the landlord's negligence clearly increased the odds that a crime would occur. In one case, an apartment was empty while the tenants went on vacation. The refrigerator in the apartment next door went on the blink. The landlord gave the next-door neighbor the key to the empty apartment so that she could use the refrigerator there. One thing led to another. It seems that the neighbor's boyfriend got hold of the key, and, rather than content himself with just taking ice cubes, he burglarized the empty apartment.

When the vacationers returned, they sued the landlord for negligence. The court had no trouble connecting the landlord's negligence with the burglary: "The use of the key in these circumstances even for a criminal purpose is a use which we may reasonably say is a foreseeable one. The intervening force, that is to say the action of [the burglar], is a force which could reasonably have been anticipated; it is an incident of the risk which the landlord himself created.'' The tenants were awarded thirteen hundred dollars in damages against their landlord.

In a 1974 case, an apartment on Manhattan's Upper West Side was burglarized. The landlord had entered the tenant's apartment, while she was away, in order to do some electrical work. When he left, the landlord failed to lock the apartment door. ''No reasonably prudent person would have acted that way,'' observed the court. ''It was reasonably foreseeable that an unlocked apartment on the west side of Manhattan in this day and age would be burglarized. It was the landlord's affirmative act in unlocking the . . . door and leaving it unlocked that was the . . . cause of the foreseeable criminal act, because a person obviously locks his door to protect himself against burglars.''

The most important case, and one that casts doubt upon the continuing authority of *Smith* v. *ABC Realty,* is *Sherman* v. *Concourse Realty Corporation.* (It was decided in 1975 by the appellate division of the state supreme court.) The landlord of 1555 Grand Concourse in the Bronx had installed a bell and buzzer system, for which he collected a rent increase. Sometime later, a critical part of that security system (the cylinder in the lock of the building's front door) broke. The landlord removed the cylinder for repair, leaving the system inoperative and the front door wide open. The landlord was well aware of the risk to which he was exposing tenants; indeed, he had posted a notice warning them of strangers and thieves who were getting in through the front door.

The cylinder was still out for repairs, after a week, when one of the tenants was mugged and robbed in the lobby by an intruder who followed him in through the unlocked front door. The tenant sued the landlord for personal injuries and property loss. At the trial, the judge found that the landlord had been negligent in the way he attempted to fix the bell and buzzer system. Nevertheless, the judge dismissed the tenant's complaint, because there was insufficient proof that the landlord's negligence was the legal cause of the tenant's injury.

In a landmark decision, the trial court was reversed by the appellate division. The appeals court rejected the proposition that a landlord's negligence can never be viewed as the legal cause for the acts of a criminal intruder: ''In the instant case the landlord had actual knowledge of the criminal activities which occurred and were likely to reoccur within the building. For a monetary consideration, i.e., increased rent, the landlord assumed a limited duty of protection by the installation of the bell and buzzer system which was permitted to fall into disrepair. The fact that the immediate cause of the tenant's injury was the act of a third party, i.e., a criminal intruder, does not prevent the landlord's negligence from being regarded in contemplation of law as the . . . cause. . . . The landlord's neglect here 'gave rise to a stream of events that culminated in' the tenant's injuries." The appellate division ruled that the tenant was entitled to a new trial.

So you can see that New York courts are becoming much more receptive to negligence claims filed by crime victims. Do you believe that negligence on your landlord's part is enhancing the likelihood of criminals entering your building? If so, complain to the landlord *in writing*. Describe the conditions that the landlord is carelessly neglecting to eliminate. Bring to the landlord's attention any actual or attempted crimes that have occurred in or near the building. Point out that if the landlord does not act promptly, criminal intrusions are reasonably foreseeable. Send your complaint via certified mail, return receipt requested, and keep a copy of the complaint for yourself.

If you've already been hit by a criminal in your building, and you think the landlord's negligence may have facilitated the criminal's entry, consider seeing an attorney. He will be able to appraise how sound a case of negligence you actually have against your landlord. If the loss that you've suffered seems not to merit legal fees, you can always sue the landlord on your own in New York City Small Claims Court. In one such case, discussed in the last section of this chapter, a tenant who was burglarized won a thousand dollars from her landlord.

THE WARRANTY OF HABITABILITY

The warranty of habitability law is normally invoked by tenants as a defense in an action brought by the landlord for nonpayment of rent. Recently, however, a few judges have ruled that tenants can use the law affirmatively. In other words, if a landlord has breached the warranty of habitability, causing a tenant to suffer some ascertainable loss, the tenant can sue the landlord for money damages. While this sort of lawsuit is only in its infancy, enterprising lawyers are bound to bring it to maturity in the near future.

Three cases are worth looking at. In none of them did the tenants actually win damages. All that these cases decided was the basic issue of whether the warranty of habitability law could be used affirmatively. On this issue, all three cases said yes, which suggests that someday a tenant may conceivably win some money.

In 1975 *Groner* v. *Lakeview Management Corporation* was decided in New York City Small Claims Court. The tenant sued her landlord for five hundred dollars, alleging: (1) breakdown in elevator service for forty-five days; (2) lack of access to the laundry room; (3) lack of intercom service; (4) no heat and hot water for sixteen days; (5) the absence of a lock on the rooftop door. Judge Arthur Blyn decided that deprivation of these services breached the warranty of habitability, for which the tenant could sue her landlord. The only catch was that she did not present sufficient evidence to enable the court to place a monetary value on the services that she had not received. Reluctantly, Judge Blyn was compelled to hand the tenant a hollow victory; she won in principle but was awarded only six cents as nominal damages.

Principle triumphed again in the 1976 case *Pekelner* v. *Park West Management Corporation*. Alan Pekelner was a tenant at Park West Village, on Central Park West and Ninety-seventh Street. One dark day, an "illegal" tenant took over the apartment next to Pekelner's. This new occupant practiced on her piano incessantly, early in the morning and late at night. She vacuumed at unreasonable hours and hosted boisterous social gatherings. As a result of these disturbances, Pekelner was subjected to physical and mental torment. Although he and other tenants complained to the landlord, no action was taken to control the noisy tenant.

So, Pekelner sued the landlord for damages, based on his pain and suffering. Among several legal grounds for this suit was breach of warranty. The landlord made a motion to dismiss Pekelner's complaint for failure to state a legal cause of action. This motion was denied by Justice Edward Greenfield of the state supreme court. He ruled that an affirmative suit for damages could be brought for breach of warranty—the breach in this case consisting of the landlord's failure to take effective measures to control the noisy tenant. (Having won this important point of law, Pekelner later dropped the case entirely and moved out of Park West Village.)

The third case is *Kaplan* v. *Coulston,* decided in New York City Civil Court in 1976. The tenant was injured when a kitchen cabinet fell and struck her. She sued the landlord for both negligence and breach of warranty. The court ruled that the latter grounds could be a basis for the lawsuit. By employing these grounds in the lawsuit, the tenant won an important tactical advantage. She was in a position to invoke the legal doctrine of *strict liability* (under which the landlord might be held liable even though he had no knowledge of the defect that had caused the tenant's injury).

Taking these three cases together, the message that emerges is: The warranty of habitability law holds obvious potential for bringing damage suits against landlords. One place where such suits might be won—assuming a tenant is able to prove the amount of his loss—is in New York City Small Claims Court (discussed in the next section).

SMALL CLAIMS COURT

The New York City Small Claims Court is a "people's court," which can be immensely useful to the aggrieved tenant. In small claims court you can sue your landlord on your own. *You don't need a lawyer.* And you can sue on almost any grounds. Some of the more common ones are those discussed in the preceding sections of this chapter.

On September 1, 1975, the jurisdiction of the small claims court was increased from $500 to $1,000; so, you can sue your landlord for up to $1,000. At present, your expense for bringing such a suit is $4.48, which covers filing your complaint and having your landlord served.

To file a small claims case, simply visit the branch of the court located in your borough (see Appendix B). Tell the clerk whom you want to sue and why. He will fill out the official complaint for you. And he will send a copy of it to whomever you are suing. You will have to pay $4.48.

You will then be told when to appear in court for the trial. The trial will always be held in the evening in order not to interfere with your work. The idea of going to trial might scare you. Don't let it. Every complainant in small claims court is in the same position as you: they are ordinary citizens, without lawyers, who are a little nervous.

Use common sense when preparing for the trial. Gather together any pieces of evidence that may help to substantiate the claim that you're making against the landlord. For example, in a repair-and-deduct type of case, where you made some of your own repairs, and now you're suing the landlord for your expenses, you will obviously want to bring with you any relevant receipts—say, a bill from a plumber or electrician. Or, suppose you're suing the landlord because his negligence resulted in damage to your personal belongings. Then you will want to bring along a copy of any relevant letter in which you warned the landlord about a threatening condition that he should have taken care of. You'll also want to present any evidence of the value of your damaged property—such as sales slips—as well as evidence of the extent of the damage—for instance, color photographs of the damaged area. Generally speaking, you should always bring along a copy of your lease and any canceled checks that are relevant.

At the trial, you will simply be asked (by a judge or arbitrator) to tell "your side of the story." There are no tricky rules of evidence to worry about. The atmosphere is completely informal, and the judge will help you present your case. You can present witnesses if you wish; for instance, a next-door neighbor or friend might testify regarding conditions in your apartment or building.

Shortly after the trial, you will be notified of the decision and the amount of any judgment you may have won. Contact the court clerk regarding the steps you must take in order to collect on the judgment. In the past, some claimants have had difficulty collecting on the judgments that they won. If you encounter such problems, there is a new organization that you can contact:

Small Claims Action Center
5 Beekman Street (suite 428)
New York, N.Y. 10038
Tel.: 212-349-2995

The center is a project of the New York Public Interest Research Group (NYPIRG), which is located at the same address. Besides offering general counseling on how to bring small claims actions, the center has attorneys and law students who will apply legal pressure to assist in the collection of judgments.

There is another possibility if you have trouble collecting on your judgment against the landlord. You may be able to withhold rent and then, when your landlord sues you for nonpayment, raise your unsatisfied judgment as a setoff against the rent due. A 1975 case, *Myack* v. *Aruca,* held that a tenant could do just that. The tenant had won a small claims judgment for $223.20 against his landlord, based on the landlord's failure to provide certain essential services. When the sheriff failed to collect the judgment, and the tenant got tired of chasing after the landlord, he simply withheld rent amounting to $298.36. Naturally, the landlord brought a nonpayment action.

In Queens housing court, the tenant said that he was willing to consent to a judgment in favor of the landlord for $75.16—the difference between the rent due ($298.36) and the unsatisfied small claims judgment ($223.20). Judge Maurice Harbater ruled that the judgment should be deducted from the rent due: "This court equates the tenant's judgment of the Small Claims Court against the landlord as partial payment of the rent due. . . . Where you have the same landlord and tenant involved in both cases and where the tenant has a judgment . . . equal to or *less* than the amount of the rent due, such judgment may be applied by the court as a set-off against the rent."

Now, let's look at a few cases in which tenants have successfully sued their landlords in small claims court:

• *Painting* In 1970 Jose Garcia was living with his family at 423 East 115th Street, in East Harlem. The apartment had once been painted with dangerous lead-based paint, which was peeling off the walls. Two of Jose's children were eating the paint flakes, which posed a serious threat of lead poisoning. When the landlord refused to remove this hazardous condition, Jose brought the necessary materials and, on his own, replastered and repainted the apartment.

Then Jose sued his landlord in the small claims court case of *Garcia* v. *Freeland Realty, Inc.* The judge ruled that, in the face of danger, the tenant did not have to sit idly by but had a right to help himself. Jose won a judgment for $45.53. Part of this amount—namely, $29.53—represented reimbursement for materials. The remaining $16.00 compensated Jose for his ten hours of labor (the judge had resorted to the then prevailing minimum wage for unskilled labor, $1.60 per hour).

• *Air-conditioners* In 1974 Herbert Harwood, Wendy Evans, and Millie Shogan were all tenants in Manhattan's Lincoln Square apartments. During that summer, the building's central air-conditioning went on the blink for six weeks. The three tenants went out and rented air-conditioners for their apartments. Then they sued the landlord to recoup their rental expenses in the case of *Harwood* v. *Lincoln Square Apartments.*

Judge Stanley Danzig ruled that the landlord had failed to uphold his lease obligations to provide air-conditioning: "I think that honest and fair-minded people expect to get what they pay for and to return that for which they have given nothing. The tenants paid for six weeks of air-conditioning and the landlord did not furnish six weeks of air-conditioning." Therefore, Judge Danzig awarded each tenant the amount of his air-conditioner rental fees: $101.65 to Herbert, and $197.95 to Wendy and to Millie.

• *Rent overcharge* In 1967 Charlotte Johnson and her mother moved into a rent-controlled apartment at 215 West 101st Street in Manhattan. The landlord told them that the rent was $170.00, which they paid. A year later, however, Charlotte learned from the Office of Rent Control that the maximum rent on the apartment was really $165.50. So Charlotte sued the landlord for the total overcharge.

In *Johnson* v. *Block,* Judge Irving Younger held that Charlotte had been willfully overcharged $58.50. Since a willful overcharge under rent control can result in treble damages, Judge Younger awarded Charlotte $175.50.

• *Burglary* In August 1976 Marla Honekman was living in a four-story apartment building at 10 Argyle Road in Brooklyn. For three weeks the lock on the front door of the building had been broken, giving intruders easy access. Despite complaints by the tenants, and two burglaries in the building, the landlady neglected to fix the lock. On August 26, Marla's apartment was burglarized to the tune of $2,885, $1,200 of which Marla recouped through insurance. That left a $1,685 loss.

Rather than waste several hundred dollars or more on a lawyer just to collect $1,685, Marla decided it made more sense to sue in small claims court for the full jurisdictional amount, $1,000. In her case, *Honekman* v. *Kuszer,* Marla brought to the court's attention the precedent set in *Sherman* v. *Concourse Realty Corporation* (discussed on page 225). After listening to her evidence, the judge awarded Marla $1,000.

These four cases should give you some idea of the variety of claims that may be brought against a landlord. Probably the most fertile area for small claims cases encompasses: (1) negligence actions; (2) repair-and-deduct type cases (like the painting case); (3) other similar self-help type cases (like the air-conditioner case); (4) warranty of habitability cases. Don't worry too much about legal niceties, though, or pigeonholing your case under some neat legal theory. All you have to do is present a justifiable claim against your landlord; it's then up to the judge to do substantial justice.

CHAPTER 17

Eviction

Basically, there are two kinds of eviction cases. One is the *nonpayment action*. As its name suggests, this action can arise when you fail to pay the rent that you owe. Although the ultimate goal of a nonpayment suit is eviction, the landlord is usually more interested in squeezing the rent out of you. And, in fact, you will not be evicted if you come up with the money before the judge actually orders your eviction.

The second kind of eviction action is the *holdover proceeding*. In this case, the landlord really means business. He's not just after your money; he wants the apartment back. The holdover proceeding gets its name from the fact that you are holding over in your apartment, after the landlord has declared that you have no right to remain. He wants you out, even though you may be willing to keep on paying rent.

NONPAYMENT OF RENT

A nonpayment action may be brought against any tenant who fails to pay his rent—regardless of whether he is rent controlled, rent stabilized, or uncontrolled. The message in a nonpayment action is not "Get out"; it is, instead, "Pay up or get out." This distinction is important: You can always defeat a nonpayment action, and avoid eviction, by paying the rent at any time before the judge issues an official warrant of eviction to the city marshal. (You will also have to pay the court costs, which are currently $17.50.)

Before a nonpayment action can be started, the landlord must make a demand on you for the rent. This demand may be made on an important-looking piece of paper called the *three-day notice*. The notice states how much rent the landlord is demanding. As the name of the notice suggests, you are given three days to pay. And you are warned that if you don't pay by the deadline, the landlord will bring an eviction action (i.e., a nonpayment action).

The notice should alert you—but not alarm you. It does not mean that you are being evicted. It does not even mean that an eviction action has been started. All it means is: Pay the rent or else a nonpayment action will be brought against you.

If you don't pay on the landlord's demand, you will be served with a notice of petition, better known as the *dispossess*. Unlike the three-day notice, the dispossess signals the actual beginning of a nonpayment action against you. If you lose that case and the judge issues a warrant of eviction, you will lose your apartment.

The dispossess itself does not mean that you are being evicted. (Only the warrant of eviction means you will be evicted.) So, you still have time to act when you get a dispossess. If you want to defeat the nonpayment action, you can still pay the rent. Give it to the landlord (plus $17.50 in court costs); or, if he won't take it, you can pay it to the clerk at the New York City Civil Court. (The court's addresses are in Appendix B.)

Of course, you may prefer to go to court and fight the landlord's demand for your rent. In that case, you'd better seek legal aid as soon as you get the dispossess. A lawyer can advise you on how to defend yourself in court against the nonpayment suit. Quite possibly, you may even want to turn the tables on your landlord and claim that he owes you money. (This tactic is the *counterclaim*.) Usually, the grounds for defending yourself, or counterclaiming, or seeking a rent reduction have to do with the condition of your apartment or the building. Put simply, the place is run-down. It needs repair and maintenance, which are the landlord's duties. In fact, the landlord's failure to do his duty may be the very reason why you did not pay your rent. In court, your lawyer will raise your landlord's shortcomings to support your side of the case. (Various grounds for deliberately withholding rent, and then defending your action in court, are discussed in chapter 14.)

As your lawyer will tell you, if you defeat the nonpayment action, you can wind up collecting money from the landlord, or paying less rent than had been demanded, or paying your rent into court. If you lose, you will not be evicted—at least, not immediately. First, the judge has to issue a warrant of eviction to the city marshal. Usually, this moment of truth is put off by the judge for five days or more. (The judge stays the issuance of a warrant of eviction, even though the landlord has won the nonpayment action.) At any time before the warrant of eviction is issued, you can still pay your rent plus the court costs. If the landlord won't accept it, you can pay it to the clerk of the court. *Payment at any time before the warrant is issued defeats the nonpayment action.* Payment means no warrant will be issued. Hence, there will be no eviction. However, if you do not pay during the judge's stay, and the stay ends, and the judge issues a warrant of eviction, that's the ball game. It's too late to pay your rent. You face eviction.

GROUNDS FOR EVICTION

• *Holdover tenants* The second kind of eviction action is the *holdover*. The tenant is holding over in his apartment after the end of his tenancy. The landlord has declared the lease to be terminated. This trick is usually accomplished by serving a notice to vacate on the tenant. The notice says the landlord has decided to terminate the tenancy. A specific date is given in the notice. By this date the tenant must leave the apartment. Otherwise, the notice warns him, the landlord will begin a summary proceeding (i.e., a holdover action). *The notice to vacate is not itself an eviction order. It does not mean that you will be evicted on the date specified in the notice.* Indeed, you cannot be. Any eviction will have to await a judge's decision to issue a warrant of eviction (as in a nonpayment action).

Before a judge can issue a warrant, there will have to be a court case. And before there can be a court case, you must be served with a notice of petition, better known as a dispossess. Once you have been served with the dispossess, you will know the fat's in the fire. Just as the landlord said he would do in the notice to vacate, he has begun a holdover action to evict. The dispossess will specify a date on which you must show up in court to defend yourself.

You should seek legal counsel immediately. The dispossess is serious business. *It is not in and of itself an eviction order*—just as the notice to vacate was not an eviction order. But the dispossess does signal that the court case, which can lead to eviction, has been started by the landlord. The dispossess will also specify the grounds on which the landlord is seeking your eviction. The most common grounds for a holdover action are discussed below.

• *Expiration of your lease* Expiration of your lease can turn you into a holdover tenant. The lease defines the term of your occupancy—say, from October 1, 1976, through September 30, 1978. After September 30, 1978, you will no longer have the right to remain in your apartment (assuming, of course, that your lease has not been renewed). If you are still in occupancy as of October 1, 1978, you will be holding over, and you can be evicted.

Holding over after the end of a lease affects only tenants who do not have the protection of rent control or rent stabilization. A rent-controlled tenant doesn't need a lease. He may have entered his apartment without a lease, or his last lease may have expired long ago. In either case he is not an illegal holdover tenant; instead, he is a protected statutory tenant. *A statutory tenant has the right to remain in his apartment indefinitely*. He can't be evicted as a holdover unless he commits some wrong that gives the landlord grounds for terminating the statutory tenancy (discussed in the following pages).

A slightly different form of protection is afforded to a rent-stabilized tenant. He does not become a statutory tenant. Instead, he has the right to renew his lease prior to its expiration.

A rent-stabilized tenant will never turn into a holdover tenant unless he commits some wrong that gives the landlord grounds for terminating the lease or refusing to renew it (discussed in the following pages).

If you are neither rent controlled nor rent stabilized, and your lease expires, you may become a *month-to-month tenant,* rather than a holdover tenant. Instead of evicting you, the landlord goes on accepting your rent each month. You do not have the right to remain indefinitely, as a statutory tenant would. But, before the landlord can evict you as a holdover, he must give you thirty days' notice of the termination of your month-to-month tenancy.

• *Violation of your lease* A substantial violation of a lease is grounds for a holdover action. The key word here is *substantial.* A mere technical violation is not good enough.

Most tenants—be they rent controlled, rent stabilized, uncontrolled, or cooperative—want to know if their particular activities are substantial violations. For example, is remodeling your apartment, or playing the piano, or having guests visit, or keeping a pet, a substantial violation? To find out, consult chapters 2, 3, 4, and 6. There, you will read about many eviction cases that arose when a tenant's lifestyle came in conflict with his lease and his landlord. In those cases where no lease violation was found—or only a technical and insubstantial one—the courts refused to order an eviction.

• *Late payment of rent* As you know, the failure to pay rent on time is grounds for a nonpayment action. In certain aggravated cases, late payment can also lead to a holdover action. A chronic failure to pay rent on time, which forces a landlord to bring repeated nonpayment actions (say nine or ten in one year), will probably constitute a substantial violation of your lease.

• *Nuisance* If you make of yourself what is legally considered a nuisance, the landlord may terminate your tenancy and try to evict you as a holdover tenant. Most nuisance cases erupt over noisemaking or a tenant's objectionable lifestyle. If you consult chapter 3 you'll discover just how far you can push things before your conduct amounts to a nuisance.

• *Damaging your apartment* If you start damaging your apartment, the landlord may terminate your tenancy and try to evict you as a holdover tenant. Serious damage is known legally as *waste.* In discussing remodeling an apartment, chapter 4 explains what waste is and when it occurs.

• *Illegal occupancy* If you carry on some illegal pursuit in your apartment, the landlord may terminate your tenancy and try to evict you as a holdover tenant. Your misconduct must be habitual before you will be in jeopardy (see page 40).

• *Refusing entry to your landlord* Every tenant has a duty to permit the landlord to enter his apartment when reasonably necessary (see page 39). If a tenant refuses entry unreasonably, he may face eviction.

EVICTION OF RENT CONTROLLED TENANTS

Even if you rent-controlled tenants do not give your landlord grounds for a holdover action, he may still be able to evict you. Under a limited number of circumstances, the Office of Rent Control will issue a certificate of eviction to your landlord. *The certificate is not an actual eviction order.* But it is the first step toward one. It permits the landlord to treat you like a run-of-the-mill holdover tenant once your lease has expired. You lose your protection as a statutory tenant.

In effect, the certificate affords a landlord exceptional relief from the rent-control system. Needless to say, the grounds for a certificate are extraordinary in nature (discussed in the following pages). You may have to dispute them before the Office of Rent Control. The office will notify you whenever your landlord applies for a certificate of eviction. At that point, you would be wise to seek legal counsel, because you will have to fight the granting of a certificate, and your battle may take you beyond the Office of Rent Control and into court.

• *Owner-occupancy* A certificate of eviction may be granted if the landlord needs your apartment for his own use. If the landlord happens to be a corporation, it cannot get a certificate on the grounds that it needs an apartment.

Assuming your landlord is not incorporated, he may be able to get a certificate if he can prove that he needs your apartment for either (1) "his own personal use and occupancy," or (2) "the use and occupancy of his immediate family." Rent control defines *immediate family* as: landlord's mother, father, son, daughter, grandfather, grandmother, grandson, granddaughter, mother-in-law, father-in-law, stepfather, stepmother, stepson, or stepdaughter.

Suppose the landlord decides to go after a rent-controlled apartment for his own use or that of his immediate family. Before he can get a certificate, he must prove to the Office of Rent Control that he is acting (1) in good faith and (2) out of an immediate and compelling necessity. If either test is failed, a certificate of eviction will be denied. (In buildings with fewer than twelve apartments, the landlord may be relieved of having to prove an immediate and compelling necessity; but he still must establish that he is acting in good faith.)

• *Other grounds* A certificate of eviction may be granted on five other grounds: (1) A statutory tenant is subletting his apartment without authorization. (2) The landlord intends to alter a rent-controlled apartment substantially, by subdividing it into two or more self-contained family units. (3) The landlord intends to demolish the rent-controlled apartment. (4) The landlord intends to withdraw his apartments permanently from the rental market. (5) Acting in good faith, the landlord has an immediate and compelling necessity to use a rent-controlled apartment for housing the building's resident super.

EVICTION OF RENT STABILIZED TENANTS

Earlier, you rent-stabilized tenants reviewed several grounds on which you might be evicted—namely: nonpayment, substantial violation, nuisance, illegal occupancy, waste, and refusal to admit the landlord. If you avoid these acts and keep paying your rent, you will not be evicted. Rent stabilization gives you the right to go on renewing your lease indefinitely. Only under a limited set of circumstances can the landlord refuse to renew your lease and evict you as a holdover tenant.

• *Grounds for nonrenewal* There are some situations in which the landlord does not have to renew your lease. He can then treat you like a holdover tenant and evict you.

The first situation can arise, ironically enough, after you have refused to sign the renewal lease offered by the landlord. Certain clauses in the lease may be objectionable to you—even though they are perfectly legitimate. Should you turn down a renewal lease because of the presence of these clauses, you may wind up with no lease at all. You will have given the landlord grounds for denying you a renewal altogether.

Therefore, you must watch out for those clauses that do not justify your rejection of a renewal lease. One such clause affects possible rent increases pursuant to any order that may be issued by the Conciliation and Appeals Board. That clause is permissible in a renewal lease. You cannot reject the lease because of the clause and still expect to get a renewal.

Another permissible clause states that you and your landlord agree to be bound by any determination of the Conciliation and Appeals Board affecting your tenancy during the term of the lease. In other words, if the board should have to settle some dispute between you and your landlord, both of you must abide by the decision.

A third permisssible clause may appear in a renewal lease after the landlord has submitted to the New York State attorney general a cooperative or condominium plan for the building. The clause says that the lease may be canceled after giving the tenant ninety days' notice that the plan has been declared effective.

In general, these three clauses are the only ones you cannot use to justify your refusal to renew. But, exceptions may arise. So before you turn down a renewal in haste, get some advice. You can either complain to the Conciliation and Appeals Board or seek legal counsel.

The second situation that can block a renewal arises when the landlord wants your apartment for himself. Rent stabilization allows the denial of a renewal lease when the landlord "seeks in good faith to recover possession of a dwelling unit for his own personal use and occupancy or for the use and occupancy of his immediate family." The landlord's immediate family includes a husband, wife, son, daughter, stepson, stepdaughter, father, mother, father-in-law, or mother-in-law.

The third and final situation that can stop a renewal concerns the withdrawal of your building from the rental market. Your landlord has to convince the Conciliation and Appeals Board that he seeks in "good faith" to withdraw apartments from both the housing and nonhousing rental markets.

RETALIATORY EVICTION

Strained relations between landlord and tenant sometimes result in the landlord seeking to evict the tenant as a means of retaliation. This form of vengeance is *retaliatory eviction,* and New York courts have ruled it to be illegal.

In *Markese* v. *Cooper,* the tenant's complaints about dilapidated housing conditions resulted in violations being placed against the landlord. When the landlord sought to evict the tenant, the defense of retaliatory eviction was raised, and the court sustained it. "It is apparent," said the court, "that without a defense [to retaliatory eviction] the threat of eviction would coerce the most justifiable complaints into submissive silence."

The defense to retaliatory eviction has also been sustained on constitutional grounds. You are exercising your first-amendment right to free speech and free association when you complain to public authorities and join in organized tenant activities. To the extent that retaliation by the landlord inhibits you, it may be ruled unconstitutional. In *Church* v. *Allen Meadows Apartments,* the state supreme court refused to allow an eviction of two tenant activists, because the landlord was clearly trying to penalize them for asserting their constitutional rights.

Establishing the defense of retaliatory eviction often calls for difficult proof regarding the landlord's motivation. So you would be well advised to consult an attorney if you think that you are the victim of a vengeful landlord.

Appendix

Appendix A

CITY AGENCIES

Office of Rent Control

Main Office of Rent Control
110 Church Street
New York, N.Y. 10007
tel: 566-5054

District Rent Office for Upper Manhattan (above 110th Street)
215 West 125th Street
New York, N.Y. 10027
tel: 678-2201

District Rent Office for Lower Manhattan (below 110th Street)
2 Lafayette Street
New York, N.Y. 10007
tel: 566-7970

District Rent Office for Brooklyn
625 Fulton Street
Brooklyn, N.Y. 11201
tel: 643-7570

District Rent Office for Bronx
260 East 161st Street
Bronx, N.Y. 10451
tel: 585-2600

District Rent Office for Queens
164-19 Hillside Avenue
Jamaica, N.Y. 11432
tel: 526-2040

District Rent Office for Staten Island
350 St. Mark's Place
Staten Island, N.Y. 10301
tel: 447-8122

Rent Stabilization Agencies

Rent Stabilization Association
477 Madison Avenue
New York, N.Y. 10022
tel: 421-5613

Conciliation and Appeals Board
N.Y.C. Rent Stabilization Law of 1969
666 Fifth Avenue
New York, N.Y. 10019
tel: 265-5105

Office of Code Enforcement

Main Office
100 Gold Street
New York, N.Y. 10038
tel: 566-3919

Manhattan Office
1851 Municipal Building
Room 1841
New York, N.Y. 10007
tel: 566-6884

Brooklyn Office
Municipal Building, 8th Floor
Brooklyn, N.Y. 11201
tel: 643-4091

Bronx Office
1932 Arthur Avenue
Bronx, N.Y. 10457
tel: 583-5520

Queens Office
126-06 Queens Blvd.
Kew Gardens, N.Y. 11415
tel: 520-3403

Staten Island Office
Borough Hall, Room 224
Staten Island, N.Y. 10301
tel: 390-5200

Central Complaint Bureau
215 West 125th Street
New York, N.Y. 10027
tel: 960-4800

Appendix B

COURTS

In each of the boroughs, the housing court and the small claims court are located at the same address.

Manhattan Courts*
111 Centre Street
New York, N.Y. 10013
Housing court tel: 374-8407
Small claims court tel: 374-8402

Bronx Courts
851 Grand Concourse
Bronx, N.Y. 10451
Housing court tel: 293-6500
Small claims court tel: 293-6500, ext. 11

Brooklyn Courts
141 Livingston Street
Brooklyn, N.Y. 11201
Housing court tel: 643-7528
Small claims court tel: 643-8180

Queens Courts
120-55 Queens Blvd.
Kew Gardens, N.Y. 11424
Housing court and small claims court tel: 520-3613

Staten Island Courts
927 Castleton Avenue
Staten Island, N.Y. 10310
Housing court and small claims court tel: 442-8000

* There is an additional branch of the Manhattan small claims court, in Harlem, at 170 East 121st Street, New York, N.Y. 10035. The telephone number is 369-8811.

Appendix C

TENANT ORGANIZATIONS

All tenants have the right to organize and hold tenants' meetings in their buildings. This right is contained in Section 230 of the state's Real Property Law, which provides:

"1. No landlord shall interfere with the right of a tenant to form, join or participate in the lawful activities of any group, committee or other organization formed to protect the rights of tenants; nor shall any landlord harass, punish, penalize, diminish, or withhold any right, benefit or privilege of a tenant under his tenancy for exercising such right.

"2. Tenants' groups, committees or other tenants' organizations shall have the right to meet in any location on the premises which is devoted to the common use of all tenants in a peaceful manner, at reasonable hours and without obstructing access to the premises or facilities. No landlord shall deny such right."

If you want assistance in organizing tenants in your building, contact the People's Housing Network, Inc., at 29 East 22d Street, New York, N.Y. 10010 (tel: 212-533-5650). This group conducts training seminars for organizers. It also publishes a magazine for organizers, titled *Network*.

The New York State Tenants' Coalition lobbies for tenants' rights. The coalition usually works through tenants' organizations. Any tenants' group interested in more information about the coalition may write to the New York State Tenants' Coalition at 29 East 22d Street, New York, N.Y. 10010 (tel: 212-533-5650).

Senior citizens seeking assistance for a housing problem may contact the Department of the Aging of the City of New York. The Information and Referral Bureau will provide the name, address, and telephone number of the nearest office with personnel able to help solve housing problems. The telephone number of the Information and Referral Bureau is 212-577-0800.

There are three major tenant organizations in New York City, which maintain up-to-date lists of other tenant organizations in the city. They also publish newsletters available by subscription. While all three organizations counsel tenants with housing problems, they will also refer tenants to other organizations around the city.

Queens Presidents' Council
43-47 45th Street
Sunnyside, N.Y. 11104
Call: 361-8854, Mon. to Fri.,
1:00 P.M. to 5:00 P.M.,
7:00 P.M. to 9:00 P.M.,
except Fri.

Flatbush Tenants Council
1702 Church Avenue
New York, N.Y. 11226
Call: 287-3850, Mon. to Sat.,
10:30 A.M. to 4:00 P.M.

Metropolitan Council on Housing
24 West 30th Street
New York, N.Y. 10001
Call: 725-4800, Mon. to Fri.,
1:30 P.M. to 6:00 P.M.

There are many local tenant organizations around the city helping tenants in the neighborhood to solve housing problems. The list that follows is a sampling of these organizations. We suggest you call the nearest organization to find out when you may visit its office.

Associated Communities East, Inc.
2082 Madison Avenue
New York, N.Y. 10037
Call: 281-8822, Mon. to Fri.,
9:00 A.M. to 4:30 P.M.

Boro Park Tenants Council
3722 15th Avenue
Brooklyn, N.Y. 11218
Call: 853-4218, Mon. to Fri.,
9:00 A.M. to 5:00 P.M.

Citizens Advice Bureau
2103 Grand Concourse
Bronx, N.Y. 10453
Call: 298-5902, Mon. to Fri.,
9:00 A.M. to 5:00 P.M., except Wed.,
1:00 P.M. to 5:00 P.M.

City-Wide Anti-Poverty Committee on Housing
349 Broadway
New York, N.Y.
Call: 433-2201, Mon. to Fri.,
9:00 A.M. to 5:00 P.M.

District Service Office
Community Board #10
621 86th Street
Brooklyn, N.Y. 11209
Call: 745-6827, Mon. to Fri.,
9:30 A.M. to 4:30 P.M.

Faro Puertorriqueneo
1514 Amsterdam Avenue
New York, N.Y. 10031
Call: 234-5358, Mon. to Fri.,
9:00 A.M. to 5:00 P.M.

Fifteen Churches United for a Better Manhattan
4271 Broadway
New York, N.Y. 10024
Call: 795-6860, Mon. to Fri.,
9:30 A.M. to 4:30 P.M.

Knickerbocker-Wyckoff
219 Irving Avenue
Brooklyn, N.Y. 11237
Call: 381-7983, Mon. to Fri.,
9:00 A.M. to 5:00 P.M.

La Casa Service Center
167 Columbia Street
Brooklyn, N.Y. 11231
Call: 852-7260, Mon. to Fri., 9:00 A.M. to 5:00 P.M.

Office of Assemblyman Edward H. Lehner
4915 Broadway
New York, N.Y. 10034
Call: 942-1065, Mon. to Fri., 10:00 A.M. to 5:00 P.M.

Neighborhood Board #5, Inc.
238 West 116th Street
New York, N.Y. 10026
Call: 666-3935, Mon. to Fri., 8:00 A.M. to 5:00 P.M.

PLACE-C.M.A.
858 Tenth Avenue
New York, N.Y. 10019
Call: 581-3088, Mon. to Fri., 10:00 A.M. to 5:00 P.M.

Trinity Avenue Block Association
751 East 160th Street
Bronx, N.Y. 10456
Call: 292-4693, Mon. to Fri., 9:00 A.M. to 5:00 P.M.

United Jewish Council of the East Side
235 Broadway
New York, N.Y. 10002
Call: 233-6037, Mon. to Fri., 9:00 A.M. to 5:00 P.M.

League of Autonomous Bronx Organizations for Renewal (LABOR)
941 Washington Avenue
Bronx, N.Y. 10456
Call: 292-1606, Mon. to Fri., 9:00 A.M. to 8:00 P.M.

Lenox Hill Neighborhood Association
331 East 70th Street
New York, N.Y. 10021
Call: 744-5022, Mon. to Fri., 9:00 A.M. to 6:00 P.M.

Neighborhood Preservation Program
Federation of Jewish Philanthropies of New York
Forest Hills Community House
108-25 62d Drive, Forest Hills, N.Y. 11375
Call: 592-5757, Mon. to Fri., 10:00 A.M. to 7:00 P.M.

Riverside Edgecombe Neighborhood Association (RENA)
556 West 158th Street
New York, N.Y. 10032
Call: 923-8771, Mon. to Fri., 10:00 A.M. to 5:00 P.M.

United Leadership of 98th Street
1268 Park Avenue
New York, N.Y. 10029
Call: 860-3944, Mon. to Fri., 9:00 A.M. to 6:00 P.M.

West Side Tenants Union
155 West 72d Street, Room 605
New York, N.Y. 10023
Call: 595-1274, anytime

Appendix D

LIST OF FREE LEGAL SERVICES

Free legal aid is available for low-income New York City tenants. In order to qualify a tenant should meet the following income standards:

Legal Aid Society
Single person—Income of not more than $85/week
Two-person family—Income of not more than $100/week
Three-person family—Income of not more than $115/week
Four-person family—Income of not more than $130/week

All Other Programs
Single person—Income of not more than $4,000/year
Two-person family—Income of not more than $4,600/year
Three-person family—Income of not more than $5,200/year
For each additional person in the family, the income level can increase by $600/year.

MANHATTAN

Legal Office	*Area Covered*
Harlem Assertion of Rights, Inc. 35-43 West 125th Street New York, N.Y. 10027 tel: 860-9292	Boundaries: North: Harlem River South: 110th Street East: Fifth Avenue West: Hudson River
Legal Aid Society Chelsea Office 267 West 17th Street New York, N.Y. 10011 tel: 255-6673	West Side Manhattan from 110th Street to 72d Street and from 34th Street all the way to the Battery—West only
Legal Aid Society Harlem Office 2090 Seventh Avenue (125th Street) New York, N.Y. 10027 tel: 663-3293	110th Street to 169th Street, Fifth Avenue to Riverside Drive

Legal Office	*Area Covered*
Legal Services for the Elderly Poor 2095 Broadway, Room 304 New York, N.Y. 10023 tel: 595-1340	Serves all elderly in Manhattan
Manhattan Legal Services Corp. East Harlem Office 170 East 116th Street New York, N.Y. 10029 tel: 427-0693	East Harlem (East 95th Street to East 135th Street)
Moblization for Youth Main Office 214 East 2d Street New York, N.Y. 10009 tel: 777-5250	Houston Street to 14th Street, East River to Bowery
Mobilization for Youth 759 Tenth Avenue (bet. 51st & 52d) New York, N.Y. 10019 tel: 581-2810	14th Street to 79th Street, Hudson River to Broadway and then to Central Park West
Mobilization for Youth 95 Delancy Street (near Ludlow) New York, N.Y. 10002 tel: 533-8310	Grand Street to Houston Street, East River to Bowery
Mobilization for Youth 45 Canal Street (Essex) New York, N.Y. 10002 tel: 966-7410	Brooklyn Bridge to Grand Street, East River to Broadway

BROOKLYN

Bedford Stuyvesant Legal Services Corp. 1368-90 Fulton Street Brooklyn, N.Y. 11216 tel: 636-7600	Zip code areas 11213, 11216, 11221, 11225, 11233

Legal Office	*Area Covered*
Brooklyn Legal Services Corporation A East Brooklyn Office 80 Jamaica Avenue Brooklyn, N.Y. 11207 tel: 345-6200	Zip code areas 11203, 11207, 11208, 11212, 11236
Brooklyn Legal Services Corporation A Williamsburg Office 260 Broadway Brooklyn, N.Y. 11211 tel: 782-6195	Zip code areas 11206, 11211, 11222, 11237
Brooklyn Legal Services Corporation B South Brooklyn Office 152 Court Street Brooklyn, N.Y. 11201 tel: 855-8003	Zip code areas 11201, 11205, 11209, 11210, 11214, 11215, 11217, 11218, 11219, 11220, 11223, 11224, 11226, 11228, 11229, 11230, 11231, 11232, 11234, 11235, 11238
Community Action for Legal Services, Inc. Brooklyn Branch 186 Joralemon Street Brooklyn, N.Y. 11201 tel: 834-6666	Zip code areas 11204, 11211, 11219, 11235
Legal Aid Society Downtown Manhattan Office 11 Park Place New York, N.Y. 10007 tel: 227-2755	Serves all Brooklyn *except* for zip code areas 11201, 11203, 11204, 11206, 11207, 11208, 11211, 11212, 11216, 11217, 11219, 11221
Legal Aid Society Office of the Aging 1685 East 15th Street Brooklyn, N.Y. 11229 tel: 645-3111	Serves all elderly in Brooklyn

BRONX

Legal Office	*Area Covered*
Bronx Legal Services Corporation C Morrisania Office 1438 Boston Road Bronx, N.Y. 10460 tel: 842-5300	Bronx
Bronx Legal Services Corporation C Landlord/Tenant Unit 579 Courtlandt Avenue Bronx, N.Y. 10451 tel: 993-8200	Bronx
Legal Aid Society Bronx Office 1029 East 163d Street Bronx, N.Y. 10459 tel: 991-4600	Bronx

QUEENS

Queens Legal Services Corporation Long Island City Office 29-42 Northern Blvd. Long Island City, N.Y. 11101 tel: 392-5646	Queens
Queens Legal Services Corporation South Jamaica Office 89-02 Sutphin Blvd. Jamaica, N.Y. 11435 tel: 657-8611	Queens
Legal Aid Society Rockaway Office 20-11 Mott Avenue Far Rockaway, N.Y. 11691 tel: 337-4900	The Rockaways

STATEN ISLAND

Legal Office	*Area Covered*
Legal Aid Society Staten Island Office 42 Richmond Terrace Staten Island, N.Y. 10301 tel: 273-6677	Staten Island

Appendix E

RENT STABILIZATION COMPLAINT FORM

CAB Docket No.

NEW YORK CITY CONCILIATION AND APPEALS BOARD
666 FIFTH AVENUE, NEW YORK, N.Y. 10019
265-5105

You will be advised in writing by the Conciliation and Appeals Board about the disposition of the application.

TENANT'S COMPLAINT OF RENT OVERCHARGES AND/OR EXCESS SECURITY DEPOSIT AND/OR OWNER'S FAILURE TO RENEW LEASE

PART I – GENERAL INFORMATION

1. MAILING ADDRESS OF TENANT: HOME TEL. # ....

NAME.. BUSINESS TEL. # ....

NUMBER AND STREET .... APT. #.....

CITY, STATE AND ZIP CODE..

2. MAILING ADDRESS OF OWNER:

NAME.. TEL. NO. ....

NUMBER AND STREET ....

CITY, STATE AND ZIP CODE..

3. ADDRESS OF PREMISES: If same as tenant's mailing address listed above, just indicate "same"

__________ (Number and Street) __________ (Apartment No.) __________ (Borough and Zip Code)

PART II – INSTRUCTIONS

WHERE YOUR APPLICATION REQUIRES A DETERMINATION OF THE STABILIZATION RENT, SECURITY DEPOSIT OR LEASE TERMS AND CONDITIONS, WE WILL NOT BE ABLE TO PROCESS YOUR APPLICATION WITHOUT COPIES OF ALL OF YOUR LEASES IN EFFECT **ON AND AFTER MAY 31, 1968**, OR SINCE YOU TOOK OCCUPANCY, IF AFTER MAY 31, 1968.

To file this application, you must mail a completed **original and one copy** of this form to the Conciliation and Appeals Board at 666 Fifth Avenue, New York, New York 10019.

PART III – RENTAL HISTORY

4. Terms of initial rental: [complete (a) or (b)]

(a) I moved into this apartment on __________ (date) pursuant to a written lease of ____ years, commencing on __________ (date) and expiring on __________ (date) at a rental of $________ per month.

(b) I moved into this apartment on __________ (date) without a written lease at an initial rental of $________ per month.

5. Thereafter, my rent changed as follows:

RENT INCREASED TO:	DATE OF INCREASE	LENGTH OF LEASE TERM (1, 2 OR 3 YEARS) OR OTHER GROUNDS FOR INCREASE, SUCH AS ADDITIONAL EQUIPMENT, NEW SERVICES OR A BUILDING-WIDE MAJOR CAPITAL IMPROVEMENT, ETC.

6. **Extra charges:** List any additional rent or other charges paid to the owner in addition to the rent recited above and the reason for such extra charge (i.e., garage space, swimming pool, electricity, etc.). If the charge is made for a season or any period longer than one month, please so indicate.

ADDITIONAL CHARGE	REASON FOR CHARGE
$________ per month	
$________ per month	
$________ per month	
$________ per month	

7. (This item is to be answered only if you are a subtenant.)
I pay my rent to: __________ name and address

He/She is: ☐ the owner of the building. ☐ the prime tenant of the apartment. ☐ other (please specify) ________

(over)

PART IV – NATURE OF COMPLAINT

(Check appropriate box – fill in the blanks and explain if necessary in Part VI.)

8. ☐ The owner refused to show me prior leases. I requested same on ____________ (date(s))

9. ☐ I believe the owner is overcharging me as follows: (Set forth the amount of rent you believe to be the lawful stabilized rent and the basis for your calculations as well as the date or dates on which the alleged overcharge(s) occurred.)

10. ☐ The owner is asking $________ as an additional charge for: (state item or reason for charge) ____________ ____________ and I believe that charge is unlawful because: ____________

11. ☐ The owner has collected or is demanding $________ which is more than one month's security deposit. The security deposit was given to the owner on ____________ (attach copies of leases showing payment of security deposits or other evidence of payment of security deposit).

12. ☐ The owner refuses to give me a new lease because ____________

13. ☐ The owner refuses to give me a lease for_____years as I requested. He offers a lease for_____years.

14. ☐ The owner refuses to offer me a renewal lease on the same conditions as were contained in my old lease. He had made the following changes: (Identify the clauses by number and describe alleged differences between the language contained in such clauses in the old and new leases. Attach copies of the old and new leases.) ____________

PART V – OTHER PROCEEDINGS

15. List any other Conciliation and Appeals Board proceedings concerning your apartment of which you have knowledge and set forth the CAB Docket No. and Opinion No., if any: ____________

PART VI – ADDITIONAL COMMENTS

PART VII – TENANT'S AFFIRMATION

I have read the above statements and I affirm that my statements are true to my own knowledge except for those statements which I have stated to be based on information and belief, and as to those matters, I believe them to be true.

____________ (Signature of Tenant)

It is not necessary that the foregoing be sworn to but false statements may subject you to the penalties provided by law.

Dated ____________ 19___

THIS FORM MUST BE FILED IN DUPLICATE

(FOR CONCILIATION AND APPEALS BOARD USE ONLY)

Tenant's Application Received ____________ (date)

Notice of Commencement mailed to both owner and tenant ____________ (date)

Owner's Answer Received ____________ (date)

Owner's Answer Mailed to Tenant ____________ (date)

(CAB-§ 20A.23.42.60.63-7/75)

11

Appendix F

RENT GUIDELINES RIDER

The parties hereto agree as follows:

Par. 1—That where the owner has proper cause and ground to apply to the Conciliation and Appeals Board for relief, and where, upon due application, the owner is found to be entitled to an increase in rent over and above the amount set forth in this lease, the parties agree:

(a) To be bound by the determination of the Conciliation and Appeals Board.

(b) That where the Conciliation and Appeals Board has granted an increase in rent, the tenant agrees to pay such increase in the manner set forth by the Conciliation and Appeals Board.

(c) Anything contained in Paragraphs 1 (a) and (b) to the contrary notwithstanding, it is distinctly understood and agreed that in the event that an order is issued increasing the stabilization rent because of owner hardship, the tenant may, within thirty (30) days of his receipt of a copy of the order by the Conciliation and Appeals Board, cancel his lease on sixty (60) days written notice to the owner. During said period, the cancelling tenant may continue in occupancy at no increase in rent.

Par. 2—In the event the guidelines established and adopted by the Rent Guidelines Board for levels of rent increases applicable to this lease are increased or decreased, the owner and tenant agree to be bound thereby, and the rent payable under this lease as of the first day of the first month of the commencement of the lease, shall be the rent so increased or decreased.

Par. 3—That the rent provided for in this lease may be increased or decreased as of the first day of the first month of the commencement of the lease, to conform to the lawful Rent Guidelines applicable to this lease as promulgated by the New York City Rent Guidelines Board.

Par. 4—In all other respects, this lease and any and all riders thereto shall continue in full force and effect, and except as modified hereinabove, shall in no way be effected hereby.

Appendix G

LIST OF RENT IMPAIRING VIOLATIONS

Order Number		
051	Discontinue the storage of combustible material	12 MDL
069	Discontinue use unless and until an approved application is filed and a certificate of occupancy is obtained	61 MDL
072	Discontinue the manufacturing business	61 MDL
080	Provide legal second means of egress and file application for approval before doing work	231 MDL
081B	Provide sprinkler heads in all class B rooms and file application for approval before doing work	194 MDL
135	Close the unnecessary opening in fire escape [*Explanation:* When the vertical ladder is removed from a fire escape there remains a hole where the ladder used to be. This hole must be covered.]	53, 187, 231 MDL
142	Brace and support balcony with suitable tie rods or suspension rods [*Explanation:* A fire escape is held to the side of a building by tie rods and suspension rods.]	53, 187, 231 MDL
176	Provide means of egress from yard to street by a fire-proof passageway for which application must be filed for approval, or by an unlocked door or gate in fence to the adjoining premises with consent of adjacent owner	53, 187, 231 MDL
181	Provide a fireproof passageway from the fire escapes at rear to street and file application for approval before doing this work	53, 187, 231 MDL
188	Properly fire retard in accordance with the rule and regulations of this department the cellar ceiling [*Explanation:* Certain tenements must have fireproofed ceilings in the cellar.]	185, 240 MDL
209	Remove door from closet leading to scuttle opening in roof [*Explanation:* The scuttle is a hole in the roof with a cover and a ladder leading down to the landing of the top floor of the building. On occasion, the ladder will lead down into a closet. In such cases the door to the closet must be removed.]	233 MDL
213	Seal with fire retarding material or provide with fireproof self-closing door and assembly, the opening leading from store to public hall [*Explanation:* Where the building includes a store, the door between the store and the building's residential area must be fire retardant and self-closing.]	61 MDL
214	Remove sash in partition between rooms and public hall and seal opening with material similar to adjacent wall [*Explanation:* In some buildings windows were installed between public hallways and individual apartments. Where such a window exists it must be removed and the area filled in with suitable material.]	189(5) MDL
222	Provide under completed permit, a proper enclosure with fireproof self-closing doors and assemblies at the top and the bottom of cellar stairs	242 MDL
494	Requires the filing of plans and compliance with Section 67 of the Multiple Dwelling Law for heretofore erected existing multiple dwellings	4, 8, 25, 67 MDL
503	Make safe by properly repairing the structural defect [*Explanation:* This is a catchall violation. Any structural defect is covered.]	D26-10.01
507	Repair the roof so that it will not leak	D26-10.01

MDL = Multiple Dwelling Law D26 = Housing Maintenance Code

511 Repair and operate the gas appliance so as to prevent carbon monoxide D26-10.01

512 Fire escape defective. Replace with new the broken, defective and/or missing [*Explanation:* This is a catchall violation. Any structural defect is covered.] D26-10.01

513 Fire escape defective. Adjust the dropladder so that it will slide easily in the guide rods D26-10.01

514 Fire escape defective. Properly secure D26-10.01

516 Fire escape defective. Reset the braces of the brackets so that they shall bear against the wall [*Explanation:* A fire escape must not be loosely held against the wall. The braces holding the fire escape to the wall must cause the brackets to come flush with the side of the wall.] D26-10.01

517 Fire escape defective. Remove and replace with new the broken and defective bracket and leave all anchorages uncovered for inspection [*Explanation:* A fire escape is anchored to the wall by sinking bolts through the wall with a nut or other securing device on the inside of the building. The nut or other securing device must not be covered up; it must be available for inspection.] D26-10.01

518 Fire escape defective. Replace with 2 X 1/2 inch iron bar extending across and secured by 2 brackets, the broken or defective angle iron or bar at the foot of gooseneck ladder [*Explanation:* The ladder which connects the top landing of a fire escape with the roof is called a gooseneck ladder.] D26-10.01

519 Fire escape defective. Remove or make safe the additional fire escape [*Explanation:* Many years ago a landlord was allowed to use a fire escape which consisted of one long vertical ladder down the side of the building. This type of fire escape is no longer legal. However, if it remains up it must be safe. If it is not safe it must be removed.] D26-10.01

520 Fire escape defective. Remove the additional dangerous inadequate fire escape [*Explanation:* See order number 519.] D26-10.01

523 Fire escape defective. Restore egress by removing locking device and arrange to open readily the gate in fence at the lot line [*Explanation:* In some tenements the fire escape leads to a lot behind the building. There must be a way out of this lot. If there is a fence surrounding the lot there must be a gate in the fence allowing an exit. There may not be any locking devices on this gate.] D26-10.01, 10.05

524 Fire egress defective. Remove the obstruction in fireproof passageway [*Explanation:* Where a building has a fire escape there must be a clear passage from the bottom of the fire escape to the street.] D26-10.01, 10.05

526 Remove the illegal fastening at roof, bulkhead door, scuttle cover, etc. [*Explanation:* These doors and hatches may not have locking devices on the outside. And only certain closing devices are permitted on the inside.] D26-10.01, 10.05

538 Remove all encumbrances [*Explanation:* This is a catchall violation. Any objects lying around are covered.] D26-10.01, 10.05

551 Cleanse and disinfect to the satisfaction of this department after removing the sewage, etc. [*Explanation:* This violation refers to the requirements following a sewer backup and the resulting overflow of sewage.] D26-11.01, 11.03, 11.05

567 Abate the nuisance consisting of rodents D26-13.03

576 Provide adequate supply of cold water for the fixtures D26-15.01

577 Provide adequate supply of hot water for the fixtures D26-15.01
578 Repair the leaky and/or defective water supply pipe D26-16.01
580 Provide suitable tight cover made of metal or wood covered with metal for water supply tank on roof D26-15.01
581 Empty and thoroughly cleanse the interior sides and bottom of water supply tank on roof D26-15.01
586 Provide a separate house sewer and house drain properly connected to plumbing system of the building and to main sewer and file an application for approval before doing the work D26-16.01
587 Remove cesspool and all sewage saturated earth, disinfect site and fill with fresh earth. Connect plumbing system of building to main sewer by installing house sewer and drain. File application for approval before doing this work D26-16.01
590 Requires a separate water closet for each family within old law tenement buildings D26-31.07
592 Replace with new the defective flush pipe of water closet [*Explanation:* The flush pipe connects the water tank of the toilet with the toilet itself.] D26-16.01
593 Repair the flushing apparatus and maintain same so as to flush effectively the water closet D26-16.01
594 Repair the leaky water closet flush pipe connection [*Explanation:* See Order Number 592.] D26-16.01
595 Remove all obstruction from water closet [*Explanation:* This violation covers any obstruction in the pipes in the bathroom such as a stopped up toilet or sink.] D26-16.01
596 Replace the broken or defective plumbing facility [*Explanation:* This is a catchall violation. Any defective plumbing is covered.] D26-16.01
599 Repair by closing so as to be gas-tight all openings [*Explanation:* The gas referred to is sewer gas. All plumbing containing sewer gas must be air-tight.] D26-16.01
600 Provide a proper screw cap for the cleanout of trap [*Explanation:* The screw cap is a large screw on a waste pipe which may be opened in order to clean out accumulated debris.] D26-16.01
646 Properly close and seal opening as described below [*Explanation:* All disused pipes in a building must be capped, i.e., there may not be an open pipe anywhere even though it is not in use.] D26-16.01
647 Properly close and seal the hub opening after removing the disused broken or defective [*Explanation:* The hub opening is the access used to the main sewer pipe in the basement. It is opened to clean out any debris in the main sewer line which might obstruct the free passage of sewage D26-16.01
648 Properly ream out, tap and plug, with screw plugs, the holes [*Explanation:* When a pipe has a leak it may be fixed by plugging the hole.] D26-16.01
649 Remove all obstructions and repair all defects [*Explanation:* This is a catchall violation. Any obstruction in a plumbing pipe must be cleaned out and any defects must be repaired.] D26-16.01
665 Install central heating system, or, if lawfully feasible, individual space heaters, and file an application for approval before doing work D26-17.01
666 Provide an adequate supply of heat for the apartment D26-17.03
668 Repair and operate the heating appliance so as to prevent coal gas D26-17.05

669 Install central hot water system or, if feasible, individual hot water heaters, and file an application for approval before doing work D26-17.07
670 Provide hot water at all hot water fixtures D26-17.07
675 Requires discontinuance of illegal space or hot water heater or obtain approval for use D26-17.09
676 Requires discontinuance of room used for sleeping in which space heater is not provided with an air intake from outside the building D26-18.01
677 Discontinue the use of the gas fired refrigerator D26-18.03
680 Provide adequate lighting for the laundry room D26-19.01, 19.05
682 Provide adequate lighting for public halls and stairs, etc. D26-19.03
695 Remove unlawful sash in partition separating apartment from public halls and seal opening with fire retarded material [*Explanation:* See Order Number 214.] D26-20.07
696 Properly fire-retard in accordance with the rules and regulations of this department, the cellar ceiling D26-20.07
710 File with the borough chief inspector of this department a sprinkler test report for the current year D26-21.07
714 Seal in open position the O.S.Y. valve of the sprinkler system in accordance with the rules and regulations of this department D26-21.07
716 Provide a manager who shall be responsible for the conduct, operation and maintenance of premises and who shall live on premises or be regularly present therein D26-21.09
721 Provide dwelling with a janitor or responsible person or janitorial service D26-22.03
741 Discontinue unlawful cooking space or file plans and application with this department to legalize same, if lawfully feasible D26-32.01
742 Provide an adequate supply of gas to the fixtures D26-32.01
753 Requires the discontinuance of unlawful use for single room occupancy D26-33.09
768 Requires a certificate of occupancy be obtained before a vacant or vacated building can be re-occupied for living purposes D26-35.01
772 File with this department a registration and occupancy statement of building D26-41.03
773 File with this department a telephone number at which the owner or a responsible person can be reached at all hours in the event of an emergency D26-41.03
774 File with the department a written designation for change in managing agent of building D26-41.09
775 File with the department registration statement for change of ownership of building D26-41.05

MDL = Multiple Dwelling Law D26 = Housing Maintenance Code

INDEX